Fundamentals of Fortran Programming: with WATFOR/WATFIV

Terry M. Walker
University of Southwestern Louisiana

Allyn and Bacon, Inc. *Boston • London • Sydney*

To my wife, ANN

Library of Congress Cataloging in Publication Data

Walker, Terry M 1938-
Fundamentals of fortran programming.

Includes index.
1. FORTRAN (Computer program language) I. Title.
QA76.73.F25W34 001.6'424 75-11791
ISBN 0-205-04885-4

CONTENTS

PREFACE

This book is designed as a text for a one-semester introductory course in FORTRAN language programming for students majoring in any subject area. It is completely self-contained and can therefore be used without additional materials. However, the book is also designed to teach FORTRAN to students who are learning problem-solving concepts from *Fundamentals of Computer Science* (Allyn and Bacon, Inc., 1975).

Emphasis in this book is placed on making FORTRAN programming easy for a student to learn. For instance, numerous examples have been included in Section 4.4 on the often troublesome input and output aspects of FORTRAN. Included are a number of examples of common errors in input and output statements so that students will not fall into the many traps that exist. There is also an extensive section on finding and correcting program errors. Again, this section contains numerous examples to illustrate the techniques to be used in program debugging. Another important feature is the discussion on program and data preparation contained in Chapter 3. In addition, the book contains a large number of problems for students to solve.

Another important philosophy adopted is that only those FORTRAN features necessary to program most problems encountered would be discussed. For example, only logical IF statements are included in the main part of the text, with arithmetic IF statements left to Appendix D. The reason for taking this non-encyclopedic approach is to avoid burying the student under a mountain of detail while at the same time providing all of the tools needed to program almost any problem that might need solution.

Because the purpose of the book is to teach FORTRAN programming, very little detail has been provided on problem-solving and algorithm design concepts. Instead, every program is preceded by an algorithm flowchart that presents the logic for problem solution. Thus, the student will be primarily involved with coding programs from flowcharts that have already been developed. For the case where the concepts of problem solving and algorithm design are also to be taught, the book *Fundamentals of Computer Science* is recommended.

Chapter 1 contains a brief introduction to computer hardware and software systems. It should be omitted by persons using this book in parallel with the main text *(Fundamentals of Computer Science)* and may be omitted by those using this text by itself. Chapter 2 gives a very brief introduction to flowcharting. For those using only this book, this chapter is required so that the flowcharts in later chapters can be understood. However, those using the main text should omit Chapter 2.

Chapter 3 introduces the concepts of program and data preparation and processing. Included in this chapter are instructions on the use of a keypunch, which is very important for beginning students. Chapters 4 and 5 introduce the important features of the FORTRAN lanuguage and programming. They contain numerous examples, not only of correct programs but also of ones with errors. The solved problems used for examples represent a mixture of problems from many areas rather than being exclusively mathematical in nature. In addition, they have been selected because they are easy to understand and should be familiar to most students. Complete coverage of Chapters 4 and 5 is mandatory.

Chapters 6 through 8 contain solved problems from several disciplines. These chapters are included to provide students with experience in programming using the FORTRAN features presented in Chapters 4 and 5. Parts or all of any of these chapters may be omitted without any loss of continuity.

The important concept of subprograms is introduced in Chapter 9. Again, simplicity has been the goal rather than introducing such concepts as secondary entry-points, which only tend to confuse most beginning students. Finally, Chapter 10 contains additional applications, including the use of subprograms.

For those using this book in conjunction with *Fundamentals of Computer Science*, Chapters 4 through 10 of the two books are keyed to each other. In certain cases references are made in this book to figures or sections in the main text. In such cases, the letter M may appear as a suffix. Thus, a reference in this book to Fig. 9.7M is a reference to Fig. 9.7 in the main text.

The author is indebted to many persons who have contributed, either directly or indirectly, prior to and during the development of this book. I would like to thank the Applied Analysis and Computer Science Department of the University of Waterloo (where the WATFOR and WATFIV comp-lers were developed) for permission to reproduce the error diagnostics that appear as appendixes to this text. Finally, I would like to thank my wife, Ann, who not only offered me encouragement and understanding during the preparation of this text, but also typed most of the manuscript. It is to her that I dedicate this book.

Terry M. Walker

CHAPTER 1

INTRODUCTION TO COMPUTER SYSTEMS

The first electronic computer was completed in 1946. Since that time, computers by the tens of thousands have gone into use in businesses, government agencies, scientific laboratories, and universities. This wide use of computers has created jobs by the hundreds of thousands. The availability of these jobs has meant that many thousands of persons have required training and education in the design and use of computers. A result of this need has been the creation of an area of study called *computer science*. This book is designed to introduce the methods needed to solve problems using a computer. The languages to be used in this book in learning to solve problems are a flowchart language and the FORTRAN programming language.

In this chapter we will learn something about how computers are organized and how they function. While this knowledge is not absolutely necessary to write computer programs in FORTRAN, it is valuable in that it reduces the notion that a computer is some sort of magical "black box." In addition, knowing something about computers will help to explain some of the things that occur when writing and running FORTRAN programs.

1.1 COMPUTERS AS INFORMATION PROCESSORS

A *computer* is an information processor. As such, it must have a memory in which to store information. It must also have a means of inputting information into the memory and outputting information from that memory. A computer also has to be able to change information by performing various operations upon it. Finally, a computer must have a set of instructions available that guide it in the solution of a problem.

The set of instructions that tell a computer how to solve a problem is called an algorithm. Thus, an *algorithm* is simply a procedure consisting of a set of unambiguous rules that specifies a sequence of operations that provides the solution to a problem in a finite number of steps. Stated simply, an algorithm represents the logic involved in arriving at the solution to a problem. Although the definition of an algorithm may sound complicated, we have all used algorithms many times. One example of an algorithm would be a recipe for making a chocolate cake. A second example of an algorithm is a set of instructions for the assembly of a model airplane.

A common error that is made when thinking about computers is that a computer consists only of the cabinets, circuitry, and other physical devices that are seen when visiting a computer center. For example, people often think that a computer consists only of the objects that you can see in the photograph in Fig. 1.1. However, this is false because the photograph shows only the *hardware* or physical components of the computer system. Not seen

Figure 1.1 IBM System/370 Computer Hardware System (Courtesy of International Business Machines Corporation)

in a computer center or in the photograph of Fig. 1.1 is the second part of a computer, a part called the computer *operating system* or *software*. The computer operating system consists of a series of algorithms that are represented in the memory of the computer. These operating system algorithms are necessary because they facilitate the processing of the algorithms people write to provide a computer with the method for solving particular types of problems. They are also used to schedule the resources (computer hardware and software components) of the computer among these user algorithms. The remainder of this chapter will be devoted to studying computer hardware and operating systems.

1.2 COMPUTER HARDWARE SYSTEMS

This section contains discussion that covers the fundamental notions of computer hardware. The concepts introduced are: (1) input devices, (2) computer memory, (3) the central processing unit, (4) output devices, and (5) hardware reliability.

1.2.1 Computer Input Devices

A computer has one or more input devices that are designed to input information into the memory of a computer. Among the types of input devices would be card readers, paper tape readers, magnetic tape drives, and typewriter terminals.

A *card reader* is a device that is designed to read punched cards, such as the one shown in Fig. 1.2. Information is represented in such a card by the hole or holes punched in the various columns of the card by a device called a *keypunch*. Thus, a card reader (Fig. 1.3) functions by sensing which columns and rows in

Figure 1.2 Hollerith Punched Card

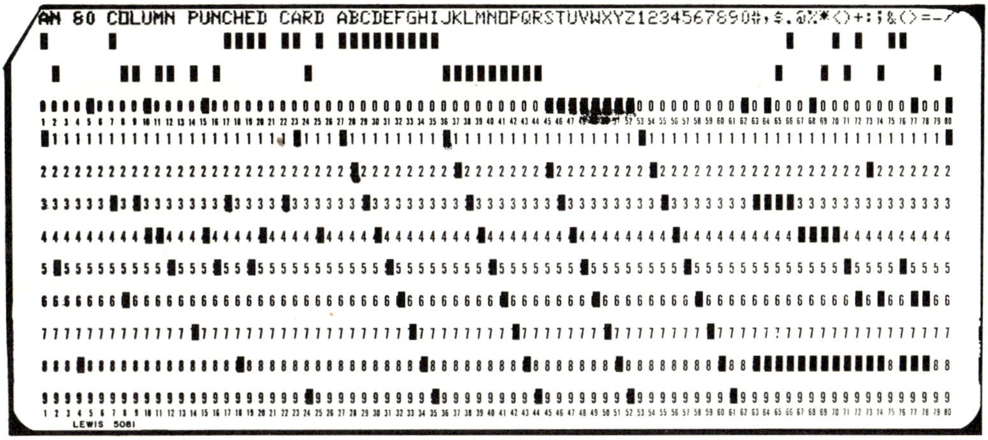

Figure 1.3 IBM 3525 Card Reader(Courtesy of International Business Machines Corporation)

a card have had holes punched in them. The result of this sensing is that the codes that represent the information in a card are electronically sent to the computer's memory. Thus, a card reader is connected directly to the computer's memory and processing unit.

Since a particular row and column on a punched card either does or does not contain a hole, the code that results is called a binary code. Thus, a *binary code* is one in which only two states are possible. An analogy to a binary code would be a conventional light switch, which must be either on or off; it cannot be in between these two states. However, even though the code is binary, the information represented in each card column is symbolic. That is, symbols, such as decimal digits and alphabetic characters, are being represented in each card column by use of a binary code.

A *punched paper tape* reader is very similar to a card reader. However, it reads information that is punched into a continuous paper tape. As in the case of punched cards, the information is represented in paper tape by the series of holes that have been punched into the tape by a paper tape punch. A *magnetic tape drive* is designed to read information that has been recorded magnetically on a coated plastic tape. The principle involved in using magnetic tape is similar to that used in recording audio messages on a tape recorder. The fundamental difference is that the information stored on a magnetic computer tape is represented using a binary code similar to the code used on punched cards. This coded information may have been written on a tape by a device that permits information to be entered manually on magnetic tape. Another possibility is that the information has been written on the magnetic tape as output from previous computer processing.

The *typewriter terminal* (Fig. 1.4) differs from the input devices discussed previously. This is because it is the only

Figure 1.4 IBM 2740 Typewriter Terminal(Courtesy of International Business Machines Corporation)

device that allows information to be entered manually directly into computer memory. That is, with punched cards, punched paper tape, and magnetic tape, the information is first entered into one of these media. Then it is read from them into computer memory. Two steps are therefore required to input information into memory. However, in the case of a typewriter terminal, the information is input directly into computer memory as it is entered into the keyboard of the terminal. In many cases this results in quite a savings of both labor and time in entering information into a computer. In addition, the chances for error may be reduced. However, no computer-readable copy of the information will be produced for future input to a computer. Thus a typewriter terminal may not always be the best device to use for the input of information. An exception to this exists in that some typewriter terminals can produce a punched paper tape while input is being made directly to computer memory. The paper tape can then be used to input that information in the future.

1.2.2 Computer Memory

The *memory* of a computer stores all information electronically in the form of a binary code. The reason that a binary code is used is that two-state electronic storage devices (remember the on-off analogy of a light switch as a two-state or binary device) are much easier to construct than are storage devices that allow three or more states. Thus, for purposes of engineering efficiency and to reduce costs, computer memory devices store information using a binary code.

The memory of a computer is usually not singular, but rather is *plural;* that is, each computer usually has more than one memory. These memories are usually segmented into two classes--*main memory* and *auxiliary memory*. The primary distinction between these two classes of memory is the source and destination of information placed in or taken from the respective memories. Thus all information placed in auxiliary memory must come from main memory, while information in main memory may come from input devices, auxiliary memory, or the central processing unit. Similarly, information output from auxiliary memory must go into main memory, while information in main memory may go to output devices, auxiliary memory, or the central processing unit. These relationships between memory classes and input/output are displayed in the information-flow diagram in Fig. 1.5. The primary reason for the distinction between main memory and auxiliary memory is cost. That is, the storage devices used for main memory are much more expensive per unit of information stored than are the devices used for auxiliary memory. Therefore, a relatively small but costly main memory is used together with a relatively large but inexpensive auxiliary memory to form the memory system of the computer.

The capacity of the typical computer main memory is between

Figure 1.5 Information Flow Between Main and Auxiliary Memories and Input/Output Devices

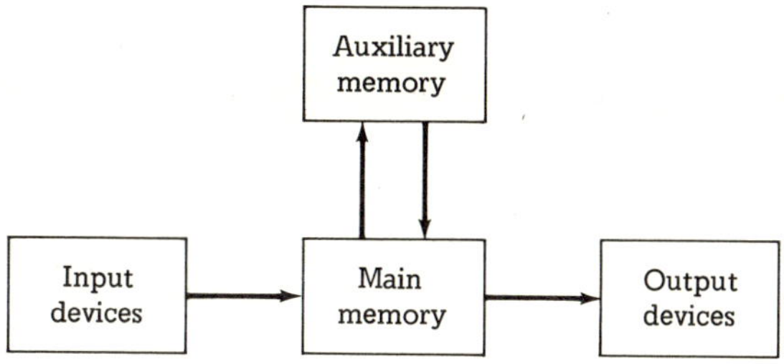

100,000 and 1,000,000 bytes (the unit of memory capable of storing one character is called a *byte*) of information. However, computers with both smaller and larger main memory capacities do exist. The amount of time required to access information stored in the typical main memory is measured in billionths of a second (one billionth of a second is called a nanosecond). Thus, many millions of characters of information can be stored and/or retrieved from main memory every second.

Main memory on a computer is broken up into units called *locations*. Depending on the particular model of computer, one main memory location will usually consist of from one to ten bytes of storage. Consequently, a particular piece of information may require more than one location for storage. For example, three locations would be needed to store a name consisting of eighteen letters on a computer in which each location allowed six bytes to be stored. The contents of a location will always be a binary or a binary-coded number. Certain binary codes are used to represent symbols other than numbers, such as alphabetic characters and punctuation marks. For example, the binary code 11000001 is used in IBM System/360 and 370 computers to represent the letter A of the English alphabet. Similarly, the code 01011011 is taken to represent a dollar sign ($). Thus, any information that can be represented using a binary code can be stored in a computer's main memory.

Because information that has been stored in a main memory location must be retrieved later, each location in main memory is given a unique location number. This location number is usually a binary integer and is called an *address*. It is very important not to confuse the contents of a location with the address of that location. That is, the address of a location tells us in which location of main memory the information is stored. The *contents* of a location, on the other hand, tell us what that information is. Furthermore, in general there is no relationship between the address of a location and the contents of that location. We might draw an analogy here with a post office box: the number on the box in general tells us nothing about the number of letters in that box, the size of the letters, or the contents of those letters. In the same way, the address of a main memory location tells us nothing about the contents of that location.

Several different types of storage devices are used for auxiliary memory. Among these are magnetic disc (Fig. 1.6), magnetic drum, magnetic core, data cells, and magnetic tape. Frequently, two or more of these types of storage devices are used on one computer system to provide the auxiliary memory.

The capacity of auxiliary memory on a typical computer system ranges from several million to hundreds of millions of characters. In fact, it is not uncommon for the auxiliary memory capacity of one computer to exceed one billion characters. The amount of time required to access information in auxiliary memory ranges from in the millionths of a second to several

Figure 1.6 Univac 8440 Disc Drive(Courtesy of Sperry Univac, A Division of Sperry Rand Corporation)

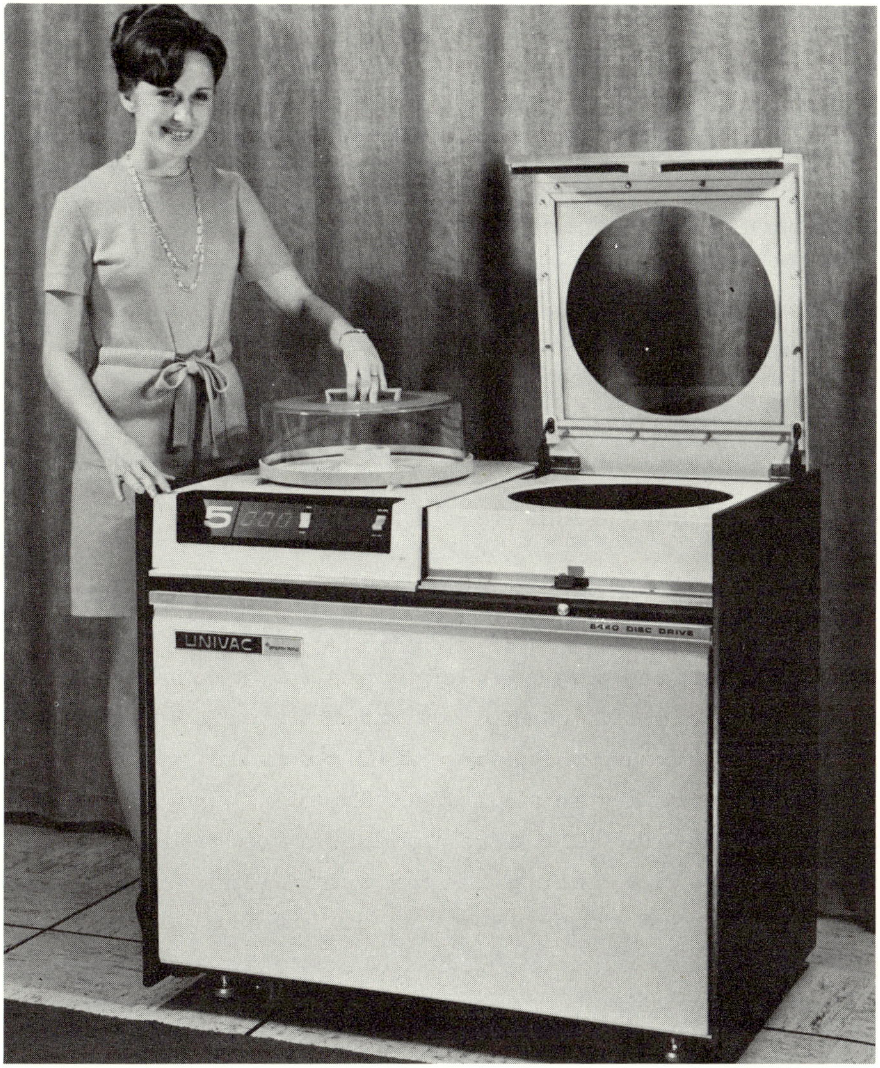

minutes, depending on the type of storage device. Moreover, the rate at which information can be transferred between auxiliary memory and main memory is generally in excess of 100,000 characters per second.

The method used to access information stored in auxiliary memory varies according to the type of device. For example, magnetic disc storage is addressable, thus allowing direct access to any item of information on a disc storage device. On the other hand, magnetic tape is generally searched serially in an associative manner. By associative, we mean that a label that describes the information we want is compared with a label contained in each group of information on the magnetic tape. This process of reading a group of information items and comparing the labels continues until a match of the labels occurs. The size of a group of information generally ranges from less than a hundred to several thousand characters.

1.2.3 Computer Central Processing Unit

The computer equivalent of the processing and control portions of the human brain is called the *central processing unit.* Thus, the central processing unit consists of components that perform such things as arithmetic and comparison operations. In addition, the central processing unit controls the operation of all of the other components of the computer hardware system. The component of the CPU (CPU is a common abbreviation for *central processing unit*) that performs operations, such as those of arithmetic and comparison, is called the *arithmetic and logical unit.* The portion of the arithmetic and logical unit that performs arithmetic operations might be thought of as an extremely fast desk calculator. This is because most computers can form the sum of several hundred thousand numbers in one second.

The portion of the CPU that controls the operation of the remainder of the computer hardware is called the *control unit.*

The control unit assures that the steps in an algorithm are executed in the proper sequence. It does this by the sequence in which the algorithm steps or instructions* are brought to the CPU for execution. This sequence is determined by the algorithm being executed. Note that the steps of an algorithm being executed by the CPU are stored in computer memory, not in the CPU. Thus, only the instruction currently being executed is generally in the CPU at any point in time. Therefore, the sequence in which instructions are executed is controlled by the order in which the CPU fetches instructions from main memory to the control portion of the CPU for execution. This sequence is determined by the instructions themselves.

1.2.4 Computer Output Devices

The output of information from main memory is performed using a variety of *output devices*. Among the types of output devices used are line printers, card punches, paper tape punches, magnetic tape drives, audio devices, CRT (cathode-ray-tube) terminals, and typewriter terminals. *Line printers* (Fig. 1.7) are devices that print numeric and alphabetic information on sheets of paper. They generally print an entire line, consisting of from 120 to 136 or more characters, in one operation. Such printers are capable of printing from 100 to 2000 lines per minute, with about 1200 being a fairly typical speed. *Card punches* and *paper tape punches* are used to punch the output information into punched cards and punched paper tape, respectively. The output produced by these devices can be used for

---

* *Instructions* are the steps of an algorithm written in a computer language. The concept of instructions and computer languages will be explained in Section 1.3.1.

Figure 1.7 Univac Series 0770 High-Speed Line Printer(Courtesy of Sperry Univac, A Division of Sperry Rand Corporation)

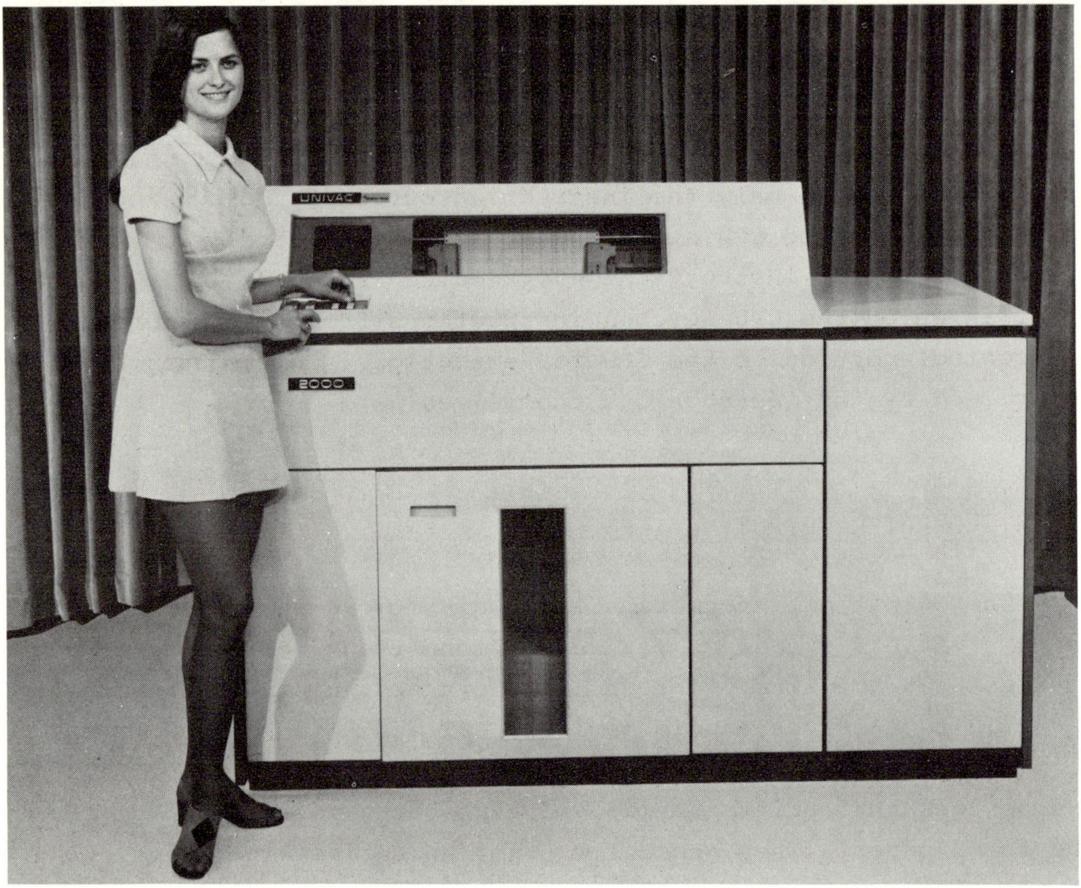

input to the computer at a later time. *Magnetic tape drives* write information on magnetic tape. These magnetic tapes can be removed from the computer and saved as future sources of input information.

Audio devices are not often used; however, they are useful in that they produce a spoken message. A common application of audio output devices is to produce things like changes in telephone numbers and stock market price quotations. They are generally best used when the response consists of numbers. *CRT terminals* provide output that may be graphical or alphabetic in nature on devices that are built around cathode-ray tubes similar to the ones used in television sets. Finally, *typewriter terminals* are used for output when a person is working at a terminal device alternating input to the computer with output from the computer. Typewriter terminals are generally fairly slow output devices when compared with such devices as line printers. However, they are much more versatile than most other types of devices because they permit both input to the computer and output from the computer.

Let us *summarize* what we have learned about computer hardware systems (Fig. 1.8). Every computer must get information into its main memory in order for that information to be available for

Figure 1.8 Major Component Subsystems of a Computer Hardware System

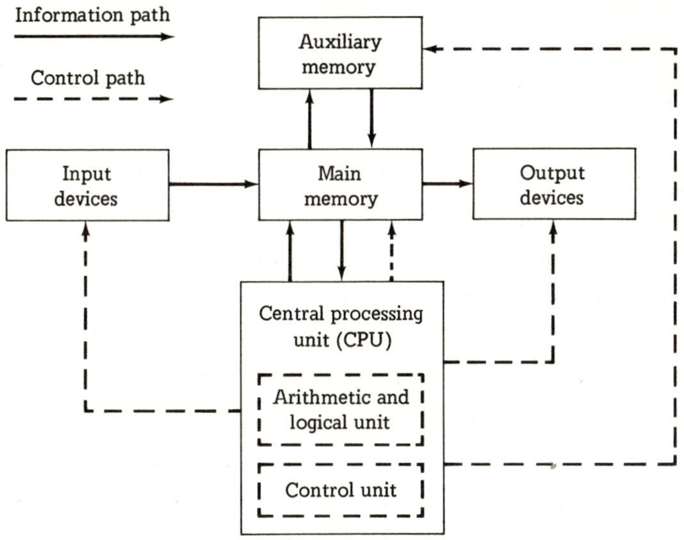

processing. An input operation is one in which information is sensed by an input device that is directly connected to the computer. Frequently used input devices include punched card readers and typewriter terminals. The information that is input goes into main memory. Main memory is organized into locations, with each location having an address. Because of the limited size of main memory, almost all computers have an auxiliary memory. Information can only be transferred between the auxiliary memory and the main memory. All processing is performed by the central processing unit. In addition, the CPU controls all parts of the computer hardware system. Finally, the information in the computer's main memory can be output through the use of output devices. The most commonly used types of output devices are line printers and typewriter terminals.

1.2.5 HARDWARE RELIABILITY

A final topic that relates to computer hardware is *reliability*. Most contemporary computer hardware systems have very few failures and thus are quite reliable. Moreover, the majority of failures that do occur relate to mechanical devices, such as card readers, rather than to the electronic components. Since incorrect answers resulting from failures in the electronic components could go for a while without discovery, computer hardware incorporates many kinds of self-checking components. Thus, should a part of main memory fail, the computer would probably stop and signal the type of failure. Some computers now available even have the capacity to correct certain kinds of errors caused by hardware failure. This is done so that processing can continue when minor hardware problems occur. Therefore, we can have a great deal of confidence that the results produced by a computer are what we expect for the algorithms that we provide it with.

1.3 COMPUTER OPERATING SYSTEMS

In this section we are going to discuss the features of an operating system. Before exploring computer operating systems, however, it will be useful to introduce the concept of a program and the various levels of programming languages.

1.3.1 Computer Programs and Programming Languages

An algorithm that is in a form that a computer can execute is called a *program*. The rules for writing programs and the operations that result from executing the various program steps define a computer programming language. Just as there are many natural languages (e.g., English, French, Spanish), there also exist numerous computer programming languages. The central processing unit of a computer is generally designed so that it can directly execute programs written in only one language. This language is called *machine language* (Fig. 1.9). The machine language that a particular model of computer is designed to execute will probably not be understood by another model of computer. Therefore there is not just one machine language; instead there exist many machine languages. Thus, an algorithm written in the machine language for one computer cannot be executed on a different model of computer. This lack of compatability creates many problems.

In addition to the problems caused by the large variety of machine languages, it is not convenient or efficient for a person to write programs in machine language. One reason for this is

Figure 1.9 Simple Machine-Language Program

```
LOC    OBJECT CODE     ADDR1 ADDR2  STMT   SOURCE STATEMENT

000000                                 1 BEGIN     START 0
000000 05C0                            2           BALR  12,0
000002                                 3           USING *,12
000002 5850 C00E             00010     4           L     5,A
000006 5A50 C012             00014     5           A     5,B
00000A 5050 C016             00018     6           ST    5,C
00000E 0000                            7           DC    X'0000'
000010 00000007                        8 A         DC    F'7'
000014 FFFFFFFC                        9 B         DC    F'-4'
000018                                10 C         DS    F
000000                                11           END   BEGIN
```

that the steps in a machine language program must generally be written using entirely octal or entirely hexadecimal numbers.* Since we are not used to writing numbers using other than the decimal system, machine language programs would be quite difficult to develop. Another problem with machine language is that a person using it must keep track of where in main memory various information has been stored. Yet another difficulty is caused by the primitive nature of the things a computer can do in one step of a machine language program. For example, three steps are required in most machine languages to add two numbers that are in main memory and leave the sum in main memory. Thus the development of machine language programs is a major task that generally requires the writing of thousands of program steps. All of these difficulties can be summarized by stating that machine language programs must be written

*Octal and hexadecimal numbers are written using eight and sixteen symbols, respectively. This is compared with the ten symbols used in writing decimal numbers. The decimal number 27, for example, would be written in octal as 33 and in hexadecimal as 1B. Octal and hexadecimal numbers are discussed in Appendix A of the main text.

using rules that conform to the design of the computer hardware.

As a result of the problems associated with the writing of machine language programs, machine-independent procedure-oriented computer languages have been developed. These languages allow programs to be written using a notation similar to the one used to describe the algorithm for solving a particular class of problems. Examples of these procedure-oriented languages would be FORTRAN, COBOL, BASIC, and PL/I. A result of using these languages is that it becomes quite easy to express an algorithm in a computer language. This is because all of the algorithm steps are written in symbolic rather than numeric form. In addition, these procedure-oriented languages do not require that the location of information in main memory be maintained in developing the algorithm.

A consequence associated with procedural languages is that computers cannot directly execute algorithms written using them. That is, algorithms represented using a procedure-oriented language must be translated into machine language programs before the computer can execute them. This translation process is performed by a computer program called a *compiler*. The use of a compiler for translating programs from a procedural language to machine language is analogous to an interpreter translating a book written in Russian into English. With this background, we are now ready to discuss computer operating systems.

1.3.2 Operating System Concepts

Earlier in this chapter we stated that a computer *operating system* consists of a series of algorithms (often called software) that: (1) *facilitate* the processing of the algorithms that people write to tell a computer how to solve a type of problem and (2) *schedule* the resources of the computer among these user algorithms.

We have already learned in this section that an algorithm in a form that can be executed by a computer is called a program. Therefore, an operating system can be defined as a collection of computer programs. Since users very rarely write their programs for problem solution in machine language, some of the programs that make up an operating system are the compilers. Recall that these compilers are used to translate programs that users have written in procedural languages, such as FORTRAN or COBOL, into machine language programs.

Another type of program contained in an operating system is the utility package. These *utility packages* contain programs that are written to handle frequently performed user tasks. Examples of such tasks would be sorting a list of names into alphabetical order, or the output of a group of information contained in computer auxiliary memory. These utility programs are very useful because they allow a user to obtain the solution to a particular type of problem without actually developing the appropriate algorithm. Thus utility programs often result in a considerable time savings for the user. In addition, a savings in computer time is often realized because the utility programs are usually written by experts that have developed the best algorithms for the particular task.

In addition to the above functions, the operating system contains programs with the responsibility of *scheduling* computer system resources* among the users' and operating system's programs. For example, there is a scheduling program that determines in what order user jobs are to be processed. Smaller computers generally do not have a scheduling problem in that one job at a time is processed until completion. Therefore, processing of another job will not start until the previous task has been completed. This type of job scheduling is called *sequential batch processing.*

---

*Computer system resources may be defined as the various computer hardware and software components that together comprise a computer.

In medium- and large-scale computers, the resources of a computer are shared by a number of jobs at one time. Such an arrangement is known as multiprogramming. In *multiprogramming*, the operating system usually inputs programs to the computer's auxiliary memory as soon as a request for processing is received. This is sometimes called a *spooling* process. At the same time, processing of programs that had been previously input is continuing. When the computer detects that it is ready to begin processing another job, the scheduling program determines which job that is waiting in auxiliary memory is to be processed next. Sometimes this is determined strictly on a first-come, first-served basis. In many systems, however, jobs are attached priorities based on such things as how much the user is willing or able to pay, or how much time will be required to process the job. Under the priority scheduling arrangement, jobs with the highest priority will be processed before jobs with a lower priority.

In addition to scheduling jobs, operating systems must include *error-recovery programs*. These are necessary in order for the computer to recover from program-caused errors that might otherwise cause the computer to come to a halt or allow incorrect results.

Another task handled by the operating system is that of *accounting* for the use of computer resources. This accounting is required so that users of the computer can be charged for the amount of computer resources they use. In addition, the accounting system is used as a screening device to prevent unauthorized users from processing jobs. This is accomplished by assigning an account number to each user for purposes of identification. These account numbers are kept in computer memory. When a user job is input, the account number of the user must appear as one of the first input items. This number is matched against the authorized account numbers in the table in computer memory. If the account number for the input job is not found in the table, the job is rejected by the computer.

A final topic that needs to be discussed under operating systems is that of *interactive* usage (also called conversational usage or *time-sharing*). In an interactive situation, a person usually enters the information to be processed through a terminal device (such as the one shown in Fig. 1.4). Should errors occur while entering this information, the computer would immediately respond with an error message. This allows the user to correct the error and continue processing of the job. An interactive user can save programs and data that are input through a terminal. The information is saved in the computer's auxiliary memory. The saved information is called a *file*. All time-sharing operating systems have an editing program that allows a user to modify portions of the file and to make additions and deletions on the file contents.

Interactive processing is becoming more popular as time passes. In fact, today time-sharing finds wide application in both education and industry. For example, in education it is used in computer-assisted instruction; in industry airline reservations would be a widely used application.

SUMMARY

1. A computer system consists of two primary components:
   a. A computer hardware system.
   b. A computer operating system.
2. Information to be processed by a computer must first be input into the main memory of the computer. This operation is performed using input devices.
3. Card readers and typewriter terminals are two of the most widely used input devices.
4. The memory of a computer stores all information electronically in the form of a binary code.
5. There are two classes of computer memory:
   a. Main memory.
   b. Auxiliary memory.

6. Computer main memory is divided into addressable units called locations. Each location in main memory has a unique address to permit access to information.
7. Information stored in a main memory location is called the contents of the location. A typical main memory location has the capacity to store from one to ten characters of information.
8. Three of the more widely used devices for auxiliary memory are magnetic disc, magnetic drum, and magnetic tape.
9. The capacity of main memory usually ranges from 100,000 to 1,000,000 characters. Auxiliary memory capacity on most computers varies from several million to hundreds of millions of characters.
10. The arithmetic and logical unit is the computer component in which the processing of information takes place.
11. The control of all components in a computer hardware system is performed by the control unit.
12. The control unit and the arithmetic and logical unit are organized into the central processing unit of a computer.
13. Information is output from computer main memory using a variety of output devices.
14. Line printers and typewriter terminals are two of the most widely used output devices.
15. Computer hardware systems are very reliable because they include self-checking components that either signal or correct errors that might occur.
16. An algorithm in a form that a computer can execute is called a program. Programs are written using programming languages.
17. The central processing unit of a computer is capable of executing only those programs that are written using its machine language.
18. Most users write their programs using a procedure-oriented programming language because of the difficulties associated with the use of machine language.
19. Programs written in procedural languages must be translated into machine language using computer programs called compilers.
20. A computer operating system consists of a collection of computer programs that:
    a. Facilitate the processing of the algorithms that people write to tell a computer how to solve a problem.
    b. Schedule the resources of a computer among these user algorithms.

21. Among the types of programs contained in an operating system are:
    a. Compilers
    b. Utility programs.
    c. Schedulers.
    d. Error recovery.
    e. Accounting.

22. Multiprogramming is the scheduling strategy in which more than one user program is being processed at one time.

23. Time-sharing or interactive computing is performed using a terminal device. This type of processing exists when the computer responds immediately to user information inputs.

CHAPTER 2

PROBLEM SOLVING AND ALGORITHM DEVELOPMENT

In Chapter 1 we learned about computer systems, including both computer hardware and software. In this chapter we are going to discuss concepts of problem solving and flowchart development. The reason for discussing flowcharts is that they provide a means of displaying algorithm logic in a graphical form. In addition, they are often used for documenting computer programs.

2.1 PROBLEM SOLVING CONCEPTS

Three separate phases can be identified in the process of *problem solving*. These three phases are:

1. Analysis of the problem.
2. Design of an algorithm for solving the problem.
3. Computer implementation of the algorithm.

In the *problem analysis* phase there are five distinct steps. They are:

1. Precisely define the problem.
2. Identify the inputs and variables of the problem.
3. Identify the outputs desired from the algorithm.
4. Determine whether or not a computer is needed to solve the problem.
5. Obtain all other information required for algorithm development.

Definition of the problem to be solved is often assumed to be a trivial step. Nothing could be further from the truth. In fact, a careful and precise definition of the problem is an absolute necessity in the process of solving a problem. It is important to note that the definition of a problem does not usually consist of just one sentence. Instead, problem definitions often require one or more pages. In addition, problem definitions often include many sub-problems, which also must be precisely defined. A well-organized approach to problem definition does not exist. The main rule to apply is to attempt to consider every possible aspect of each problem. In conclusion, problem definition is an art that is learned through experience gained from having defined many problems.

Identifying the inputs and the variables needed to solve a problem can often be done during the problem-definition step. The *inputs* for a problem consist of the data to be processed by the algorithm in arriving at a problem solution. The problem *variables* are such things as the inputs and outputs of a problem, together with any constants and intermediate results that may be needed. *Outputs* are also closely related to problem definition. A considerable amount of judgement is required in identifying problem output because producing more output than is necessary is a waste of resources. However, producing too little output will often result in the algorithm not producing a correct solution to the problem.

The question of whether or not a computer is needed to solve a problem is important for several reasons. First, computer time is expensive. Second, developing an algorithm a computer can use to solve a problem may often require more time than solving the problem by hand. So it may require more time and may cost more to solve a problem by use of a computer than to solve the problem manually. The primary purpose for including the step of obtaining all other information is to cover anything that may not have been included in the other four problem analysis steps.

2.2 ALGORITHM DEVELOPMENT

After the problem has been analyzed, we are ready to begin the development of an algorithm. Algorithms to be executed on computers are often developed using a flowchart language. After the algorithm has been designed as a flowchart, it can be coded into a FORTRAN program to be executed by a computer. In this section, we will learn the fundamentals of the flowchart language that will be used in this book.

2.2.1 THE ALPHABET, CONSTANTS, AND VARIABLES

As in any language, our flowchart language requires an *alphabet* of symbols. The one for our flowchart language consists of:

1. The symbols for the 26 uppercase and 26 lowercase letters of the English alphabet.
2. The following punctuation and grouping symbols:
   .) , (' *blank* ; % :] ? [- $ &
3. The symbols for the ten decimal digits and the following mathematical symbols:
   $+ \quad - \quad \cdot \quad / \quad \leftarrow \quad = \quad \neq \quad < \quad \leq \quad > \quad \geq$
4. The set of eight standard flowchart symbols (six of which we will call *flowchart boxes*) shown in Fig. 2.1.

Some of these symbols are used to form words. These words are then combined using operators and punctuation and grouping symbols to form statements.

A very important kind of word in the flowchart language is called a *constant*. Two types of constants are permitted in our flowchart language: (1) numeric constants and (2) string constants. A *numeric constant* always consists of a string of decimal digits that may or may not: (1) contain a decimal point and (2) be preceded by a plus sign (+) or a minus sign (-). Examples of numeric constants are:

+123	467.523
-78	-0.000012
46532	56700000

Notice that numeric constants may not contain a comma.

String constants consist of any sequence of symbols in the flowchart language (except for the eight standard flowcharting symbols) enclosed in apostrophes ('). Since the apostrophe is used to indicate the starting and ending point of a string constant, an

Figure 2.1 Flowchart Symbols

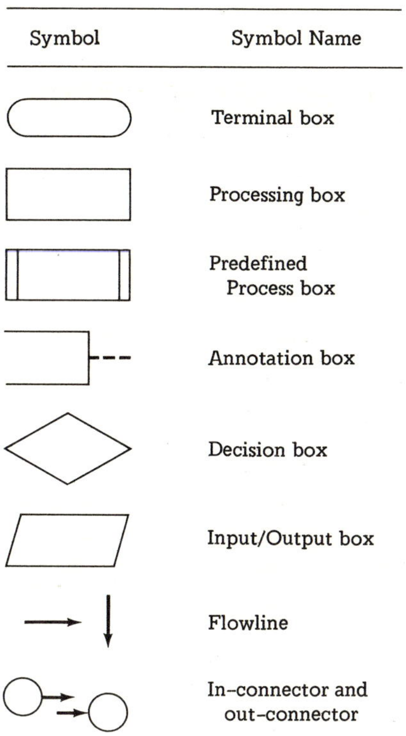

apostrophe may not appear as a character in a flowchart language string constant. In addition, the number of blank spaces in a string constant is often difficult to determine. Therefore, we will adopt the convention in this text of using an *underline* to indicate each *blank space* in a flowchart language string constant.

Examples of string constants would be:

'THIS_IS_A_STRING_CONSTANT.'
'This_is_a_string_constant.'
'Dont_you_do_it!'

Note that the only thing that matters in writing a string constant is whether or not the sequence of characters that make up the constant is enclosed within apostrophes.

Another important kind of word in our flowchart language is called a variable name. A *variable name* is a sequence of symbols that consists of uppercase and/or lowercase and/or decimal digits. The first character in a word that is a variable name must be alphabetic. Examples of valid variable names are:

A *Alpha* *FICATax* *Spiritof76*

A variable name is used to refer to a place* in main memory where a constant is stored. Since constants may be numeric or string constants, variables may be numeric or string variables. We assume in the flowchart language that the number of memory locations required to represent the numeric or string constant associated with a variable name will be available.

At any point during the execution of an algorithm a variable will have only one value stored in its main memory location (or locations). During the execution of the algorithm, however, many values (remember, only one at a time) will usually be associated with any variable name. Care must be taken not to confuse the name of a variable with the value of the constant associated with that variable name. Another important point is that each time a variable name is given a new value, the old value of that variable name is no longer available.

---

*A *place* is one or more consecutive main memory locations.

Finally, every variable name must always be declared as to the type of constants it may have as values. This declaration is performed by attaching an *annotation box* to the first flowchart box where that variable is used. Three keywords are used to declare the type of a variable. The keyword NUM is used to declare numeric variables, STR is used to declare string variables, and NUMINT is used to declare a variable name that can have only numeric integers as values. For example, the annotation box:

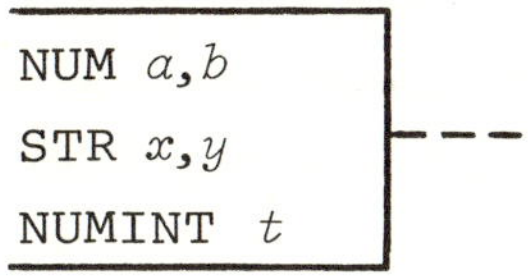

declares the variables: (1) *a* and *b* to be able to have any numeric constants as values, (2) *x* and *y* to be able to have any string constants as values, and (3) *t* to be able to have any numeric constant that is an integer as a value.

2.2.2 Flowchart Organization and Giving Values to Variables

Execution of every flowchart must begin with an oval shaped flowchart box. The flowchart box that indicates where algorithm execution begins is:

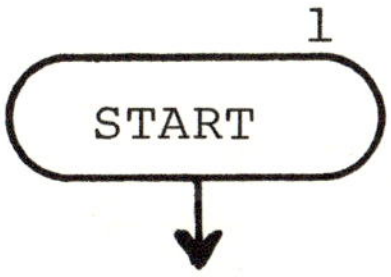

The end of algorithm execution is indicated by:

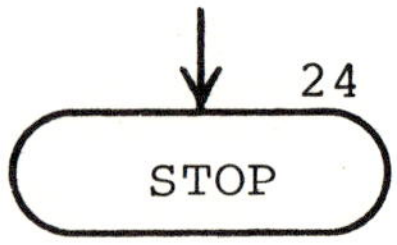

There will be only one START and one STOP operation per algorithm flowchart in our flowchart language.

Flowchart boxes are connected by using straight lines with arrowheads. These directed lines are called *flowlines*. Every type of box in a flowchart except three will always have one flowline leading to it and one flowline leading from it. Two of the exceptions are the START and STOP boxes, with the START box having no flowline leading to it and the STOP box having no flowline leading from it. The third exception is the decision box, which will always have one flowline leading to it and two flowlines leading out of it.

Variables have two ways of being given constants as values. The first is the assignment statement, which has the general form

variable ← *expression*

where: (1) *variable* is any numeric or string variable name, (2) the left-pointing arrow (←) is called the *assignment operator*, and (3) *expression* is any arithmetic or string expression. Assignment statements always appear inside of rectangular boxes, which are called *processing boxes*. Two examples of assignment statements would be:

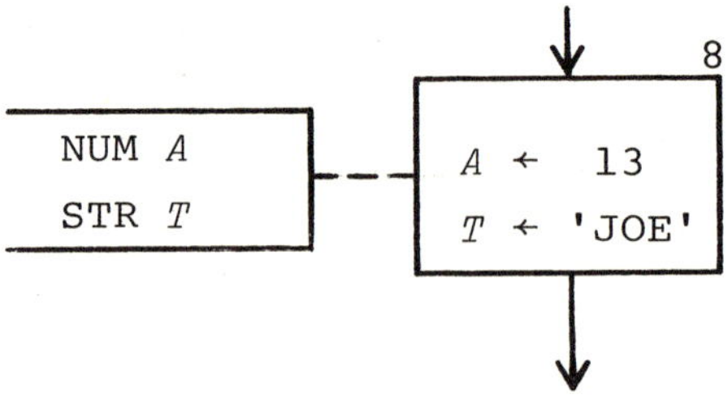

In the first of these statements the numeric variable A is being assigned the numeric constant 13 as its value. The value assigned to the string variable T in the second statement is the string constant 'JOE'. An assignment statement is the operation of moving a constant in main memory into the memory location that is associated with a variable.

More complex expressions can appear to the right of an assignment operator. A *string expression* may only consist of a string constant or a string variable. On the other hand, an *arithmetic expression* can consist of any sequence of numeric variables and constants that is formed using arithmetic operators, numeric functional operators, and an operation implied by position. Parentheses may be used in an arithmetic expression to indicate the order in which operations are to be carried out. Essentially, the flowchart version of an arithmetic expression looks much like an arithmetic expression of algebra.

The *arithmetic operators* are: (1) for addition, a plus sign (+); for subtraction, a minus sign (-); (3) for multiplication, a dot (·); (4) for division, a slash (/); and (5) for exponentiation, a superscript (e.g., a^b). The numeric functional operators shown in Fig. 2.2

Figure 2.2 Mnemonic Numeric Functional Operators

Operation	*Mathematical Functional Operator**	*Mnemonic Functional Operator**
Absolute value	$\|x\|$	**abs[x]**
Exponential	e^x	**exp[x]**
Natural logarithm	$\log_e x$	**log[x]**
Base-ten logarithm	$\log_{10} x$	**log10[x]**
Square root	$\sqrt{x}$	**sqrt[x]**
Truncate	x_{tr}	**trun[x]**

* Using x as a typical operand.

are used to find such things as square roots. Notice that square brackets are used only with numeric functional operators and never to group items into a subexpression. Also observe that implied multiplication and the division operator ÷ are not allowed.

The final topic to be discussed in relation to arithmetic expressions is the order in which they are evaluated. Evaluation is performed using the set of *precedence rules* given in Fig. 2.3. An arithmetic expression is scanned four times, with all operations on one level being carried out on each scan in the order indicated. In Fig. 2.4 examples of a number of flowchart language expressions are presented. These expressions are evaluated for the values given in the footnote to that figure. Each of these examples should be studied carefully to be certain that the precedence rules are completely understood. Finally, it is *not* really necessary to learn precedence rules. The reason is that parentheses can be used to group expressions into subexpressions. Since subexpressions are executed first, these subexpressions will determine the order in which an expression is evaluated.

The second way to give a variable a constant as a value is to *input* the value into the main memory location associated with that

Figure 2.3 Precedence Rules for Evaluating Arithmetic Expressions

Precedence Level	*Operation*	*Order of Evaluation*
1	Numeric functional reference	Any order
2	Prefix + and prefix – Exponentiation	Right to left
3	Multiplication Division	Left to right
4	Addition Subtraction	Left to right

Figure 2.4 Examples of Flowchart Language Arithmetic Expressions and Their Evaluation

Arithmetic Expression*	Value
$X + A - 2 \cdot BAD$	−29
$(X - A/C)^{Y} \cdot F$	49
$(X - A)/C^{Y} \cdot F$	5/4
$X - A/C^{Y} \cdot F$	7/2
$(X^{Y})^{E}$	729
$X^{Y^{E}}$	6,561
$(X + E)^{-\mathrm{sqrt}[C]}$	1/36
$A - B^{2}/C \cdot D \cdot \mathrm{abs}[A]$	−21/8
$\mathrm{sqrt}[2 \cdot \mathrm{log10}[D^{2} \cdot C]]$	2
X^{-A}	9

* $A = -2$, $B = 0.5$, $BAD = 15$, $C = 4$, $D = 5$, $E = 3$, $F = 4$, $X = 3$, $Y = 2$.

variable. This is done in the flowchart language by using a GET box. For example, the step

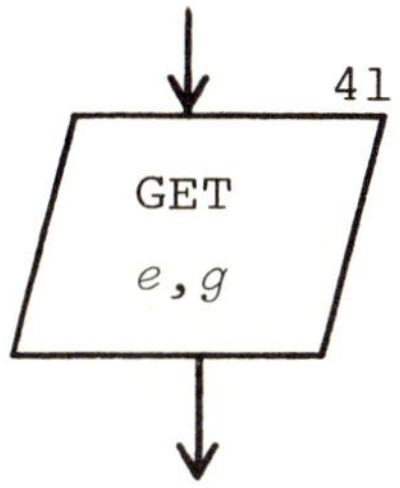

causes two constants to be input, with the first one being stored as the value of *e* and the second one being stored as the value of the variable *g*. The values input are considered to be an input data stream of constants that is coming from some input device, such as a card reader or a terminal device. Of course, this input data stream of constants must be available when the GET command is executed. Notice that only variables can appear in GET boxes since variables are the only things that can be given a value.

2.2.3 Output Operations, Algorithm Flow, and Branching Operations

For any algorithm to be meaningful, it must produce results that will be used by people or machines. Since the results produced by an algorithm will already exist in main memory, we need to have some means of outputting this information. That is, just as information to be processed needs to be input to main memory, results of processing need to be output.

In the flowchart language, this *output* is accomplished by means of a PUT box. The PUT box consists of the verb PUT followed by a list of variables and/or constants. The result of executing a PUT box is to output to some output device the constants and values of variables listed. For example, execution of the step

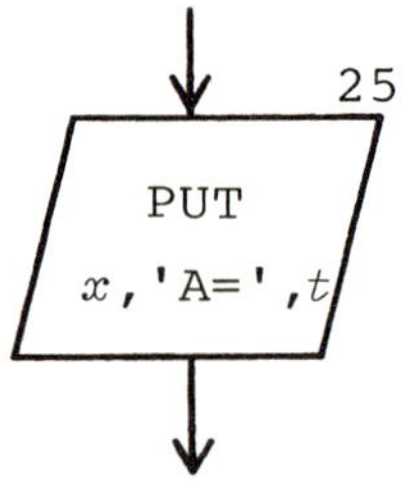

would result in the output of: (1) the value of the variable x, (2) the string constant 'A=', and (3) the value of the variable t. In general, PUT boxes are considered to generate a stream of constants, which is called the output data stream.

Earlier we discussed algorithm flow of execution by observing that *flowlines* are used to connect flowchart boxes and indicate which step is to be executed next. Sometimes, however, the bottom of a column is reached or a page is full. In such cases, we can use connectors (which are represented as small circles) to indicate the continuation of execution flow.

There are two types of connectors: (1) out-connectors and (2) in-connectors. An *out-connector* is a circle that has a flowline pointing to it. An *in-connector* is a circle that has a flowline leading from it that points to a flowchart box or another flowline. An out-connector indicates that the next flowchart box to be executed is located elsewhere in the algorithm flowchart. Out-connectors may be placed next to any flowchart box. Every out-connector will always contain a label constant, where a label constant is simply any unsigned integer constant. An in-connector indicates a place in a flowchart where flow is to resume. In-connectors may appear anywhere in a flowchart and must always contain *unique* label constants. That is, no two in-connectors in a flowchart may contain the same label constant value. In-connectors are used as reference points by out-connectors in other parts of an algorithm flowchart. That is each time during algorithm execution that an out-connector is reached, flow will resume with the in-connector pointed to by the label constant in that out-connector.

A *conditional branching operation* is one in which a decision is made to determine the next flowchart box to be executed. Conditional branches are indicated in flowcharts by the use of a diamond-shaped symbol, which is called a *decision box*. All decision boxes will have two flowlines leading from them. Which one of these two flowlines is to be followed when leaving the decision box is determined by the result of the relation or condition contained in the decision box. These relations or conditions are more or less like statements that can be answered as *true* or *false* (or *yes* or *no*). The most common type of relation is one that is used to compare two values. This comparison utilizes one of the relational operators

Figure 2.5 Flowchart Language Relational Operators

Operator	Meaning	Example
$=$	is equal to	$A = B$
$\neq$	is not equal to	$A \neq B$
$>$	is greater than	$A > B$
$\geq$	is greater than or equal to	$A \geq B$
$<$	is less than	$A < B$
$\leq$	is less than or equal to	$A \leq B$

given in Fig. 2.5. The meaning of each of the six flowchart language relational operators is given in this table and examples of their use are also included. Note that the symbols used for the relational operators are the same as those used in mathematics. As an example, execution of the decision box

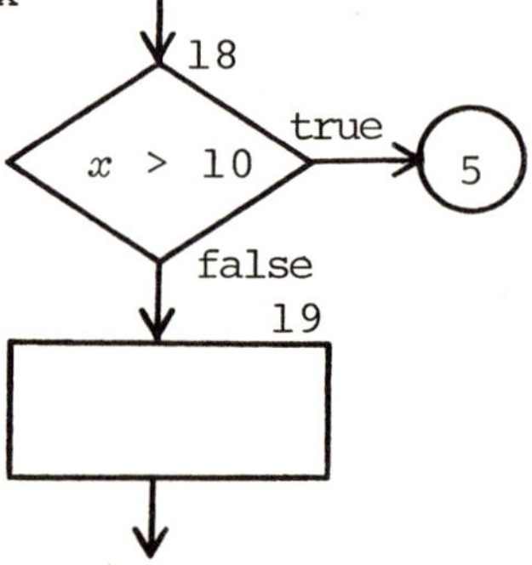

would cause: (1) a branch to the box following in-connector 5 when the value of x is greater than 10 and (2) execution of the step in box 19 when the value of x is less than or equal to 10. Note that a relation must be either true or false. Therefore, only two flow-lines can exit from flowchart box 18.

2.2.4 Algorithm Design

The process of designing an algorithm is an art learned through experience gained by designing many algorithms. In the remainder of this book, we will examine a number of algorithm flowcharts and their FORTRAN programs. Through this study of worked examples and by solving problems contained in this book, you should be in a position to use a computer to solve problems of interest to you.

In Fig. 2.6 is a flowchart for finding the largest value among a set of three data values. Notice that the first step in the flowchart is a START box. The next step to be performed is a GET box. In this box, we order the input into main memory of the next three data values. The constants input are stored as the values of the three numeric variables *V1*, *V2*, and *V3*. Flowchart box 3 is a decision box in which the end-of-file condition is tested. The end-of-file condition results in a value of true when the supply of input data values was exhausted during the last GET operation. In such a case, algorithm execution is halted by the step in flowchart box 4. When three data values were actually input, however, algorithm execution continues with flowchart box 5. Execution of this box results in the output of three string constant values, with each string constant being followed by one of the three data values input in the step in box 2. In box 6, the numeric variable *Large* is assigned the value of the first input data value. Then out-connector 2 is reached, which indicates that execution continues at the top of the righthand column of the flowchart.

Execution of flowchart box 7 results in the flow proceding to box 8 whenever the value of the variable *V2* is greater than the value of the variable *Large*. That is, if the value of the second input data value is greater than the current value of *Large*, then the value of *V2* is assigned to be the new value of the variable *Large*. Otherwise, the next step executed will be the one in box 9. This

Figure 2.6 Algorithm Flowchart for the Largest-Value Problem

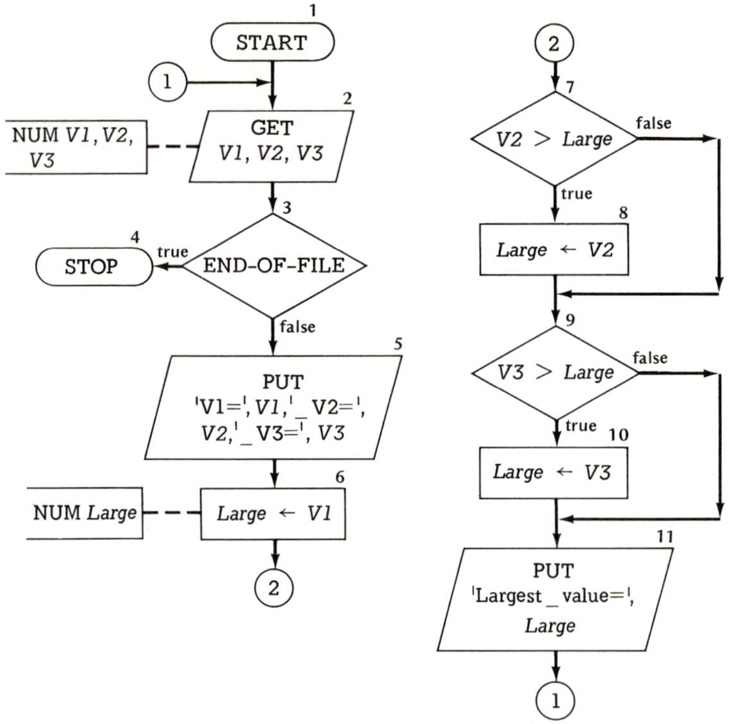

step performs an operation equivalent to the one in box 7, except this time the value of the variable *V3* is involved. Similarly, in box 10 is an operation that is much like the one in box 8. Finally, execution of flowchart box 11 causes a string constant to be output, followed by the value of the variable *Large*. Then algorithm execution continues at in-connector 1, which causes another set of three data values to be input. This process of inputting and outputting three data values, finding the largest value and outputting it will continue until the supply of input data values has been exhausted.

2.2.5 Trace Tables

A final topic to consider in algorithm development is the trace table. A *trace table* is simply a table in which the column headings may consist of:

1. The variable names used in the algorithm flowchart.
2. Conditions contained in decision boxes used in the flowchart.
3. The PUT box contents of output steps included in the flowchart.

The values contained in the trace table itself are:

1. For the columns headed by variable names, the sequence of values that have been assigned to the respective variables through either GET operations or assignment statements.
2. For the columns headed by conditions, the results of the decision for the current values of the variables. That is, these columns would contain the values of either true or false.
3. For the columns headed by PUT box contents, the sequence of values output from memory by the respective PUT operation.

The trace table is created dynamically by stepping through the algorithm flowchart one box at a time. As each step is executed, the results are entered in the appropriate column of the trace table. Thus the value assigned to a variable in an assignment statement is recorded in the column headed with the name of that variable. Similarly, a value of true or false is entered in the column with a condition as a heading each time the box for that condition is executed. Thus a trace table is created one entry at a time, with each

Figure 2.7 Trace Table for the Algorithm of Figure 2.6

V1	*V2*	*V3*	*Large*	*V2 > Large*	*V3 > Large*
5	6	7	5	true	
			6		true
			7		
5	8	3	5	true	
			8		false
4	3	2	4	false	false
9	5	15	9	false	true
			15		

entry corresponding with the result of executing one flowchart step.

The trace table for the algorithm flowchart of Fig. 2.6 is given in Fig. 2.7. In developing this trace table, the input data stream

5,6,7, 5,8,3, 4,3,2, 9,5,15

is assumed to have been used. Ideally, the input data stream values chosen in developing a trace table should be ones that cause every possible combination of branches in the algorithm to be taken. Trace tables also assume that the correct answers are known for the input data stream used to develop the table. The values the variables *V1*, *V2*, and *V3* assume in this trace table are coming from the input data stream using the GET operation in flowchart box 2. The true or false values in the condition columns are determined by the relations in boxes 7 and 9. Finally, the values in the column headed *Large* are being assigned by one of the statements in flowchart boxes 6, 8, or 10.

PROBLEMS

1. Develop an algorithm flowchart that inputs and outputs four values, finds the largest of those values, and then outputs this largest value. Also develop a trace table for the flowchart using the input data stream of Sec. 2.2.5.
2. Develop an algorithm flowchart that inputs and outputs three values, finds the smallest of those values, and then outputs this smallest value. Also develop a trace table for the flowchart using the input data stream of Sec. 2.2.5.
3. Develop an algorithm flowchart that inputs and outputs five values, forms the sum of these values adding in one value at a time to a summing variable, and then outputs the value of the summing variable. Also develop a trace table for the flowchart using the first ten values of the input data stream of Sec. 2.2.5.

SUMMARY

1. The three phases of problem solving are:
   a. Analysis of the problem.
   b. Design of an algorithm for solving the problem.
   c. Computer implementation of the algorithm.
2. The five steps of problem analysis are:
   a. Precisely define the problem.
   b. Identify the inputs and variables of the problem.
   c. Identify the outputs desired from the algorithm.
   d. Determine whether or not a computer is needed to solve the problem.
   e. Obtain all other information required for algorithm development.
3. The symbols in the alphabet of our flowchart language are:
   a. The symbols for the 26 uppercase and 26 lowercase letters of the English alphabet, associated punctuation marks, and certain special symbols.
   b. The symbols for the ten decimal digits and the other usual symbols of mathematics.
   c. A set of eight standard flowchart symbols, six of which we call flowchart boxes.
4. The words in our flowchart language consist of: (a) constants, (b) variables, and (c) certain keyword verbs.

5. The four basic types of statements in our flowchart language are:
   a. Processing statements.
   b. Control statements.
   c. Declarative statements.
   d. Input/output statements.
6. There are two types of constants and variables in our flowchart language. They are:
   a. Numeric constants and variables.
   b. String constants and variables.
7. A variable is a name that refers to a place in computer main memory where a constant is stored.
8. Information about an algorithm variable or an algorithm step is called declarative information and is enclosed in an annotation box. The annotation box is connected to a flowchart box by a broken line.
9. All variables in our flowchart language must be declared as to type. The three types of variables are:
   a. Numeric variables (declared using NUM).
   b. Integer-valued numeric variables (declared using NUMINT).
   c. String variables (declared using STR).
10. The assignment statement is of the form

    variable ← *expression*

11. Evaluation of an expression is the process of successively reducing subexpressions to constant values until the entire expression is reduced to a single constant.
12. Arithmetic expressions are evaluated using the precedence rules given in Fig. 2.3.
13. A GET box contains a list of variable names that are assigned values obtained from an input data stream that consists of a list of constant values.
14. A PUT box contains a list of constants and variables the values of which are placed in an output data stream.
15. The two basic types of connectors are: (a) in-connectors and (b) out-connectors.
16. The basic branching statement is the conditional branch, which is indicated in a flowchart by a decision box.
17. The condition contained in a decision box will be either true or false. Some of the conditions that can be tested are mathematical equality or inequality, the sequencing of string constants, and end-of-file conditions.

18. In designing an algorithm, all possible conditions that are important should be considered and tests included to determine when these conditions hold.

19. The trace table provides an effective way to test the logic of an algorithm to learn whether or not it is correct.

CHAPTER 3

PROGRAM AND DATA PREPARATION AND PROCESSING

An algorithm represented as a flowchart cannot be directly executed on a computer. Instead, the algorithm flowchart must be coded into a computer programming language representation. Such a computer programming language representation of an algorithm is called a *computer program* (or simply a *program*). In this chapter, we will examine the steps required to prepare a program and its data for computer processing. Then in the remainder of the book we will learn how to write FORTRAN programs to solve a variety of problems.

3.1 THE STEPS IN WRITING A PROGRAM

After an algorithm flowchart has been designed, we are ready to develop a FORTRAN program. The task of translating an algorithm flowchart into a FORTRAN program involves a process called coding. *Coding* is the writing out of those FORTRAN language statements that cause the same operations to be performed as are indicated by the corresponding flowchart steps. To do this coding, the person writing the program must know the rules for generating the FORTRAN statements that correspond with the various flowchart language steps. The primary purpose of this text is to present these rules and illustrate their use.

Forms, called *coding forms*, are available that help in the coding process. A coding form appears in Fig. 3.1. On this form is written the FORTRAN program that results from coding the flowchart of Fig. 2.6 Notice that a coding form has both vertical and horizontal lines. In addition, it has column numbers.

The FORTRAN language requires that statements appear in certain columns of an input record. In particular, FORTRAN statements must appear between columns 7 through 72, inclusive. To make reading a program listing easier, it is best to begin writing a new statement

Figure 3.1 Coding Form for the FORTRAN Program for Figure 2.6

80 COLUMN KEYPUNCH FORM

FOR CENTER USE ONLY

PROGRAM	DATE	JOB NO.	PUNCHING INSTRUCTIONS	GRAPHIC	PAGE OF
PROGRAMMER	PROJ. NO.	DATE		PUNCH	

```
C    *****  FØRTRAN PRØGRAM FØR THE ALGØRITHM ØF FIGURE 2.6 ****************
      REAL V1,V2,V3,LARGE
  501 FØRMAT(3E12.5)
  502 FØRMAT(/,1X,'V1=',E12.5,' V2=',E12.5,' V3=',E12.5)
  503 FØRMAT(1X,'LARGEST VALUE=',E12.5)
    1 READ(5,501,END=999) V1,V2,V3
      WRITE(6,502) V1,V2,V3
      LARGE=V1
      IF(V2.GT.LARGE) LARGE=V2
      IF(V3.GT.LARGE) LARGE=V3
      WRITE(6,503) LARGE
      GØ TØ 1
  999 STØP
      END
```

in column 7 of the input record. *Comment lines* can be used anywhere in a program to cause comments to be included in the program listing. Notice, however, that comment lines are not program statements. A FORTRAN comment line is indicated by placing the letter C in column 1 of a line. Except for being output in the listing, the information on a comment line is ignored by the FORTRAN compiler.

Sometimes the sixty-six positions between columns 7 and 72 of a line do not provide enough space for a FORTRAN statement. In this case, one or more succeeding lines can be used as *continuation lines*. To indicate that a line contains a continuation of the statement on the previous line, any character, other than a zero or a *blank*, is placed in column 6 of each such continuation line. The maximum number of continuation lines permitted for one statement varies for different dialects. All dialects permit at least five continuation lines, and most permit up to nineteen (WATFOR and WATFIV permit only five). Note that the line on which a statement *begins* must have a zero or a *blank* in column 6.

Columns 1 through 5 of a FORTRAN program line are reserved for statement labels. A statement label is simply a positive integer that is used to identify a particular statement. We will discuss statement labels and their uses in Ch. 4.

When the FORTRAN program has been completed, we are ready to *test* it on the computer to make sure that it produces correct results. To do this, two other things are required: (1) control statements and (2) input data values. These elements are also normally shown on the coding form. However, it is important to note that neither control statements or input data values are part of a FORTRAN program.

Control statements are required by computer operating systems to provide certain important information about the job to be processed. Among this information is:

1. The name and account number of the user.
2. The programming language in which that program is written.

3. Where the program ends and the input data begins.
4. Where the input data ends.

The program of Fig. 3.1 is shown again in Fig. 3.2, this time complete with control statements and input data. The control statements used are those for the popular WATFOR and WATFIV dialects of FORTRAN. These control statements are easily identified because they always have a dollar sign in column 1 of the line.

The first control statement identifies the user whose program is being run. If the account number is not one the system has recorded as the number of an authorized user, the job will not be run. Thus the $JOB control statement is used to identify users and also to keep account of how much of each of the computer resources are used by each user. The second control statement is the $ENTRY statement. This control statement has two functions. First, it indicates that there are no more program statements to be translated into machine language by the FORTRAN compiler. Second, it tells the computer that the program is to be executed and that everything that follows the $ENTRY statement is data. At this point execution is begun of the machine language program that resulted from translating the FORTRAN program. Execution of any READ statements in the FORTRAN program will cause data values to be input to main memory. Should the $IBSYS control statement be encountered when executing a READ statement, this results in an end-of-file condition.

The discussion of the previous paragraph raises an important point, which is that the solution of any problem using a computer involves two separate phases. First, a program written in FORTRAN (or some other programming language) is input to the computer and translated into a machine language program. During this time the data values have still not been input to main memory. After all of the FORTRAN program statements have been input and translated, execution of the resulting machine language program begins. During execution of this program, data values are input to the computer as

Figure 3.2 Coding Form for the Program of Figure 3.1 with Control Statements and Data

80 COLUMN KEYPUNCH FORM

```
$JØB   TERRY WALKER
C    *****  FØRTRAN PRØGRAM FØR THE ALGØRITHM ØF FIGURE 2.6 **************
      REAL V1, V2, V3, LARGE
  501 FØRMAT(3E12.5)
  502 FØRMAT(/, 1X, 'V1=',E12.5,' V2=',E12.5,' V3=',E12.5)
  503 FØRMAT(1X,'LARGEST VALUE=',E12.5)
    1 READ(5,501,END=999) V1,V2,V3
      WRITE(6,502) V1,V2,V3
      LARGE=V1
      IF(V2.GT.LARGE) LARGE=V2
      IF(V3.GT.LARGE) LARGE=V3
      WRITE(6,503) LARGE
      GØ TØ 1
  999 STØP
      END
$ENTRY
         4.5        6.87         9.5
         9.5        6.87         4.5
         9.5         4.5        6.87
$IBSYS
```

they are requested by READ statements. Therefore, data values are input to main memory only because the program contains statements which direct the computer to input data values.

As a final note on control statements, the types of control statements required vary for each model and type of computer and among computer installations. Therefore, the correct control statement information for the computer being used should be obtained from your instructor or computing center before a program is submitted for processing.

When the program, control statements, and input data values have been coded, the next step is to input them to the computer. In a student environment, the most popular method for doing this is to punch all of the statements into 80-column punched cards using a device called a keypunch. Information is represented on an 80-column punched card by the pattern of holes that is punched into a card. The widely used IBM Model 29 keypunch is pictured in Fig. 3.3. When cards are punched using a keypunch, the character represented by the holes in a column can be printed above that column. Thus, the accuracy of the information contained in a card can be visually verified by reading the printing on top of the card. After the program, control statements, and data values have been punched into cards, the cards are input to the computer using a card reader, such as the one shown in Fig. 1.3.

Other methods of inputting information to computers are gaining in popularity. One of these is to input information directly into computer memory from a typewriter terminal, such as the one pictured in Fig. 1.4. This method has the advantage of not requiring the intermediate step of inputting something onto some medium that will later be input to the computer. Other methods for inputting information are key-to-tape and key-to-disc devices. In these, information is entered into a device which writes the information on magnetic tape or magnetic disc. This information will then be input

Figure 3.3 An IBM Model 29 Keypunch(Courtesy of International Business Machines Corporation)

to the computer at a later time. Since punched cards are still the most popular method of information input in a student environment, we will devote a section of this chapter to the use of a keypunch.

As the FORTRAN program is input into the computer, all of the program statements are usually listed on an output device. In most cases, the output device used is a line printer, such as the one pictured in Fig. 1.7. After all of the program statements have been listed and the FORTRAN program has been translated into machine

Figure 3.4 Listing of Computer Output for the Program of Figure 3.2

```
$JOB R19081,10,DR WALKER      ,TIME=5,PAGES=30
C   ***** PROGRAM FOR ALGORITHM OF FIGURE 4.13M *************************
          REAL V1,V2,V3,LARGE
      501 FORMAT(3E12.5)
      502 FORMAT(/,1X,'V1=',E12.5,' V2=',E12.5,' V3=',E12.5)
      503 FORMAT(1X,'LARGEST VALUE=',E12.5)
        1 READ(5,501,END=999) V1,V2,V3
          WRITE(6,502) V1,V2,V3
          LARGE=V1
          IF(V2.GT.LARGE) LARGE=V2
          IF(V3.GT.LARGE) LARGE=V3
          WRITE(6,503) LARGE
          GO TO 1
      999 STOP
          END

$ENTRY

V1= 0.45000E 01 V2= 0.68700E 01 V3= 0.95000E 01
LARGEST VALUE= 0.95000E 01

V1= 0.95000E 01 V2= 0.68700E 01 V3= 0.45000E 01
LARGEST VALUE= 0.95000E 01

V1= 0.95000E 01 V2= 0.45000E 01 V3= 0.68700E 01
LARGEST VALUE= 0.95000E 01

COMPILATION:    CPU TIME= 0.4193 SECONDS, REAL TIME= 5 SECONDS.
EXECUTION:      CPU TIME= 0.1808 SECONDS, REAL TIME= 1 SECONDS.
CORE REQUIRED: OBJECT CODE= 624 BYTES, ARRAYS= 0 BYTES, UNUSED= 65,832 BYTES.
I/O REQUESTS:   CARDS READ= 20, CARDS PUNCHED= 0, LINES PRINTED= 28.
$IBSYS
```

language, execution of the program begins. Any output that occurs when program execution has begun is caused by execution of WRITE statements that are in the program. The output that results from the input and processing of the program and input data of Fig. 3.2 using the WATFOR compiler is shown in Fig. 3.4. Notice that the $JOB statement is output and is followed by the FORTRAN program statements. Next the $ENTRY statement is listed. The following six lines are output by the two WRITE statements in the program. Finally, there are four lines of summary statistics listed. These summary statistics tell us how much CPU time was required to compile and execute our program, how much memory was required to store our program, and how many input records were input and how many output lines were output.

3.2 USE OF A KEYPUNCH

The remainder of this chapter contains instructions on the use of IBM Model 26 and IBM Model 29 keypunches. These instructions are also generally applicable to the IBM Model 129 keypunch, although a few differences do exist. Since many cards will have to be punched during this course, you should sit down at a keypunch after reading this material and practice punching a few cards.

The *card input hopper* is located on the top right-hand side of the keypunch. This hopper contains a spring-loaded plate which holds blank cards against the feeding machanism. An adequate number of blank punched cards should be placed in the input hopper before punching begins. When a card is fed from the input hopper, it drops into what is called the *preregister station*, which is immediately below the input hopper. The card is moved left from the preregister station into a position where punching can begin. This position is called the *punch station*. As the card is punched, it moves leftward.

When the punching of a card is complete, it moves to the *read station*. The read station functions to read the punches of an already punched card during the process of duplicating a card. Notice that there are slots in the guides in the middle of the read station area. These slots permit a card to be inserted directly to the read station. When a card leaves the read station it flips upward into the *output stacker*, located in the upper left-hand portion of the keypunch.

There are several switches on the keypunch which require setting. The *on-off switch* is located under the keyboard table on the front right-hand side of the cabinet. The keypunch is turned on when this switch is in an up position. Near the upper-middle portion of the keypunch is a small rectangular window, beneath which is located the small V-shaped *program-unit switch*. For our purposes, this switch should always be set to the right. Just above the keypunch keyboard is a panel (see Fig. 3.5) which contains a series of *toggle switches*. On the Model 26 keypunch this panel contains three switches; on the Model 29 keypunch it contains six. All of these switches should be in a *down* position, except for the one labeled "print" which should be kept in an up position. On the Model 29 keypunch, pressing the rightmost switch into an up position causes all cards to be cleared out of the preregister, punch, and read

Figure 3.5 An IBM Model 29 Keypunch Switch Panel (Courtesy of International Business Machines Corporation)

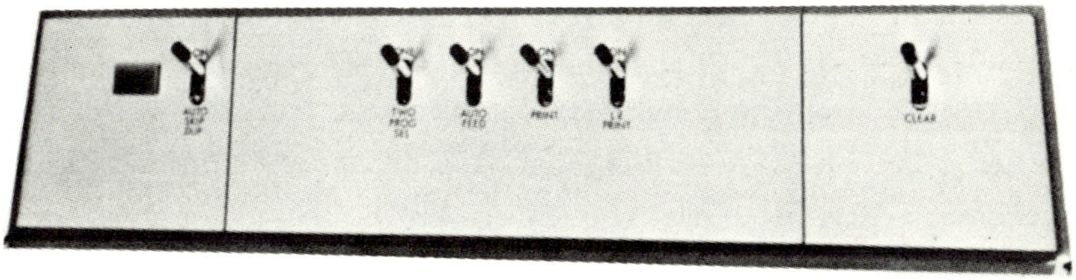

Figure 3.6 An IBM Model 29 Keypunch Keyboard(Courtesy of International Business Machines Corporation)

stations.

The *keyboard* of a keypunch is located on the keyboard table and is very similar in appearance, layout, and operation to the keyboard of a typewriter (see Fig. 3.6). The major differences are: (1) only upper-case (capital) alphabetic characters are available on a keypunch and (2) numeric and special characters are located on keys which also punch alphabetic characters. The bottom character shown on a key that contains multiple characters is punched into a card by depressing the key containing that character. The top character on such a key is punched by simultaneously depressing the NUMERIC key (labeled NUM on the Model 26) and the key containing the character to be punched. The column about to be punched can be easily determined by looking at the pointer inside the small rectangular window in the upper middle part of the keypunch. This pointer points to the number of the column which will be the next one punched.

In addition to the numeric, alphabetic, and special characters on the keyboard, there are also some *special-purpose keys*. These are:

1. DUP--Depressing this key causes the characters of the card passing through the read station to be punched into the corresponding card columns of the card passing through the punch station.
2. REL--Depressing this key causes a card to be released from the punch and read stations.
3. FEED--Depressing this key causes one card from the input hopper to be fed to the preregister stations.
4. REG--Depressing this key causes a card to be moved from the preregister to the punch station.
5. MULT PCH--Depressing this key prevents a card in the punch station from advancing, thus permitting more than one character to be punched in one column.
6. ERROR-RESET (Model 29 only)--Depressing this key releases a jammed keyboard.

The three most common types of keypunching tasks to be performed in a beginning course will be: (1) punching a series of cards, (2) punching one card, and (3) duplicating all or portions of a card. The steps to be following in *punching a series of cards* are:

1. Set the AUTO FEED toggle switch in an up position.
2. Depress the FEED key twice.
3. Begin punching information into cards. When the remainder of a card is not to be punched, simply depress the REL key. The resulting action will be to: (1) move the card in the read station to the output stacker, (2) move the card in the punch station to the read station, (3) move the card in the preregister station to the punch station, and (4) feed a blank card to the preregister station.
4. After the last card has been punched, push the rightmost toggle switch (only on the Model 29) up to clear all cards from the read, punch, and preregister stations. On the

Model 26 card punch, these stations are cleared out by setting the AUTO FEED switch in a down position and then alternately depressing the REL and REG keys three times.

For *punching only one card*, the steps to be followed are:

1. Be certain that the AUTO FEED toggle switch is in a down position.
2. Depress the FEED key followed by the REG key and punch the information into the card.
3. Perform step 4 from the above instructions for punching a series of cards.

Finally when the task is to *duplicate all or portions of a card*, the steps are:

1. Be certain that the AUTO FEED toggle switch is in a down position and that cards are cleared from all three stations.
2. Depress the FEED key.
3. Insert the card to be duplicated into the read station through the slots provided in the guides. Position this card so that its left-hand edge is about one inch to the left of the little roller.
4. Depress the REG key and duplicate any portion of the card desired by depressing the DUP key. Portions of a card may be duplicated at the same time that other portions of the same card are being punched.
5. Perform step 4 from the above instructions for punching a series of cards.

Notice that the ability to duplicate portions of a previously punched card provides an easy means of correcting an error or making a small change in a card that has already been punched. Duplicating a card is certainly to be preferred to repunching the entire card since it is a much faster procedure.

PROBLEMS

1. Using the model of keypunch available at your installation, punch a deck of cards for the program given in Fig. 3.2. Also punch the control cards for your installation and the data values and run the program on your computer.
2. Using the duplicate feature, revise the card in Fig. 3.2 containing the statement with the label 503 so that it reads

```
503 FORMAT(1X,'BIGGEST VALUE=',E14.5)
```

SUMMARY

1. The task of translating an algorithm flowchart into a FORTRAN program involves a process called coding.
2. Coding is the writing out of those FORTRAN language statements that cause the same operations to be performed as are indicated by the corresponding flowchart steps.
3. Coding forms are used for writing out the statements of a program.
4. FORTRAN statements must appear between columns 7 and 72 in an input record.
5. Control statements are required by computer operating systems to provide important information about a job to be processed.
6. The control statements and FORTRAN source statements are normally listed on the output medium along with the results produced by executing the program.
7. The important parts in the operation of a keypunch are: (a) the switch panel; (b) the card input and output hoppers; (c) the preregister, punch, and read stations; and (d) the keyboard.
8. The keyboard of a keypunch is similar to that of a typewriter.

CHAPTER 4

PROGRAM DESIGN I: FUNDAMENTAL CONCEPTS

The rules for writing programs using the FORTRAN IV programming language will be presented in this chapter and in chapters 5 and 9. A FORTRAN program, like a flowchart, is simply a way of representing an algorithm. Therefore, one method for learning how to write FORTRAN programs is to think primarily in terms of which FORTRAN statements are equivalent to the various flowchart-language steps. For example, in Sec. 4.5 you will learn that most flowchart-language decision boxes are equivalent to the FORTRAN-language IF statement.

Before beginning an examination of the FORTRAN IV programming language, several observations need to be made. First, several different versions of the FORTRAN programming language have existed: FORTRAN IV evolved in 1962 from FORTRAN II, which, in turn, evolved in 1958 from FORTRAN, the parent language introduced by IBM Corporation in 1956. In general, each successive version of FORTRAN has contained features not contained in the previous versions. Therefore, when learning FORTRAN IV, a person is also learning FORTRAN II. Anyone who knows FORTRAN IV and wants to program using FORTRAN II must simply learn which features of FORTRAN IV are not available in FORTRAN II. In this text those FORTRAN IV features which are not permitted in FORTRAN II will be identified from time to time. Throughout the remainder of this book FORTRAN IV will be called simply FORTRAN.

Second, FORTRAN programs must be translated into machine language by a computer program before they can be executed by a computer. The translator program is called a FORTRAN *compiler*, while the FORTRAN program translated and machine-language program generated are called *source* and *object programs*, respectively. Since each model of computer generally has a different machine language, it must also have a different compiler. In general, these compilers are designed so that execution of the object code generated for any legal FORTRAN program will produce the same results. However, variations in the design of different computer systems cause the results produced to vary among FORTRAN compilers. Thus, instead of one homogeneous language, there are many variations of FORTRAN. Each of these variations is called a *dialect* of the language. An attempt will be made in this text to introduce features that are common to a majority of the FORTRAN dialects currently in use. In particular, all FORTRAN features introduced in this book are accepted by the popular WATFOR and WATFIV compilers that are in use at many colleges and universities. When a question arises as to what is permitted in a particular dialect, however, the reference manual for your computer should always be consulted.

As a third point, FORTRAN contains a number of features that are included in the language for efficiency or for other special reasons. For example, there exist the COMMON statement, designed to provide for the efficient use of main memory, and the REWIND statement included to permit the control of magnetic tape drives. However, none of these special features are required for the FORTRAN implementations of the algorithms presented in this text.* A summary of the FORTRAN features introduced in this book is provided in Appendix A.

4.1 THE FORTRAN LANGUAGE

The alphabet of the FORTRAN language consists of three character classes:

1. The *alphabetic symbols*, which consist of the twenty-six upper-case letters of the English alphabet:

   A B C D E F G H I J K L M N O P Q R S T U V W X Y Z

*The FORTRAN statements introduced in this book have been restricted to those needed to program the algorithms developed in the main text, *FUNDAMENTALS OF COMPUTER SCIENCE: A PROBLEM-SOLVING APPROACH.*

2. The *numeric symbols*, which consist of the ten decimal digits:

   0 1 2 3 4 5 6 7 8 9

3. The *special symbols*, which are:

   + - * / = .) , ($ *blank* ' ;

   It should be noted that not all FORTRAN dialects permit the apostrophe and the semicolon.

In addition, two classes of symbol combinations exist in FORTRAN that replace position or single symbols in the flowchart language. These are:

1. The *exponentiation operator*, in which the symbol combination ** indicates the arithmetic operation of exponentiation (i.e., raising a value to a power).
2. *Keywords*, which are certain strings of alphabetic characters that define operations in the language.

There are several noteworthy differences between the flowchart language and FORTRAN. First, FORTRAN permits only the twenty-six upper-case letters of the English alphabet--the twenty-six lower-case letters are not allowed. Recall that in the flowchart language both upper-case and lower-case letters of the English alphabet are permitted. Second, in the flowchart language the conventional mathematical way of indicating exponentiation is used. That is, A raised to the B power is denoted by showing B as a superscript on A, thus: A^B. Since a superscript cannot be denoted on a punched card or terminal, the operation of exponentiation is denoted in FORTRAN by using a pair of asterisks: what appears as A^B in the flowchart language becomes A**B in FORTRAN. Third, keywords are used in FORTRAN to replace flowchart boxes and symbols. For example, a decision box in the flowchart language is replaced by an IF statement in FORTRAN. There are, however, more keywords in FORTRAN than flowchart symbols in the flowchart language.

As in the flowchart language, the characters of FORTRAN can be used to form words. Similarly, words can be combined to form

FORTRAN *statements*. The four basic types of statements in FORTRAN are:

1. Processing statements.
2. Control statements.
3. Declarative statements.
4. Input/Output statements.

The use of each of these statement types is the same in FORTRAN as in the flowchart language.

In FORTRAN, statements are combined to form program segments. A *program segment* is analogous to a flowchart for an algorithm or a subalgorithm. FORTRAN *programs* consist of one or more program segments. Every FORTRAN program has one program segment that is thought of as the main program segment. Any other program segments within a program must be subprograms to this main program segment. Every program developed in Chs. 4 through 8 will consist of only one program segment--the main one. Then in Ch. 9 subprograms will be introduced.

The last statement physically of every program segment must be the nonexecutable END statement. In Sec. 4.3 it is pointed out that the FORTRAN program END statement is not analogous to the STOP statement of a flowchart.

The executable statements in a FORTRAN program are normally executed in the sequence in which they appear in a program segment. Program execution always begins with the first executable statement in the main program segment. FORTRAN programs also contain nonexecutable statements. These statements are usually declarative statements. As each statement is introduced in this book, it will be designated as being an executable or nonexecutable statement. A summary of statement types and whether they are executable or nonexecutable is given in Appendix A.

Finally, a FORTRAN *statement label* is an unsigned integer

constant that, for many dialects, lies in the interval* $1 \leq \mathit{label} \leq 32767$. Statement labels may appear on any executable or FORMAT statement, and may be entered anywhere in columns 1 through 5, inclusive. A statement label attached to an executable statement is analogous to an in-connector in the flowchart language. It follows that only statements that must be referenced need to be given statement labels. In addition, statement labels need not have values that are in any particular sequence. The use of statement labels will be discussed in Sections 4.4 and 4.5.

4.2 FORTRAN CONSTANTS AND VARIABLES

4.2.1 CONSTANTS

Two basic classes of constants are permitted in FORTRAN: (1) numeric constants and (2) string constants. The two types of FORTRAN numeric constants are:† (1) integer constants and (2) real constants. In FORTRAN the difference between integer and real values is quite important because integer and real constants are represented differently in computer main storage.‡ Therefore, care must be taken in deciding when to use an integer constant and when to use a real constant.

A FORTRAN *integer constant* is any signed or unsigned decimal number that does not contain a decimal point. The following are

---

*Some dialects of FORTRAN permit statement labels to be in the interval

$$1 \leq \mathit{label} \leq 99999$$

†We will ignore hexadecimal constants in this book. Double precision constants will be covered in Sec. 10.1, while complex and logical constants are discussed in Appendix D.

‡Integer constants are generally represented in main memory as binary integers; real constants, on the other hand, are represented internally as floating-point numbers.

examples of valid integer constants:

```
+123     -12     45678923     -23482     0
```

The magnitude allowed for valid integer constants varies from dialect to dialect. For example, the IBM System/360 and 370 permit as integers any number n which lies in the interval

$$-2147483648 \leq n \leq 2147483647$$

The smallest interval permitted for integers is in IBM 1130 FORTRAN, where the value of n must lie in the interval

$$-32767 \leq n \leq 32767$$

Notice that commas are not permitted in an integer constant. Examples of invalid FORTRAN integer constants are:

```
12,356  (contains a comma)
  -2.6  (contains a decimal point)
   0.0  (contains a decimal point)
```

A *real constant* is any signed or unsigned decimal number that contains a decimal point. Examples of valid real constants are:

```
123.456    -0.0000000052    +4.63    -10.0
8652.45    -1478590000.0    0.046      0.0
```

In addition, a real constant may contain the letter E followed by a signed or unsigned integer constant. When the letter E appears as a part of a real constant, then the value to the left of the E is to be multiplied by 10 raised to the power of the integer following the E. Thus, the above examples of valid real constants can be restated, in order, as:

```
1.23456E2      -0.52E-8        +46.3E-01    -10.0E+00
0.865245E+4    -1.47859E+09    4.6E-2        0.0E0
```

Use of the optional E is particularly useful for writing a real constant which is very large or very small in magnitude. As the above examples indicate, there is quite a bit of flexibility as to the placement of the decimal point and the form of the exponent of 10 in writing a real number using the E option. A real constant written in this form is often called a floating-point constant.

The largest and smallest magnitude permitted for real constants also varies among dialects. For the IBM System/360 or 370, the magnitude m of a real number either must be zero or must lie in the approximate interval $10^{-79} \leq m \leq 10^{75}$. In the IBM 1130, Univac 1106, 1108, and 1110, and the Honeywell 6000 series computers, the magnitude m of a real number either must be zero or must lie in the approximate interval $10^{-38} \leq m \leq 10^{38}$. In addition, the number of digits in a real number, and the number of digits in the integer to the right of the E, are limited in all FORTRAN dialects. For example, no more than two decimal digits may appear to the right of the E and no more than seven significant digits may appear in a real constant in the dialect for the IBM System/360 or 370. Note that commas may not appear anywhere in a real constant. Some examples of invalid real constants are:

23	(no decimal point)
4,659.87	(contains a comma)
-2.34E2.5	(real constants not permitted to the right of the E)
465E2	(no decimal point)
2.34E	(no integer constant to the right of the E)

A *string constant* is expressed in FORTRAN in one of two ways. The first method of representing a string constant uses the letter H preceded by an unsigned positive integer constant n and followed by a string consisting of n valid FORTRAN characters. The value preceding the H must be an exact count of the number of characters in the string. Note that each blank space in a string constant also counts as one character. Examples of valid FORTRAN string constants are:

```
26HTHIS IS A STRING CONSTANT.
16HDON'T YOU DO IT.
9H-124.67E5
3H234
```

The last two string constants cannot be confused with numeric constants since they are preceded by a length count *n* and the letter H.

A second way of stating a string constant is by enclosing a string consisting of any valid FORTRAN symbols in between a pair of apostrophes.* Since an apostrophe is a valid FORTRAN symbol, two consecutive apostrophes must be used to indicate the apostrophe symbol. The above examples of valid FORTRAN string constants would be written using this second method as:

```
'THIS IS A STRING CONSTANT.'
'DON''T YOU DO IT.'
'-124.67E5'
'234'
```

The major advantage of this second method of writing string constants is that a count of the number of symbols in the string is not needed. Unfortunately, some dialects of FORTRAN do not permit string constants to be represented using the second method. In such dialects the first method for representing string constants must be used.

As a final note, the maximum number of characters permitted in a string constant varies from dialect to dialect. In fact, this will prove to be a very limiting factor in the dialect independence of certain algorithms implemented in FORTRAN. These limitations will be explored further in Sec. 4.3.2.

---

*In some CDC dialects, asterisks are used instead of apostrophes to enclose strings. Similarly, in some XDS dialects, dollar signs may be used to indicate the start and finish of a string.

4.2.2 Variables and Type Statements

A *variable name* in FORTRAN consists of a sequence of from one to six alphabetic or numeric symbols, where the first symbol must be alphabetic.[*] Examples of valid FORTRAN variable names are:

```
A      ALPHA      S23      IJ      Z45K
```

Variable names may not contain any special characters. Some examples of invalid variable names are:

5ABC	(first symbol not alphabetic)
FICATAX	(more than six characters)
PRCE/Q	(special characters not permitted)
AL FOX	(special characters not permitted)

While there are two classes of constants permitted in FORTRAN, all variable names are declared to be numeric. The *two types* of *numeric variable* names permitted in FORTRAN are: (1) integer variables and (2) real variables.[†] When discussing the *type of a variable name*, what we really mean is the *type of constants* that can be associated with that variable name. A variable name may be given a type in one of two ways: (1) explicitly or (2) implicitly.[‡] The type of a variable name may be declared *explicitly* by writing a variable name in the list of a type statement. The two kinds of FORTRAN type statements to be discussed here are INTEGER and REAL type statements. Any variable name that appears in an INTEGER statement will be defined to be an *integer variable* throughout that program segment. Similarly, any

---

[*] Some dialects permit variable names to consist of a maximum of five symbols, while other dialects permit up to eight symbols in a name.

[†] Double precision variables will be introduced in Sec. 10.1, while complex and logical variables will be discussed in Appendix D.

[‡] FORTRAN II does not permit type statements. Therefore, all variable names must be given their type implicitly.

variable name that appears in a REAL statement is defined to be of *type real* for the entire program segment. An integer or real type statement consists of the keyword REAL or the keyword INTEGER followed by a list of FORTRAN variable names. Examples of a REAL and an INTEGER type statement are:

```
REAL  IJ23,K,AB25,MNOP
INTEGER  AB5,R2,C35,I
```

Type statements must appear at the beginning of a program segment and are nonexecutable.

The type of a variable name can be declared implicitly only when the variable name has not been given in a type statement variable-name list. *Implicit* type declaration is indicated by the first letter used in a variable name. When the *first letter* of a variable name is an I, J, K, L, M, or N, then the variable name is of *type integer*. Otherwise, the variable name is of *type real*. Examples of implicitly declared integer variable names are

```
I      JKL      N      K43A      IABC
```

while examples of implicitly declared real variable names are:

```
A32      ZIJK      R      VT15      G
```

In all programs of this text, the type of a variable name will always be declared explicitly in a type statement. There are two reasons for the explicit declaration of variables. First, the beginning programmer should think explicitly about the type of values that each variable name should have associated with it. Second, the errors introduced by mixing variable names of different types are often quite difficult to discover. Explicit type declaration is one way of minimizing the frequency of these errors. In general, when values are always going to be integers, then integer variables should be used. When the possibility exists that a value may have a fractional portion, however, then variables should be declared as real variables. Thus, a variable used to count the number of repetitions of a loop or the number of items in a set should be declared as an integer variable since fractional values are not possible. Quantities such as distance and dollars, on the other hand, should be declared as type real since they often involve fractional parts.

As this point the reader might ask how string variables are going to be represented in FORTRAN since only numeric variables are allowed. The solution is easy, since string constants can be stored as the values of either real or integer variables. However, caution is needed because the variable type selected for representing string constants in a particular program must be used consistently when operations are being performed on the string values. The reason for this will be given in Sec. 4.3.2, where we further discuss the representation of string constants.

PROBLEMS

1. Identify the valid FORTRAN constants in the following list and determine the type of each valid constant.

a. 567.85	i. 'DON''T'	q. 45.3709
b. -475.8E-05	j. ''''	r. .58E-2.4
c. 'GO OUT'	k. 475E3	s. GOLLYGEE'
d. -5.76	l. +9.5E456	t. -0.0005E4
e. 'COW'	m. -5.6789E+4	u. 567,432.1E4
f. 47	n. -75,432	v. 'IT'TIS'
g. -395	o. +5.2E+85	w. 58745.E30
h. 5.6E	p. '5E40'	x. 'BUGOUT'

2. Identify the valid FORTRAN variable names in the following list.

a. C45678	f. A**2	k. M
b. JBIG	g. SUM	l. 3LABT
c. DOL/YR	h. HI BOB	m. VAL-OF
d. SYS360	i. FORTRAN	n. U/TEXS
e. A	j. SOCCER	o. SAM

3. Using the rules for implicit type declaration, identify the valid real and valid integer variables in Prob. 2.

4. Write the necessary type statements to declare the valid variables in parts *a* through *h* of Prob. 2 to be real and the valid variables in parts *i* through *o* to be integer.

4.3 FORTRAN ASSIGNMENT STATEMENT

The START statement of the flowchart language has no counterpart in FORTRAN. This is because execution of a FORTRAN program always begins with the first executable statement appearing in the main program segment. The counterpart of the flowchart-language STOP statement is the FORTRAN statement

```
STOP
```

which results in termination of program execution. While all dialects permit any number of STOP statements in a program segment, we will never have more than one in any of the programs we write. Because they are executable, STOP statements may appear anywhere in a program. Be careful not to confuse the FORTRAN language STOP statement with the END statement; they do not serve the same purpose. The END statement is nonexecutable and must physically be the last statement in a program segment. The reason for this is that the END statement is used to signal the FORTRAN compiler that there are no more statements in the program segment of which it is a part.

The FORTRAN assignment statement has a form similar to the flowchart-language assignment statement. The only difference is that in FORTRAN the equal sign (=) replaces the left-pointing arrow (←) as the *assignment operator*. Thus, the general form of a FORTRAN assignment statement is:

variable = expression

In FORTRAN, as in the flowchart language, execution of an assignment statement causes the expression on the right of the assignment operator to be evaluated to a single value. This value is then stored as the value of the variable on the left of the assignment operator. Notice that in FORTRAN the equal sign is used as the assignment operator. Therefore, it should no longer be called an equal sign, but rather is called the assignment operator.

The one major difference in implementation between flowchart-language and FORTRAN assignment statements relates to the appearance of string expressions to the right of the assignment operator. In most FORTRAN dialects, a string constant may not appear to the right of the assignment operator. Thus, only a variable which has a string constant as a value may appear to the right of the assignment operator. Methods for solving problems under this restriction will be discussed in Sec. 4.3.2.

An example of a FORTRAN assignment statement is:

```
A=13
```

Execution of this statement results in the integer constant 13 being assigned as the value of the variable A. This statement is read: *Assign the integer constant 13 to be the new value of the variable A.* As in the flowchart language, a variable in FORTRAN may have only one value at a time. Thus, execution of this statement causes the previous value of A to be lost.

Another type of expression is one that consists of a single variable. An example is:

```
A=B
```

Execution of this statement results in assigning the current value of the variable B to be the new value of A. After this assignment is completed, the variables A and B will both have the same value. This is because the assignment operation does not affect the values of variables to the right of the assignment operator. Note that there is no way of knowing whether the value assigned to A is a real, integer, or string value. It is only in the context of the entire program that this can be determined.

This leads to a very important point about FORTRAN assignment statements--a point which when ignored can cause errors that are often difficult to detect. When the type of constant that results from evaluation of the expression to the right of the assignment operator is different from the type of variable to the left of the assignment operator, FORTRAN automatically *converts* the constant to the type of the variable to the left of the assignment operator. In the case where the variable to the left is of type real and the expression to the right is of type integer, the integer value is converted to a real value before the assignment operation is completed. For example, if A is declared to be of type real, execution of the statement

```
A=13
```

causes the integer constant 13 to be converted to a real value before it is assigned to A.

When the variable to the left of the assignment operator is of type integer and the expression to the right is of type real, the real value is truncated at the decimal point and the resulting value is converted to an integer constant prior to assignment. For example, if K is declared to be of type integer, execution of the statement

```
K=13.52
```

causes truncation of the real constant, with the resulting integer value 13 being assigned as the value of K. When the value of a variable is a string constant, this conversion changes the value of the string constant in an unpredictable way. Thus, a good rule to follow in writing FORTRAN assignment statements is always to be sure that the type of the variable and expression are the same. In all examples presented in this text, the type of the variable and the type of the expression will always be the same.

As in the flowchart language, the expression on the right of the assignment operator may be more complex than the expressions in the above examples. Therefore, the formation of arithmetic expressions will now be studied in greater detail.

4.3.1 ARITHMETIC EXPRESSIONS

A FORTRAN *arithmetic expression* consists of a sequence of numeric variables and constants that are combined using arithmetic operators and numeric functional operators. Parentheses may be used in an arithmetic expression to indicate the order in which operations are to be carried out. That is, parentheses will be used to group certain sequences of operators and operands into subexpressions.

The rules for forming FORTRAN arithmetic expressions are:

1. *Addition* and *subtraction* are indicated by the operators + and -, respectively, as is the case in the flowchart language.
2. *Multiplication* is indicated by the operator *, which must always separate the two operands. Thus, an * is used in FORTRAN in the same way that a · is used in the flowchart language.
3. *Division* is indicated by the operator /, which appears between the two operands in the same way it did in the flowchart language.
4. *Exponentiation* is indicated by the operator **, where the pair of asterisks is treated as a single symbol which represents the exponentiation operator.
5. The *numeric functional operators* are indicated by the use of special names, as is the case in the flowchart language. The names used for several of the FORTRAN numeric functional

Figure 4.1 FORTRAN Numeric Functional Operators

Operation	Name	Type of Argument Expression	Type of Resulting Value
Absolute Value	ABS	Real	Real
	IABS	Integer	Integer
Exponential	EXP	Real	Real
Natural Logarithm	ALOG	Real	Real
Base-10 Logarithm	ALOG10	Real	Real
Square Root	SQRT	Real	Real
Conversion	IFIX	Real	Integer
	FLOAT	Integer	Real

operators are given in Fig. 4.1.* A complete table of the more widely used FORTRAN numeric functional operators appears in Appendix B. These FORTRAN functional operators are used in essentially the same way as are the flowchart-language functional operators. One difference, however, is that in FORTRAN parentheses are used instead of square brackets to enclose the argument expression. In general, it is a good idea not to use the names of functional operators as variable names in FORTRAN programs. Notice in the tables of numeric functional operators in Fig. 4.1 and Appendix B that several functions have two versions, one for integer arguments and one for real arguments. It is important that the proper functional operator be used for the type of operand involved.

---

*The names of most of the numeric functional operators in FORTRAN II are different from those given in this table.

6. Two operators may not appear consecutively in an expression.

Thus, the rules for forming FORTRAN arithmetic expressions are essentially the same as those for the flowchart language. To summarize, the only changes are:

1. The flowchart-language multiplication operator · is replaced by the * in FORTRAN arithmetic expressions.
2. Exponentiation is indicated implicitly in the flowchart language by the position of the exponent, while in FORTRAN it is indicated explicitly by the use of the exponentiation operator **.
3. The names of some of the numeric functional operators of the flowchart language are different in FORTRAN. In addition, argument expressions in FORTRAN are enclosed in parentheses rather than square brackets. Also, in FORTRAN the type of the argument must be considered in selecting a function to use.

The precedence rules used by most FORTRAN dialects are the same as those given for the flowchart language,* with one exception--the evaluation of consecutive exponentiation operations. That is, some FORTRAN dialects evaluate an expression of the type A**B**C from left to right while others evaluate it from right to left. Still other dialects consider this expression to be ambiguous, and therefore in error. Consequently, parentheses should always be used in such cases to make the order of evaluation explicit. Thus, the preceding expression should be written as A**(B**C) if the intent is to evaluate B**C first and use the resulting value as an exponent for A. On the other hand, the expression should be written as (A**B)**C if the intent is to raise A**B to the C power.

The precedence rules for evaluating flowchart-language arithmetic expressions should be reviewed at this point. In Fig. 4.2 the FORTRAN equivalents to the flowchart-language arithmetic expressions

---

*See Fig. 2.3 or Fig. 4.3M.

Figure 4.2 FORTRAN Equivalents of Flowchart-Language Arithmetic Expressions of Figure 2.4 (or Figure 4.4M)

Flowchart-Language Arithmetic Expression	FORTRAN Equivalent
$X + A - 2 \cdot BAD$	X+A-2*BAD
$(X - A/C)^{Y} \cdot F$	(X-A/C)**Y*F
$(X - A)/C^{Y} \cdot F$	(X-A)/C**Y*F
$X - A/C^{Y} \cdot F$	X-A/C**Y*F
$(X^{Y})^{E}$	(X**Y)**E
$X^{Y^{E}}$	X**(Y**E)
$(X + E)^{-sqrt[C]}$	(X+E)**(-SQRT(C))
$A - B^{2}/C \cdot D \cdot abs[A]$	A-B**2/C*D*ABS(A)
$sqrt[2 \cdot log10[D^{2} \cdot C]]$	SQRT(2.0*ALOG10(D**2*C))
X^{-A}	X**(-A)

of Fig. 2.4* are given. Notice that the flowchart-language expressions are also reproduced in Fig. 4.2. These examples should be studied carefully. Observe that parentheses have been included in the FORTRAN expressions in examples 7 and 10 to avoid violating the rule that two operators may not appear consecutively.

Another consideration that enters into constructing FORTRAN arithmetic expressions stems from the fact that there are both integer and real numeric constants and variables in FORTRAN. Recall from Sec. 4.3 that conversion takes place when the variable to the

---

*For those using the main text, see Fig. 4.4M.

left of an assignment operator is of a different type from the expression on the right. Similarly, there must be concern for mixing values of different types in arithmetic expressions. Some FORTRAN dialects do not permit so-called mixed-mode expressions, in which constants and variables of different types appear in the same expression. In these dialects, mixed-mode expressions result in an error message.

Many FORTRAN dialects do permit mixed-mode expressions, with automatic conversion occurring when a conflict in data types is found. To avoid difficulty, however, the rule that integer and real values will never be mixed in an arithmetic expression should be adopted. This rule will be used throughout this book. For example, let us assume that A and N are declared to be of types real and integer, respectively. Then, the flowchart statement $N \leftarrow N - 1$ should be written in FORTRAN as

```
N=N-1
```

instead of as

```
N=N-1.0
```

since 1.0 is a real constant while N is an integer variable. Similarly the flowchart assignment statement $A \leftarrow A/5$ should be written in FORTRAN as

```
A=A/5.0
```

rather than as

```
A=A/5
```

since 5 is an integer constant while A is a real variable.

There are cases, however, in which a real value and an integer value might logically be used in the same expression. For example, if A represents a sum of values and N represents the number of values the average can be computed using the statement $A \leftarrow A/N$. But in FORTRAN this would result in a mixed-mode expression. To avoid this, the FLOAT conversion numeric functional operator can be used to convert the value of N to be a real quantity. The expression should thus be written in FORTRAN as

```
A=A/FLOAT(N)
```

Notice that the variable N was not changed to a real variable nor was the value of N in main memory converted to a real constant. Instead, the value of N is fetched from memory as an integer and converted to a real constant during evaluation of the above expression. In a similar manner, the IFIX functional operator can be used to convert a real value to integer mode.

An important exception exists to the above rule on mixed-mode expressions in that an integer constant or an integer variable may be used as the exponent of a real variable or a real constant without creating a mixed-mode expression. In fact, when the exponent to which a real value is to be raised is an integer, then an integer constant or integer variable should be used. Thus, for the real variables A and B, the form

```
A=B**3
```

is to be preferred to

```
A=B**3.0
```

The reason is that in FORTRAN the first statement would be evaluated as

```
A=B*B*B
```

while the second statement would be evaluated as

```
A=EXP(3.0*ALOG(B))
```

Since any real value raised to a real power is evaluated in FORTRAN by using a logarithm, it is not legal to raise a negative value to a real power.

Another point that needs to be made relates to the results produced by integer division. Since a fractional portion cannot be represented using an integer variable or an integer constant, integer division always produces a truncated result. Thus, for the integer variable A,

```
A=7/5
```

produces a result of 1, as does

```
A=9/5
```

In other words, there is no rounding in FORTRAN integer division. As a result, the truncation functional operator of the flowchart language can be accomplished in FORTRAN simply by performing integer division.

Finally, care must be taken not to confuse an exponentiation operator with the E-type constant. Thus, 10.0**3 should not be confused with 1.0E3, since the first form is the operation of multiplying 10.0 times itself two times, while the latter is the real constant 1000.0. The results are equivalent, but it is more efficient to use the constant since no evaluation is required.

As a conclusion to this section, Fig. 4.3* contains a flowchart for the simple problem of summing three numbers, with the corresponding FORTRAN program appearing in Fig. 4.4. Notice that the type statement appears first to declare all variables used in the program. Then the four assignment statements are given which correspond with those appearing in flowchart boxes 2 and 3. Next the STOP statement is included to halt program execution. Finally, an END statement

---

*For those using the main text, this flowchart is the same one that appears in Fig. 4.5M.

Figure 4.3 Algorithm Flowchart for Summing Three Numbers

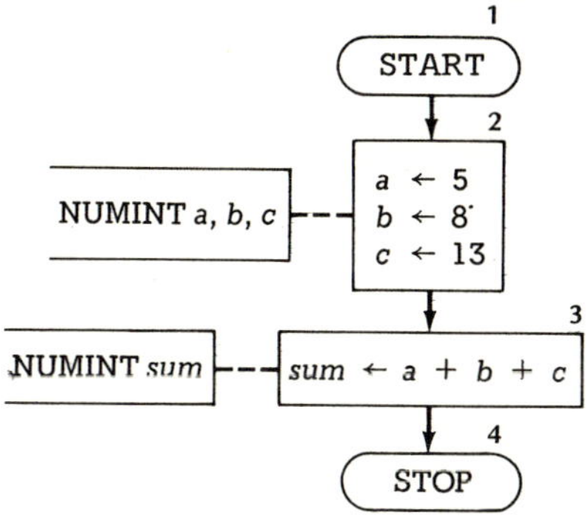

appears to signal the FORTRAN compiler that there are no other statements in this program. As was the case with the flowchart from which this program was coded, this program serves no useful purpose because it produces no output. That is, the computer will never output the sum of the three values because a statement has not been included in the program to do this.

Figure 4.4 FORTRAN Program for Flowchart of Figure 4.3

```
C   ***** PROGRAM FOR ALGORITHM OF FIGURE 4.5M ***************************
      INTEGER A,B,C,SUM
      A=5
      B=8
      C=13
      SUM=A+B+C
      STOP
      END
```

4.3.2 String Values and the DATA Statement

String values are very difficult to represent and process using FORTRAN. Moreover, most FORTRAN dialects do not allow string constants to appear in assignment statements. Therefore, in this section the problems related to the processing of strings will be discussed and the method for solving these problems will be introduced.

The first problem encountered in processing strings in FORTRAN is that string constants *cannot* appear in assignment statements. This being the case, it seems as though FORTRAN provides no way to assign string values to a variable. This is not quite true, however, in that the DATA statement does permit the assignment of string constants to variables. In addition, the input/output statements that will be discussed in Sec. 4.4 permit string values to be input and output. Also, recall from Sec. 4.3 that a real or integer variable that has a string constant as a value may appear to the right of the assignment operator. That is, a string constant that is the value of one variable can be assigned to be the value of another variable.

The DATA statement is a nonexecutable FORTRAN statement that tells the FORTRAN compiler to give variables initial values. Assuming that A, B, and C are declared to be real variables, the statement

```
DATA  A,B,C/2.3,45.2E-5,-47.8/
```

causes the compiler to assign the real constants 2.3, 45.2E-5, and -47.8 as the initial values of the variables A, B, and C, respectively Thus, a DATA statement consists of the keyword DATA followed by a list of variables and a list of constants. Notice that the list of constants in a DATA statement must be enclosed between a pair of slashes. In addition, the variable names in the variable name list and the constants in the constant list must be separated from each other by commas. Constants are associated with variables in a left-to-right order.

One DATA statement may contain more than one set of variable names and associated constant lists. In addition, variables of both integer and real types may be assigned values in the same list. For a second example, assume that A, B, and C are declared to be real variables and X, Y, and Z are declared to be integer variables. Then the statement

```
DATA  A,C,Z/-2.0,4.0E10,5/, Y,B,X/0,4.3,-4/
```

causes the variables A, B, C, X, Y, and Z to be assigned the values -2.0, 4.3, 4.0E10, -4, 0, and 5, respectively. Notice that the second variable name list is preceded by a comma. In addition, real constants are specified for real variables and integer constants for integer variables.

In general, a DATA statement may have any number of paired variable name and constant lists. Because the values are assigned by the compiler, DATA statements are not processed during program execution. Thus, the DATA statement only provides a one-time means of assigning values to variables. Many FORTRAN compilers also require that DATA statements appear at the beginning of a program segment, immediately following the type statements.

Returning to our discussion of string expressions, we now see that the DATA statement provides a means of assigning string values to a variable. For example, the value 'CAR' can be assigned to a variable named M by using* the statement

```
DATA  M/'CAR'/
```

As long as the variable M is not assigned another value during

---

*If a compiler permits only the use of H-type string constants, then this statement should be written as

```
DATA  M/3HCAR/
```

execution of the program, it continues to have the string constant 'CAR' as its value. This value can be used anywhere in the program. For example, execution of the statement

```
A=M
```

causes the string constant 'CAR' to be assigned as the value of the variable A. After execution of this assignment statement, both A and M have the string constant 'CAR' as their values.

Another problem occurs because the maximum number of symbols which a string constant may contain is limited,* and it varies for different FORTRAN dialects. The maximum number of symbols permitted in a single constant ranges from two to ten, depending on the dialect. Therefore, in writing a FORTRAN program, a programmer must either be familiar with the limit for the dialect being used, or use a number which is permitted in all dialects. When a real variable is used to hold a string constant, all FORTRAN dialects permit the storage of four-symbol string constants. Thus, no more than four symbols are used in the string constants processed in the programs in this book. When the string constants to be processed are known to consist of only one character, integer variables are used, because on some computers this reduces the amount of computer memory and the processing time required. When using integer variables, however, caution must be exercised since some dialects permit only string constants with two characters to be represented.

When there are fewer characters in a string constant than the number of characters permitted in the memory location to which that constant has been assigned, then the location is filled with blanks on the right. For example, suppose that the FORTRAN dialect being

---

*An exception to this rule is that there is no practical maximum length for string constants which appear in FORMAT statements. See the discussion in Sec. 4.4.

used permits the storage of four-symbol strings as the values of real variables. Then the value stored for ZC in the statement

```
DATA  ZC/'A'/
```

would be 'A___' (that is, the letter A followed by three blanks). Thus, string constants are placed in storage left-justified (that is, aligned vertically at the left), and are filled with blanks as necessary for justification at the right to the total length of the memory location.

PROBLEMS

5. For those using the main text, write the FORTRAN arithmetic expressions that correspond with the flowchart-language expressions developed in Prob. 4 of Ch. 4M.

6. Make the necessary changes to correct any errors that may exist in the following FORTRAN assignment statements. Assume that ABC, X, Y, and Z are real variables and I, J, and K are integer variables.

   a. `ABC=X**Y-2*Z`
   b. `X=SQRT(I*J)+4.5E3*ABC`
   c. `J=I*IFIX(ABC-4)`
   d. `Z=X**ABC**2-ALOG(X*I+5)`
   e. `K=I**2**J-5.0*ABC**4+FLOAT(K)`

7. Using a DATA statement, initialize the variables in the following statements with the values shown.

```
      REAL    A,B,C,D,E,F
      INTEGER  G,H,I,J,K,L
```

```
A=0.123E-4     B='TEST'     C='FORT'     D='RAN'
E=52.34        F=+4.2E23    G=523        H=-7658
I='LONG'       J='JOHN'     K=0          L=426783
```

4.4 FORTRAN INPUT/OUTPUT STATEMENTS

The FORTRAN equivalent to the flowchart-language GET box is the READ statement, which is executable. An example of a READ statement is:

```
READ(5,100) A,B,C
```

This statement directs the computer to read three values from input records and assign them to the variables A, B, and C, in that order. The first number in between the parentheses, the 5, indicates that the input record containing the values to be input is a punched card. The second number, the 100, is a label constant which specifies the FORMAT statement to be used in performing the READ operations.

The flowchart-language PUT box is coded in FORTRAN using the WRITE statement, which is also executable. An example of a WRITE statement is:

```
WRITE(6,105) X,Y
```

This statement causes the computer to produce an output record that contains the values of the variables X and Y. The number 6 specifies that the output record containing the values to be output is to be generated by a line printer. The value 105 specifies which FORMAT statement is to be used.

The general forms of the READ and WRITE statements are:*

READ(*device*,*format*) *variable list*
WRITE(*device*,*format*) *variable list*

In these statements, *device* is an unsigned positive integer constant or integer variable that specifies the number of the logical device

---

*Some FORTRAN dialects provide input and output statements that do not require FORMAT statements. Two of the more popular of these are discussed in Appendix C.

that is to be used for input or output. While the numbers assigned to different devices vary from computer to computer, the values 5 and 6 are fairly standard device numbers for referring to the card reader and line printer, respectively.* These values will be used throughout this manual since most beginning students currently use punched cards to input their programs and line printers for their output. Should you be using a terminal, you would simply use different device numbers to refer to the terminal you are using.

The value of *format* in a READ or WRITE statement must be the label of the FORMAT statement that is to be used in processing that READ or WRITE statement. The FORMAT statement is a nonexecutable statement that has the general form

FORMAT(*format list*)

where *format list* contains a sequence of format codes that are separated from each other by commas. The FORTRAN format codes used in this manual are given in Fig. 4.5. The purpose of the format codes is to indicate how information appears in input records (usually cards) or how it is to appear in output records (usually printed on paper forms by the line printer). For all of these specifications, *w* and *d* are unsigned integer constants. The value of *w* indicates the width in characters of a field, while *d* indicates the location of the decimal point in the number.

Let us first learn how the READ and FORMAT statements interact. The six format codes that generally might appear in a format list associated with a READ statement are I*w*, F*w*.*d*, E*w*.*d*, A*w*, *w*X, and /. The I*w*, F*w*.*d*, and E*w*.*d* codes are used to input numeric constants from input records. The numeric values must be right-justified in a field *w* columns wide in the input record.

---

*Caution should be exercised since some computers use different device numbers. For example, the IBM 1130 uses 2 and 3 for the 1442 card reader and 1132 line printer, respectively.

Figure 4.5 FORTRAN Input/Output FORMAT Codes

Format Code*	Variable Type	Data Constant Type or Other Usage
I*w*	Integer	Integer constant
F*w*.*d*	Real	Real constant
E*w*.*d*	Real	E-type real constant
A*w*	Real or integer	String constant without apostrophes
' ' or *w*H	None	String constant without apostrophes
*w*X	None	Horizontal spacing
/	None	Record terminator

*The maximum values that *w* and *d* may assume vary among dialects. Therefore, you should consult the FORTRAN reference manual for your computer to determine these maximum values.

The format list is used in processing a READ statement as follows. First, the format list is scanned from left to right until the first I, F, E, or A code is found. This code is used to specify the editing of the first data constant, which is being input as the value of the first variable of the READ statement variable list. Any non-I, non-F, non-E, and non-A codes that precede the first I, F, E, or A codes are executed as they are found. The above process is then repeated for subsequent READ statement variables until either: (1) the last variable in the list is processed and (a) an I, F, E, or A format code is found in the format list, or (b) the end of the format list is reached; or (2) all of the input records for the current program are used up, in which case an end-of-file condition occurs. However, a READ statement variable list may not be exhausted when the end of the format list has been reached. In most FORTRAN dialects this will cause the remainder of the current input record to be ignored and the scan of the format list to be resumed beginning from the rightmost left parenthesis.

The I*w* code is used to input an integer constant, which may or may not contain an algebraic sign. When the sign is omitted, the value input is assumed to be positive. For example, assuming that M, KLM, and Z are declared to be integer variables, the statements

```
      READ(5,110) M,KLM,Z
  110 FORMAT(I5,I8,I10)
```

when taken together with the input record

```
 +42    -475      63275
```

would read the values 42, -475, and 63275 into the locations associated with M, KLM, and Z, respectively. Thus, the format list is scanned from left to right as the READ statement is executed. The first variable M is associated with the format code I5 because they are the first elements in the READ statement variable list and FORMAT statement format list, respectively. The format code I5 tells the computer to input an integer constant from a field that consists of the first five columns of the next available input record. The value +42 obtained is thus input as the value of the variable M. Next, a value is input for the variable KLM from a field consisting of columns 6 through 13 of the same input record. The reason the field is taken to be input record columns 6 through 13 is that KLM is associated with the second format code, I8. Since the first format code used columns 1 through 5, the second field must start in column 6 and go through column 13. Similarly, the code I10 is used to input a value for the integer variable Z from columns 14 through 23 of the same input record.

If in error +42 had been entered in input record columns 1 through 3 in the above example, then the value input for M would be taken by most computers to be +4200 instead of +42. This is because the number was not right-justified in the five-column field specified by the first format code, I5. The I*w* code must be used only for the purpose of inputting integer constants as the values of variables that have been declared to be of type integer. When an I*w* code is used to input a real constant as the value of an integer variable, then an error occurs. Similarly, an error results when an I*w* code is used to input an integer constant to be the value of a real variable.

As a second example, assume that the FORMAT statement labeled 110 in the previous example is modified as follows:

```
110 FORMAT(I4,3X,I6,7X,I3)
```

Then, if the READ statement and input record of the above example are used, the values input for M, KLM, and Z would be 4, -475, and 275, respectively. The value input for M is +4 rather than +42 because the first format code, I4, specifies that the value of M is to be input from columns 1 through 4. Then, the format code 3X is encountered which says to skip the next three columns. This causes the value 2 in column 5 and the two blanks that follow to be ignored. Notice that the *w*X code is not associated with a variable in the READ statement variable list. Next, the constant -475 is input from card columns 8 through 13 as the value of the variable KLM. Notice that this field begins in column 8 since columns 5 through 7 are skipped by the 3X code. Before inputting the constant 275 as the value of Z, the 7X code is executed causing the five blanks in columns 14 through 18 and the value 63 in volumns 19 and 20 to be ignored. Finally, the I3 code is used to input the value 275 from columns 21 through 23 as the value of Z.

For a third example, let the FORMAT statement with the label 110 from the first example be changed to read:

```
110 FORMAT(I5,I8,/,I10)
```

This FORMAT statement, when used with the previous READ, will again cause three integer constants to be input as the values of M, KLM, and Z. However, this time the constants will be input from two input records. If these records are as follows

```
••••••••••••••••••••••••••••••••••••••••
 +42    -475
    63275
••••••••••••••••••••••••••••••••••••••••
```

then the same values would be input to M, KLM, and Z as were input in the first example. In executing the READ statement, the constants +42 and -475 would be input as the values of M and KLM under the I5 and I8 codes, as before. However, prior to finding the I10 code, the slash would be found in the format list. This slash causes the remainder of the current input record to be ignored, thus causing the I10 code to be used beginning with column 1 of the next input record in the data set. Therefore, the value of Z is input as the constant contained in columns 1 through 10 of the second input record.

A fourth example might be to write the FORMAT statement labeled 110 from the first example as

```
110 FORMAT(3I8)
```

which would be equivalent to having written:

```
110 FORMAT(I8,I8,I8)
```

Thus, an unsigned integer constant can be placed before a format code to indicate that the code is to be repeated. This constant is called a *repetition factor*. A repetition factor may also appear before a group of format codes enclosed within a pair of parentheses. Such use of the repetition factor causes the entire group of codes to be repeated. For example, the FORMAT statement

```
115 FORMAT(I5,2(I7,5X,I2),3I4)
```

is equivalent to the statement:

```
115 FORMAT(I5,I7,5X,I2,I7,5X,I2,I4,I4,I4)
```

A repetition factor may be used only before an I*w*, F*w*.*d*, E*w*.*d*, or A*w* format code, or before a group of format codes enclosed within a pair of parentheses.

The FORMAT statements used with WRITE statements differ only slightly from those associated with READ statements. The first difference is that string constants will often appear in a format statement that is used with a WRITE statement. While string constants may also appear in a FORMAT statement used with a READ statement, this usage is infrequent and will not be discussed in this book. As an example, the statements

```
    WRITE(6,120) AZ,BD
120 FORMAT(5X,'A=',I4,3X,'VALUE B=',I5)
```

would cause the output record

```
A=   25   VALUE B= -347
```

to be displayed on an output device, given that AZ and BD were declared to be integer variables and had the values 25 and -347, respectively. Thus, string constants are output as they are encountered during the search for an I*w*, F*w*.*d*, E*w*.*d*, or A*w* format code to be used in outputting a variable list value. In addition, string constants that appear in FORMAT statements may contain up to as many characters as are permitted in an output record.

Notice that the numbers in this example are output right-justified in their fields with leading blanks being placed to the left of the value to complete the field width of *w* output positions. However, had the value of *w* not been large enough to provide for the value to be output, then either *w* asterisks are output in place of the value or truncation of the number occurs on the left, depending on the dialect. For example, if the value of AZ to be output in the previous example was 58756, then either four asterisks or 8756 would be output in the I4 field following 'A='. The reason is that a four-position field is not wide enough to contain a five-digit number.

Another acceptable output form is one that uses a WRITE statement that contains an empty variable list. This form is usually used to output headings. For example, the statements

```
      WRITE(6,125)
  125 FORMAT(3X,'THIS IS AN EXAMPLE',/,6X,'OF A HEADING')
```

would produce the two output records:

```
   THIS IS AN EXAMPLE
      OF A HEADING
```

Notice that a slash used in a FORMAT statement has essentially the same result with a WRITE statement as it did with a READ statement. That is, a slash in a format list being used for output causes the remainder of the output record to be ignored. Similarly, the *w*X code causes *w* positions in a line to be skipped, which is equivalent to placing blanks in those positions.

The second difference between the FORMAT statements used with READ statements and those used with WRITE statements involves the carriage control feature, which handles the vertical spacing of output. Carriage control is handled in FORMAT statements associated with WRITE statements by the character which appears in the leftmost position of the output record. The carriage-control characters common to most dialects of FORTRAN are given in Fig. 4.6, along with their meanings. Note that these characters have meaning for carriage control only if they appear in the first position in an output record. In addition, the character placed in the first position in an output record is not actually output in most dialects since it is used only for carriage control.

Figure 4.6 Carriage-Control Characters for Vertical Spacing of Forms

Character	Action Before Printing
+	Do not advance paper forms
blank	Advance paper forms 1 line
0	Advance paper forms 2 lines
1	Advance paper forms to the top of the next page

A non-blank carriage-control character is generally introduced into a FORMAT statement as a string constant. Thus, the two statements

```
    WRITE(6,130)
130 FORMAT('1',5X,'HEADING')
```

cause the output record

```
HEADING
```

to be generated at the top of a new page. Had FORMAT statement 130 read

```
130 FORMAT('0',5X,'HEADING')
```

then the output record would have been produced two lines after the most recent line that was output. In the case where FORMAT statement 130 is

```
130 FORMAT('+',5X,'HEADING')
```

the output record would be displayed over (superimposed upon) the previous output record since the + suppresses vertical spacing before producing the record to be output.

The usual way of introducing the blank as a carriage-control character is by the *w*X code. Thus, had FORMAT statement 130 been

```
130 FORMAT(6X,'HEADING')
```

the above output record would have been displayed on the line following the most recent output record. Caution must be exercised to ensure that the correct carriage-control character is provided for every record to be output. Therefore, the first character output in a format list and after each slash must be a carriage-control character.

In addition to the I*w* format code, there are also the F*w*.*d* and E*w*.*d* format codes, which are used to input and output real numeric constants. Both F*w*.*d* and E*w*.*d* codes require that the number of decimal places in a constant be given, in addition to the width of the field. The number of decimal places is given in these codes as the value of the unsigned integer constant *d*.

On input, the F*w*.*d* code causes a real constant to be input from a field consisting of *w* columns. If a decimal point does not appear in the input constant, then the decimal point is assumed to be to the left of the *d*th digit from the right of the constant. As with integer constants, real constants must appear right-justified in the field from which they are to be input. For example, the statements

```
    READ(5,135) A,B,C
135 FORMAT(F7.2,F10.3,F5.0)
```

will cause the input record

```
••••••••••••••••••••••••••••••••••••••••
  23456     -8456 8705
••••••••••••••••••••••••••••••••••••••••
```

to be input, with the values input to A, B, and C being 234.56, -8.456, and 8705, respectively. Of course, in this example A, B, and C must be declared to be real variables; otherwise, an error will occur. When the constants do have decimal points in them, the constants will be input as they appear, with the value of *d* in the format code being ignored. Thus, had the input record in the above example been

```
.......................................
 23.456    -845.6.8705
.......................................
```

then the values input for A, B, and C would have been 23.456, -845.6, and 0.8705, respectively.

On output, an F*w.d* code causes a real value to be output right-justified in a field *w* print positions in width, with a decimal point appearing to the left of the *d*th digit from the right of the constant. Thus, the statements

```
    WRITE(6,140) DX,J,R
140 FORMAT(5X,F8.3,2X,F9.1,F7.3)
```

would cause the following output record to be produced

```
     5.600        -72.8  0.734
```

given that DX, J, and R are declared to be real variables with the values 5.6, -72.8, and 0.734, respectively. As in the case of an I*w* code, *w* must be large enough to provide a field that will contain the constant which is to be output. If it is not, then either *w* asterisks are output in place of the constant or the constant is truncated on the left, depending on the dialect.

The E*w.d* format code is used to input and output E-type real constants. On input, the E*w.d* code is used to input an E-type real constant from a field consisting of *w* columns. If a decimal point does not appear in the constant, the decimal point is assumed to be to the left of the *d*th digit to the left of the E in the constant. Again, the constant must be right-justified in the field. Assuming that DX, J, and RR are declared to be real variables, the statements

```
    READ(5,145) DX,J,RR
145 FORMAT(E13.5,E12.3,E7.0)
```

would cause the input record

```
.....................................
   -654321E+5  987324E-05  567E5
.....................................
```

to be input, with the values assigned to DX, J, and RR being -6.54321E5, 987.324E-5, and 567.0E5, respectively. Notice that the *d* decimal places are taken counting from the E, not from the rightmost column of the field. When the constants do contain decimal points, then the value of *d* in the format code is ignored. Thus, had the input record in the above example been

```
.....................................
  -.654321E+5 9.87324E-05 5.67E5
.....................................
```

then the values assigned to DX, J, and RR would have been -0.654321E5, 9.87324E-5, and 5.67E5, respectively. As with the F*w.d* format code, only real variables may be associated with an E*w.d* format code; otherwise an error will occur.

When an E*w.d* code is used for output, a real value will be displayed as an E-type real constant, right-justified in a *w*-position field. The constant will have a decimal point appearing to the left of the *d*th digit to the left of the E. In addition, most dialects place all significant digits to the right of the decimal point. Therefore, *d* represents a count of the number of significant digits that are to appear in an E-type constant. Thus the statements

```
      WRITE(6,150) X,Y,ZZ
  150 FORMAT(E13.5,E14.6,3X,E12.3)
```

would cause the following record to be output*

---

*In some dialects, the form of an E-type constant may vary slightly from that shown above, but the above form holds for the vast majority of dialects.

```
0.56700E-04 -0.427500E 17      0.783E 05
```

given that X, Y, and ZZ are declared to be real variables and have the values 5.67E-5, -42.75E15, and 0.78334E5. In order to ensure that the field is wide enough to hold an E-type constant, w should be chosen such that $w \geq d + 7$. The seven extra positions are needed to hold the two signs, leading zero, decimal point, E, and two-digit exponent.

The final format code to be inspected is the Aw code, which is used to input and output string constants. On input, the Aw code indicates that the next w columns contain a string constant.* This constant is to be placed left-justified into the memory location of the input variable given in the variable list. If the location cannot hold all w characters, then the characters will be lost from the left side of the string constant. That is, only the n rightmost characters of the string constant will be stored, where n is the capacity in characters of the location in which the constant is to be stored. Recall from Sec. 4.3.2 that in all dialects the locations for real variables can contain at least four-character string constants. Therefore, four is a safe number to use for w. In the case where $n > w$, then the $(n - w)$ unfilled positions of the memory location to the right of the w characters of the input string constant are filled with blanks. As an example, execution of the statements

```
      READ(5,155) A,B,C
  155 FORMAT(A4,3X,A7,2X,A2)
```

*The treatment of string constants on input and output varies among dialects. This discussion provides an explanation which holds for most dialects.

would cause the record

```
.......................................
ABCD   EFGHIJK  LM
.......................................
```

to be input, with the real variables A, B, and C having the values (after execution of the above READ statement) of 'ABCD', 'HIJK', and 'LM__', respectively. In this example, each variable is assumed to hold one four-character string constant. Notice that string constants are not enclosed within a pair of apostrophes in an input record.

Use of the A*w* format code for output causes the value of the variable in the WRITE statement variable list to be displayed right-justified as a string constant made up of *w* characters. Should the length of the string in computer memory be greater than *w* characters, the *w* leftmost characters of the constant will be output. When the field width *w* is greater then the number of characters in the memory location, then blanks will be used to fill the leftmost portion of the field. For example, the statements

```
    WRITE(6,160) A,B,C
160 FORMAT(2X,A4,A7,5X,A2)
```

would produce the output record

```
  KLMN   OPQR     ST
```

given that A, B, and C are real variables that have as their values 'KLMN', 'OPQR', and 'STUV', respectively. Notice that string constants are not enclosed in a pair of apostrophes when output.

Two easy-to-remember rules for A*w* format codes are: (1) external string constants are right-justified and (2) string constants are stored in main memory locations left-justified. Always be cautious when using A*w* format codes to avoid the loss of characters from a string.

The format codes mentioned in this section may appear in a FORMAT statement in any order. There are no restrictions on the mixing of format codes within a format list. The only requirements are that only integer variables be associated with I*w* codes and only real variables be used with F*w*.*d* and E*w*.*d* format codes.

Finally, we must note that: (1) punched cards generally have 80 columns each and (2) a line on a line printer usually contains 133 print positions (including the position used for carriage control), although on some printers there may be as few as 121 print positions per line. Therefore, caution must be exercised in constructing FORMAT statements so that no more than the maximum number of characters are specified for each input and output record.

In Fig. 4.7* is a flowchart that simply performs a number of input and output operations. The FORTRAN program that corresponds with this flowchart appears in Fig. 4.8. Also listed (below the program itself) is sample output produced by the computer using the input records:

```
........................................
0.12-485 HOWDY
 GUMBO4102
20 A STRING
........................................
```

The row of periods above and below the input records are included to help in determining the columns in which the values appear. The leftmost period in these lines should be assumed to be column 1 of the input record. Let us examine this program in detail.

First, notice that the FORTRAN equivalents to the flowchart variables *A*, *S*, *T*, and *Temp* have been declared to be of type REAL. The reason for declaring them to be REAL variables is that they can assume any real values. In a similar way, the flowchart variables

---

*For those using the main text, this flowchart is the same one that appears in Fig. 4.6M.

Figure 4.7 Algorithm Flowchart for Input and Output

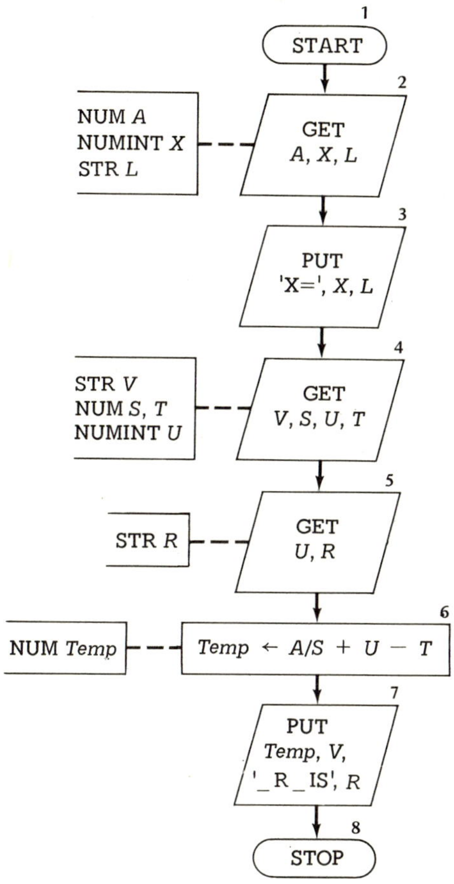

declared NUMINT (*X* and *U*) have been declared in the program to be of type INTEGER. Also observe that the string variables *L*, *V*, and *R* have been declared to be of type INTEGER. This may seem confusing at first; however, recall from Section 4.2.2 that only numeric variables are permitted in FORTRAN. Also notice in the program that there is not just one variable L, but instead there are four

Figure 4.8 FORTRAN Program for Flowchart of Figure 4.7

```
C   ***** PROGRAM FOR ALGORITHM OF FIGURE 4.6M ****************************
      REAL A,S,T,TEMP
      INTEGER X,L1,L2,L3,L4,U,V1,V2,V3,R1,R2,R3,R4,R5
  501 FORMAT(F4.0,I4,4A2)
  502 FORMAT('1','X=',I4,4A2)
  503 FORMAT(3A2,F1.0,I2,F1.0)
  504 FORMAT(I2,5A2)
  505 FORMAT(1X,F5.2,3A2,' R IS',5A2)
      READ(5,501) A,X,L1,L2,L3,L4
      WRITE(6,502) X,L1,L2,L3,L4
      READ(5,503) V1,V2,V3,S,U,T
      READ(5,504) U,R1,R2,R3,R4,R5
      TEMP=A/S+FLOAT(U)-T
      WRITE(6,505) TEMP,V1,V2,V3,R1,R2,R3,R4,R5
      STOP
      END
```

```
X=-485 HOWDY
18.03 GUMBO R IS A STRING
```

(L1, L2, L3, and L4). The reason is that in the flowchart example we used *L* to hold a string constant with seven characters. Since FORTRAN integer variables in many dialects can hold no more than two-character string constants, we must use four variables to represent seven characters. Thus, the FORTRAN variables L1, L2, and L3 are used to hold two characters each, while L4 is used to hold the seventh character. Similarly, since the string variables *V* and *R* of the flowchart were used to hold six and nine characters, respectively, we have declared three FORTRAN variables (V1, V2, and V3) and five FORTRAN variables (R1, R2, R3, R4, and R5). Notice that had we declared the variables for *L*, *V*, and *R* to be of type

REAL, only two *L* (L1 and L2), two *V* (V1 and V2), and three *R* (R1, R2, and R3) variables would have been needed. The reason is that all FORTRAN dialects allow at least four-character string constants to be stored as the value of each real variable.

The first executable statement in this program

```
READ(5,501) A,X,L1,L2,L3,L4
```

causes the first input record to be read, with six constants from the record being assigned to the six variables in the variable list. This input is performed under the control of FORMAT statement 501. Therefore, the value for A (0.12) is taken as a real constant from the leftmost four columns in the input record because the format code F4.0 is associated with A. Similarly, the value for X (-485) is input from columns five through eight of the input record because the format code I4 is associated with X. Next, the contents of columns nine through sixteen are input as four two-character string constants into the variables L1, L2, L3, and L4. The reason is that the format list item 4A2 indicates a format code of A2 repeated four times. Thus, L1 will be assigned '_H', L2 will be assigned 'OW', L3 will be assigned 'DY', and L4 will be assigned '__'. Notice that string constants in input records are not placed within apostrophes as they were in the input data streams of the flowchart language. The reason is that the A*w* format code tells FORTRAN that these are string constants.

The next statement to be executed

```
WRITE(6,502) X,L1,L2,L3,L4
```

performs an output operation under the control of format statement 502. The first variable in the variable list, X, is output under an I4 format in the third through seventh positions of the output record. Notice that before outputting the value of X, the paper forms (assuming the use of a line printer) were advanced to the top of the next page and the string constant 'X=' was output in the first and second positions. Also observe that while string constants appear in flowchart PUT boxes, they must not be used in WRITE statement variable lists. Instead, string constants to be output must be placed in the FORMAT statement associated with some WRITE statement. Finally, the values of L1, L2, L3, and L4 are output to positions 8 through 15 of the output record using the 4A2 format code. This results in the output of the string of characters (recall that L1='_H', L2='OW', L3='DY', and L4='__')

```
HOWDY
```

to the same output record that contains the string constant 'X=' and the value of X. Notice that in the case of 'X=' and the values of L1, L2, L3, and L4 that apostrophes are not included in the output that is produced.

The next two statements executed will be:

```
READ(5,503) V1,V2,V3,S,U,T
READ(5,504) U,R1,R2,R3,R4,R5
```

The first of these statements causes three two-character string constants to be input from the first six columns of the second input record. This is because the first three format codes in FORMAT statement 503 and A2 (the first format list item is 3A2, which is a shorthand form for A2, A2, A2). Notice that execution of a READ statement always starts with column one of a new input record. After inputting the three string constants, the real constant 4.0 is input for the variable S from column seven of the second input record. Similarly, the integer constant 10 and the real constant 2.0 are input (as the values of U and T) from columns eight through nine and column ten, respectively, of the same input record. Execution of the statement that begins READ(5,504) causes six constants to be input from the third input record in a similar manner. In the next statement an expression is evaluated, with the resulting constant being assigned as the value of the real variable TEMP. Next, the statement

```
WRITE(6,505) TEMP,V1,V2,V3,R1,R2,R3,R4,R5
```

is executed, with the result being the output record that appears as the last line in Fig. 4.8. Again, notice that string constants must be placed in the format list rather than in the variable list of the WRITE statement. Finally, execution of the STOP statement causes execution of the program to halt.

A more extensive input/output program example is given in Fig. 4.9. Again, the top portion of the figure contains a listing of the FORTRAN program statements, while in the bottom part is the output produced when this program was executed by the computer using the input records:

```
..........................................................................
 -198765E-2    32.098E4            734265 -2.4      TESTCASE
 234-7658          6234   SUPERTEST
 7864E+05 186429SUPERMAN
..........................................................................
```

There is no flowchart for this program since the program does not solve any particular problem but rather is designed to illustrate FORTRAN input/output. Examining the program, the statement

```
WRITE(6,501)
```

causes two heading lines to be output at the top of a new page. The reason output began at the top of a new page is that FORMAT statement 501 begins with a '1', which indicates that the forms should be advanced to the top of a new page before output begins. Notice that the presence of a slash after the first string constant causes the remainder of the first output record to be skipped. Thus, the second string constant was output as the second output record.

Figure 4.9 FORTRAN Program to Illustrate Input/Output and FORMAT Statements

```
C    ***** PROGRAM TO ILLUSTRATE INPUT/OUTPUT AND FORMAT *****************
      REAL A,B,C,D,E,F
      INTEGER G,H,I,J,K,L
  501 FORMAT('1',16X,'THIS IS A HEADING',/,10X,'FOR THE I/O-FORMAT TES',
     * 'T PROGRAM')
  502 FORMAT(2E12.5,6X,F10.2,F5.3,5X,2A4,/,2I5,5X,I7,3X,A4,A3,A2)
  503 FORMAT(1X,2E15.5,F12.2,F8.3,/,1X,2A4,I8,2I9,5X,A4,A3,A2)
  504 FORMAT(3X,'A=',F10.3,E10.4,E10.7,/,3X,'D=',F9.5,F5.3,E14.6,/,3X,
     * 'E=',A7,2X,A3,2X,A1,/,3X,'H=',I7,2X,I5,2X,I3,/,3X,'J=',A7,2X,A2,
     * A4)
  505 FORMAT(E10.3,F7.4,2A4)
  506 FORMAT(5X,'A=',F12.2,3X,'B=',E12.5,/,5X,'G+H=',2A5,3X,'I=',I6,3X,
     * 'J=',I5)
      WRITE(6,501)
      READ(5,502) A,B,C,D,E,F,G,H,I,J,K,L
      WRITE(6,503) A,B,C,D,E,F,G,H,I,J,K,L
      WRITE(6,504) A,A,A,D,D,D,E,E,E,H,H,H,J,J,J
      READ(5,505) A,B,G,H
      WRITE(6,506) A,B,G,H,I,J
      STOP
      END
```

```
                THIS IS A HEADING
          FOR THE I/O-FORMAT TEST PROGRAM
  -0.19876E-01     0.32098E 06        7342.65  -2.400
TESTCASE      234      -7658       6234        SUPERTEST
  A=-0.199E-01********************
  D= -2.40000***** -0.240000E 01
  E=    TEST   TES    T
  H=  -7658   -7658   ***
  J=    SUPE   SUSUPE
    A=     786400.00     B= 0.18643E 02
    G+H= SUPE RMAN     I=    6234     J=*****
```

Notice the use of a continuation line for this FORMAT statement. Also notice the use of the format codes 16X and 10X for the purpose of centering the two string constants in their respective output records. Finally, observe that the WRITE statement has an empty variable list (i.e., there are no variables whose values are to be printed by this statement). This illustrates how WRITE statements can be used to output headings and other descriptive information.

The second statement to be executed is

```
READ(5,502) A,B,C,D,E,F,G,H,I,J,K,L
```

which causes twelve constants to be input from the first two input records as the values of these twelve variables. The variables A and B are assigned the real constants -1.98765E-2 and 32.098E4, which are obtained from the first 24 columns of the input record using the format code E12.5 twice. Then the specification 6X causes columns 25 through 30 to be skipped. Next, the constant 7342.65 is input for C from columns 31 through 40 of the first input record. Following this, a value of -2.4 is input for D from columns 41 through 45. Columns 46 through 50 are then skipped over because of the 5X format code. Then the string constants 'TEST' and 'CASE' are input as the values of E and F, using an A4 format code for both variables. At this point in the format list a slash is encountered. This causes the remainder of the first input record to be ignored. Thus, the value of G is input from columns 1 through 5 of the second input record. The remainder of this READ statement should be easy to understand and therefore will not be discussed.

The third and fourth output records are the result of executing the statement

```
WRITE(6,503) A,B,C,D,E,F,G,H,I,J,K,L
```

This statement is included to simply list the values input for these twelve variables. The statement

```
WRITE(6,504) A,A,A,D,D,D,E,E,E,H,H,H,J,J,J
```

is included to illustrate errors that can be made in selecting format codes. The value of the real variable A is output three times on the fifth output line using the E*w*.*d* format code. The use of E10.3 illustrates that when a smaller number of decimal positions (3 in this case) are used on output than will allow all of the significant digits to be displayed, the number is rounded. In this example, the fractional part -0.19876 was rounded to -0.199. The use of E10.4 and E10.7 caused two groups of ten asterisks each to be output. This is because the field width *w* allowed was not at least 7 greater than the number of decimal places *d*. Thus, rather than lose the sign and/or some of the significant digits, FORTRAN printed out a string of asterisks to indicate that it could not output the constant in the space provided.

The value of the real constant D is output three times on the sixth output line. In the first case, we see that asking for more decimal places to be output than the input constant contained simply results in as many righthand zeros as are required. Using F5.3 causes five asterisks to be output because 3 decimal places and a decimal point require four printing positions. Thus a five-column field cannot contain the real constant -2.400, which is six characters in length. Since six characters cannot be output in a five-position field, FORTRAN outputs asterisks instead. Next, notice that even though the value of D was input under an F5.3 format code, we output it using an E*w*.*d* format code. This illustrates that the input and output format codes do not have to be the same in dealing with real constants. The reason is that all real values are stored in memory as floating-point constants regardless of the format code used for the input.

The seventh output line contains the value of the variable E, output three times. Under an A7 format code, the value of E is right-justified in the next seven output record positions. Since E is a string constant with only four characters, this means that three blank spaces are produced to the left of the constant. The second time the value of E is output, an A3 format code is used. Since the value of E consists of four characters, this causes the rightmost character to be lost. Similarly, the use of A1 as the format code on the third output of E causes the rightmost three characters of the constant to be lost on output.

The eighth output line has the results of outputting the value of H three times. The first two times this value is output right-justified in a field 7 and 5 characters wide. On the third output, however, three asterisks are output because a five character constant (-7658) cannot fit in the three-character field specified by the I3 format code. The ninth print line shows the results of outputting the value of J three times. It should now be easy to understand how the format codes affect the output.

The final READ statement

```
READ(5,505) A,B,G,H
```

is used to input the constants 786400.0, 18.643, 'SUPE', and 'RMAN' to the variables in the variable list. Then the statement

```
WRITE(6,506) A,B,G,H,I,J
```

is used to output the tenth and eleventh output records. Both of these statements should be easy to understnad and thus will not be discussed. However, note that even though J has had a string constant as its value, we have tried to output it as an integer constant. This did not produce an error but instead resulted in five asterisks being output. Thus FORTRAN is willing to treat a string constant as a number since J is declared to be an integer variable. Therefore, caution must be used in selecting format codes.

PROBLEMS

8. Using the type statements

```
REAL A,B,C,D
INTEGER E,F,G
```

write the necessary READ and FORMAT statements to read the values from the following input records. Assume that all declared variables will appear in the READ statements in the order of their appearance in the type statements.

a.
```
..........................................................
 +0.123E-05     1.2345 ABCD 4.5  HI   -847  63
..........................................................
```

b.
```
.......................................
 +0.123E-05     1.2345 ABCD
 4.5
 HI    -847        63
.......................................
```

9. Using the type statements and values given in Prob. 8, write the necessary WRITE and FORMAT statements to generate the following output. The periods in the top line of each printout are included in order for you to judge spacing.

a.
```
..........................................................
   0.12300E-05  1.2345 ABCD 4.5  HI    -847      63
```

b.
```
..........................................................
   0.12300E-05  0.12345E 01    ABC        0.450E 01
 HI                     -847          63
```

c.
```
..........................................................
 0.00000123     1.2345000


ABCD            4.5000        H            -847
                         63
```

4.5 FORTRAN BRANCHING STATEMENTS

The two basic types of branch statements in FORTRAN are the IF and GO TO statements. One form of the GO TO statement and one form of the IF statement will be presented in this section, with both types being executable statements. Two additional forms of the GO TO statement and another version of the IF statement are discussed in Appendix D.

The FORTRAN unconditional branch instruction is the GO TO statement. Its general form is

GO TO *label*

where *label* is an unsigned positive integer constant. The value of *label* is that of a label on some executable statement within the program segment in which the GO TO statement appears. The GO TO statement is equivalent to an out-connector or a change in flow direction in the flowchart language. Therefore, execution of a GO TO statement always causes the program statement indicated by *label* to be the next one executed. An example of a GO TO statement is

```
GO TO 23
```

which is equivalent to the flowchart out-connector:

A GO TO statement always causes a branch to occur. Therefore, the first executable statement following a GO TO statement must always have a label on it so that it can be reached by some other branch statement.

The conditional branch statement in FORTRAN is the IF statement, which is the equivalent of the flowchart-language decision box. In this text we will use the logical IF statement for all of the programs we develop. A second version, the arithmetic IF statement, is discussed in Appendix D. The general form of the logical IF statement is

IF (*logical expression*) *statement*

where *logical expression* is a logical expression, and *statement* is any executable FORTRAN statement, except for a DO statement or another logical IF statement. A logical expression evaluates to a value of either *true* or *false*. If the value that results from evaluating the logical expression is true, then *statement* is executed; otherwise it is ignored. Whether or not *statement* is executed, the first executable statement following the logical IF will ordinarily be the next statement executed. The one exception to this is when *statement* is a statement that causes a branch to another point in the program. The only such statement used as *statement* in this book will be the GO TO.

The form of a logical expression is

$$expression_1.relational\ operator.expression_2$$

where $expression_1$ and $expression_2$ are any legal FORTRAN expressions (as defined in Section 4.3 of this text), *relational operator* is one of the FORTRAN relational operators appearing in Fig. 4.10, and the

Figure 4.10 FORTRAN Relational Operators

Symbol for FORTRAN Operator	Flowchart Language Equivalent	Meaning	Example
LT	$<$	Less than	A.LT.B
GT	$>$	Greater than	A.GT.B
EQ	$=$	Equal to	A.EQ.B
NE	$\neq$	Not equal to	A.NE.B
LE	$\leq$	Less than or equal to	A.LE.B
GE	$\geq$	Greater than or equal to	A.GE.B

two periods used to separate the expressions from the relational operator are required. Notice that a FORTRAN logical IF statement is similar in function to a flowchart language decision box. That is, a flowchart decision box contains a logical expression that produces a result of true or false. Based on whether the value is true or false, one of two exits is made from the decision box. Similarly, a logical IF statement contains a logical expression that evaluates to a value of true or false. Then *statement* is either executed or not, depending on whether the logical expression resulted in a value of true or a value of false.

An example of a logical IF statement is:

```
IF(A.LT.10.0) N=N+1
```

When the value of A is less than 10.0, then the logical expression is true. In that case the assignment statement N=N+1 is executed. However, when the value of A is greater than or equal to 10.0, the logical expression is false. When the value is false, the assignment statement N=N+1 is not executed. In either case, the next statement to be executed will be the one following this IF statement. The flowchart language equivalent of this example would be:

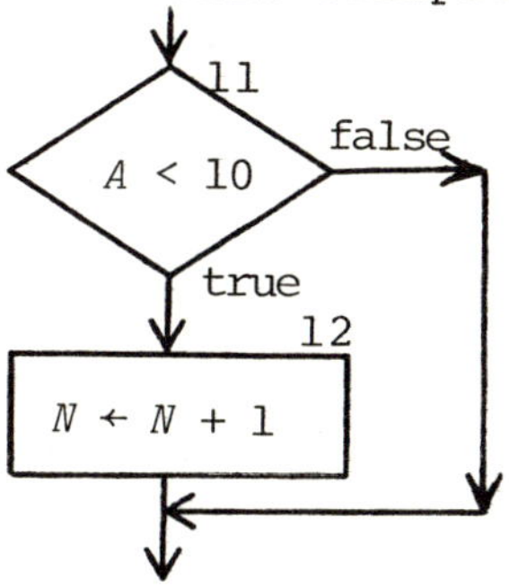

For a second example, we have:

```
IF(A.GE.B) GO TO 20
```

Execution of this logical IF statement causes a branch to the statement labeled 20 whenever the value of A is greater than or equal to the value of B. However, when the value of A is less than that of B, the next statement executed will be the one following this IF statement. The flowchart equivalent to this example is

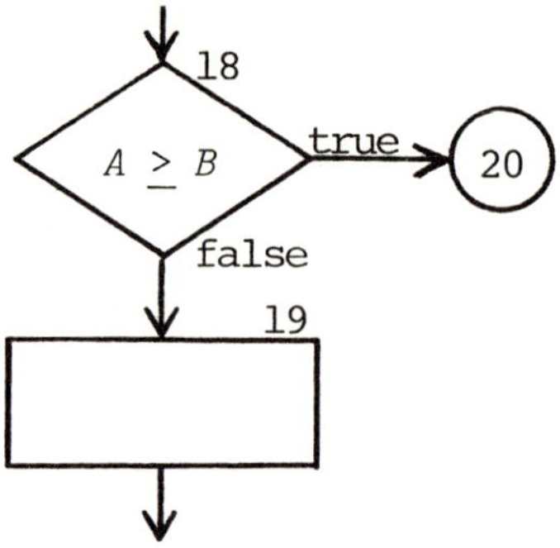

where the processing box below the decision box represents the flowchart statement that is equivalent to the FORTRAN statement that follows the IF statement.

Since we also will want to make decisions about string values, let us examine the use of the IF statement for this purpose. Recall from Section 4.2.2 that in FORTRAN all string constants are stored as the values of either integer or real variables. Therefore, in all dialects of FORTRAN, two string values can be compared to determine whether or not they are equal to each other by simply considering them as numeric values. In making such comparisons, two variables will always be used. This is because string constants may not appear in any executable FORTRAN statement. In addition, the two variables always must be of the same type. As an example, assume that G and H are two integer variables whose values are string constants. In such a case, the statement

```
IF(G.EQ.H) GO TO 20
```

will result in a branch to statement 20 if the string constant associated with G is equal to the one that is the value of H. If the two string values are not equal, then the statement following this IF statement will be executed next.

All problems we solve in this text involve making decisions only about the equality of two string values. Therefore, it does not matter whether the two variables used in the IF statement are both real or both integer. However, in most FORTRAN dialects it can be determined whether one string value is less than or greater than another string value. Such decisions generally yield valid results, however, only when the string values being compared are stored using integer variables. This can be verified by listing the integer values that result from storing a list of string constants as the values of string variables. Problem 11 at the end of this section provides this as an exercise.

Finally, let us examine how end-of-file decisions are handled in FORTRAN. The easiest way is to use the END= option of the READ statement, which is available in many FORTRAN dialects. This option simply involves including a third element in between the set of parentheses used for listing the device number and the format statement number. The element consists of the four characters END=, followed by a statement label. The value of the statement label tells which statement is to be executed when execution of the READ statement results in an end-of-file condition. As an example, execution of the statement

```
READ(5,502,END=30) X
```

will result in a branch to statement 30 if no more values are available to be input. However, when a value for X is input, the statement following this READ is executed next and the END=30 option is ignored. The end-of-file test will be implemented in all of our programs in this book using the END= option.

For FORTRAN dialects that do not permit the END= option, we can use the trailer card (also called the sentinel card) method. In this method, a value that is not a valid data value for the problem being solved is placed after the last value in the data set. Then an IF statement is placed after the READ statement in which end-of-file could occur. For example, in a certain problem we might know that none of the values input for X will ever be as large as 1.0E30. The end-of-file can be signalled in this case by including the value 1.0E30 in a record that follows the last valid data record. Then the end-of-file test will consist of checking each value input for X to determine whether or not it is greater than or equal to 1.0E30. This can be done with the statements

```
READ(5,502) X
IF(X.GE.1.0E30) GO TO 30
```

where the format statement has not been given, and a branch is made to statement 30 when the end-of-file record has been reached. When the end-of-file has not occurred, program execution will continue with the statement following this IF statement.

PROBLEMS

10. Using the declarations

```
REAL A,B,C,D
INTEGER SW
DATA A,B,C,D,SW/10.0,20.0,1.0E30,-5.0,2/
```

determine the statement number to which the branch will be taken in each of the following cases.

a.

```
IF(A.GT.B) GO TO 15
IF(A.EQ.B) GO TO 10
GO TO 5
```

b.

```
IF(D.LT.0.0) GO TO 4
IF(D.EQ.0.0) GO TO 3
GO TO 2
```

c.

```
IF(SW.NE.1) GO TO 25
GO TO 20
```

d.
```
      IF(2.0*A-B.LT.0.0) GO TO 5
      GO TO 8
```

e.
```
      IF(A**30.GE.C) GO TO 19
      GO TO 22
```

f.
```
      SW=5-SW
      IF(SW.EQ.3) GO TO 35
      GO TO 36
```

11. Write a FORTRAN program in which eleven integer variables are initialized with the string constant values: 'A', 'AA', 'AB', 'AC', 'B', 'BA', 'BB', 'BC', 'C', 'D', and 'E'. Then cause the program to print the values of each of the variables twice--once each under the A4 and I12 format specifications. The integer values printed should be in increasing order, since the string constants given above are in increasing order. If they are not in order, this would mean that your FORTRAN dialect does not store string constants in a manner that permits their comparison in a less than or greater than sense.

4.6 CODING ALGORITHMS IN FORTRAN

In this section, the FORTRAN code is presented that corresponds with the algorithms designed in Sec. 4.6 of the main text. For those not using the main text, the flowcharts for these algorithms are reproduced in this book. The conventions adopted in writing these programs are:

1. All type statements will appear first in a program segment.
2. The DATA statement (if one is used) will appear immediately following the type statements.
3. All FORMAT statements will appear next, usually in the order in which they are referenced in the program. In addition, all FORMAT statements will have labels in the 500s so that they can be easily identified.

4. The remainder of the program segment (except for the END statement) will generally consist of executable statements. Recall that the END statement is always the last statement in a program segment.
5. Statements labeled from 1 through 9 correspond to like-numbered in-connectors of the algorithm flowchart for which the program is coded. All statement labels 10 and greater are labels required because of the linear nature of FORTRAN, and thus do not have corresponding in-connectors in the flowchart. A STOP statement that requires a label will be given 999 as the value of the statement label.
6. At the beginning of each program segment, a comment line will provide the figure number of the algorithm flowchart in the main text with which that program corresponds.
7. All variable names and string constants in FORTRAN must be written using only capital letters. Therefore, whenever lower-case letters are used in a flowchart variable name or string constant, they will be replaced with the same upper-case letters.
8. Continuation lines will always be indicated by an asterisk in column 6.
9. Display of the input records used to produce sample output for the various programs will be accomplished by showing a listing of the records. So that the columns in which data appear can be easily determined, a line with a series of periods will appear above and below each input record listing. The leftmost period in such lines will always be used to indicate column 1 of the input record.

While not all of the above ordering and statement numbering rules are a part of FORTRAN, they have been set up to facilitate the comparison between FORTRAN programs and their corresponding flowcharts. Placing all of the nonexecutable statements at the beginning of a program segment makes program logic easier to follow. In addition, FORMAT statements have no counterpart in the flowchart language. Thus, it is reasonable to group them together and give them special labels. Finally, output statements are included in the programs for which there are no corresponding PUT boxes. These are included to provide headings and descriptive information with the output.

4.6.1 The Largest-Value Programs

For out first problem, let us write a FORTRAN program to find the largest value in a set of numbers. An algorithm flowchart that describes the logic required to solve this problem for the limited case of only two data values in a set appears in Fig. 4.11.*

Recall from Section 4.3 that the flowchart START box has no counterpart in a FORTRAN program. This is because FORTRAN assumes that execution of a program will always begin with the topmost executable statement in the main program segment. Thus, the first statements to appear in a FORTRAN program are the REAL and/or INTEGER type statements. These are used to declare the types of all of the variables in the program. Coding these type statements is accomplished by scanning the algorithm flowchart for the annotation boxes in which variables are declared. Any flowchart variable declared NUM is placed in a REAL type statement while any flowchart variable specified as NUMINT should appear in an INTEGER statement. Flowchart variables declared to be STR may be declared to be either REAL or INTEGER in a FORTRAN program. Which choice to make was discussed in Section 4.3.2. For the flowchart of Fig. 4.11, the type statement

---

*For those using the main text, this flowchart is the same one that appears in Fig. 4.9M.

Figure 4.11 Algorithm Flowchart for the Largest-Value Problem in the Case of Two Data Values

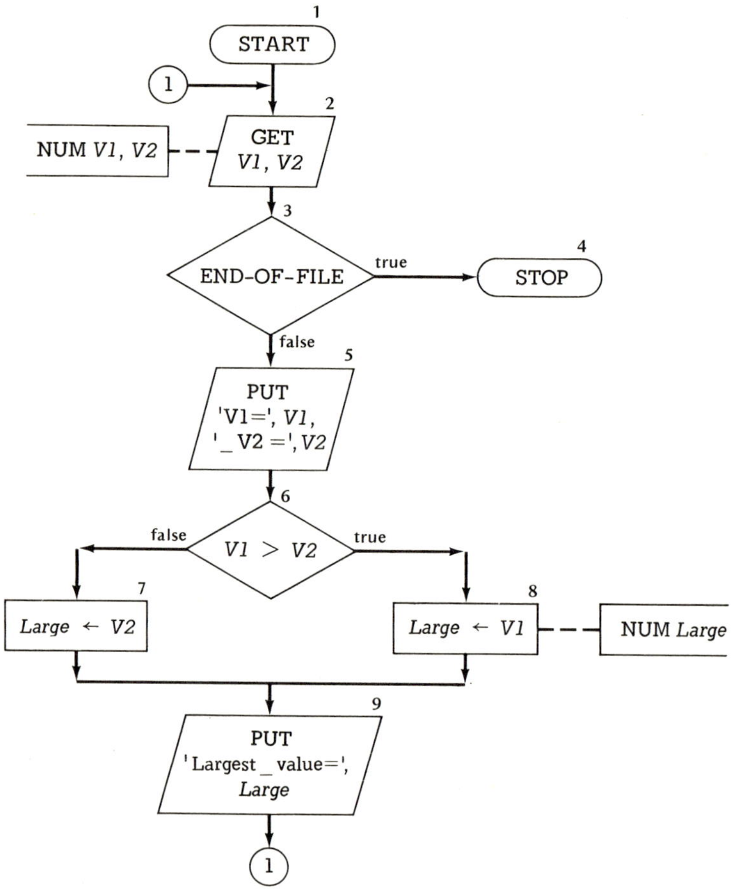

in the FORTRAN program will be:

```
REAL V1,V2,LARGE
```

Notice that there will not be an INTEGER type statement in this program because there were no flowchart variables declared to be NUMINT.

After declaring program variables, we are ready to begin coding the steps of the flowchart. The GET operation of flowchart box 2 and end-of-file test of flowchart box 3 are coded into the FORTRAN statement:

```
1 READ(5,501,END=999) V1,V2
```

This is because flowchart GET operations are coded in FORTRAN as READ statements, with the END= option being included whenever an end-of-file test immediately follows the GET box. In this case, the READ statement has been labeled 1 because in the flowchart in-connector 1 points to the flowline leading into box 2. Notice that on end-of-file, the END= option will cause a branch to the statement labeled 999. The FORMAT statement used by this READ statement is:

```
501 FORMAT(2E12.5)
```

This statement specifies that the two values input will be contained in columns 1 through 12 and 13 through 24 of the next input record. Moreover, the input values will appear as real constants and will be assumed to have a decimal point to the left of the fifth digit to the left of the E whenever a decimal point does not appear in the constant. The choice of twelve-column input fields and five implied decimal positions was somewhat arbitrary. However, twelve columns does allow for six fractional digits, which should be satisfactory in most cases. The E*w*.*d* format code was chosen instead of F*w*.*d* because E*w*.*d* allows a wider range of input values. In some cases F*w*.*d* would be appropriate, but only when a reasonably narrow range of input values is expected.

Some FORTRAN dialects do not include the END= option in a READ statement. In this case, an IF statement must be included to test for end-of-file. Flowchart boxes 2 and 3 would be coded in such dialects as

```
1 READ(5,501) V1,V2
  IF(V1.GE.1.0E35) GO TO 999
```

where we have assumed that a value of V1 will never be as large as 10^{35}. If larger values are possible, then a value larger than the largest possible value should be used. Notice that in this case an extra input record will be needed following the input record for the last valid data set. The reason is that a value greater than or equal to 10^{35} must be input to signal end-of-file.

The next statement in the program should be

```
WRITE(6,502) V1,V2
```

which corresponds with flowchart box 5. Notice that there is no statement label on this statement since there is only one way to reach flowchart box 5. The FORMAT statement used by the above WRITE statement is:

```
502 FORMAT(/,1X,'V1=',E12.5,'  V2=',E12.5)
```

Observe that string constants in flowchart box 5 appear in the format list rather than in the variable list of the WRITE statement. The reason is that most FORTRAN dialects do not allow constants to appear in WRITE statement variable lists but they all permit string constants to appear in format lists. Also notice that a slash is used to begin the format list. The reason is that the slash causes a blank line to appear before the line in which the input values are output so that the output for this data set is separated from that of any preceding data set. Following the slash is a 1X format code, which is used for carriage control. Since 1X produces a blank as output, this means that the next line output will be single spaced. Finally, the values of V1 and V2 will be output under E12.5 format codes. This means that the values output will be floating-point constants in twelve-column fields, with five fractional digits. The reason E*w*.*d* was chosen rather than F*w*.*d* is that E*w*.*d* was used on input, thus permitting a broad range of input data values.

The decision box (numbered as box 6) and two processing boxes (numbered as boxes 7 and 8) are coded as:

```
      IF(V1.GT.V2) GO TO 10
      LARGE=V2
      GO TO 15
   10 LARGE=V1
```

Notice that the logical expression in the IF statement is the same as the condition contained in the flowchart decision box. When the condition is true (which is when the value of V1 is greater than the value of V2) then statement 10 is the next one executed, where statement 10 corresponds with flowchart box 8. However, when the IF statement condition is false then the statement LARGE=V2 is executed next (this statement corresponds with flowchart box 7). Then the statement GO TO 15 is executed to cause a branch around statement 10. Notice that either LARGE=V2 or LARGE=V1 will be executed, but not both. Thus, this sequence of four statements agrees with the logic of flowchart boxes 6, 7, and 8.

The next statement to be executed is:

```
   15 WRITE(6,503) LARGE
```

Observe that this statement has been labeled as statement 15 because there are really two ways to reach it. These two ways correspond with the flow coming from either flowchart box 7 or flowchart box 8. The FORMAT statement needed for this WRITE statement is:

```
  503 FORMAT(1X,'LARGEST VALUE=',E12.5)
```

Again, the 1X format code causes the forms to be single-spaced before output of the line begins. In addition, the string constant of flowchart box 9 appears in the format list rather than the output list because of the FORTRAN restrictions mentioned above. Finally, E12.5

was used as the format code to output the value of the variable LARGE for the same reason it was used to output the values of V1 and V2.

Finally, the last three program statements are:

```
      GO TO 1
  999 STOP
      END
```

The first of these statements corresponds with out-connector 1 that follows flowchart box 9. It causes a branch to be taken to the READ statement that corresponds with flowchart box 2. The second statement above causes program execution to stop. Thus, it corresponds with flowchart box 4. Recall that this statement will be reached only when an end-of-file has been detected when executing the READ statement. Finally, the END statement does not correspond with any of the flowchart steps. Instead, it is included to signal FORTRAN that there are no more statements in the main program segment. Notice that the END statement must be the last statement in a program segment.

All of these program statements are brought together in the listing that appears in Fig. 4.12. Notice that all of the FORMAT statements have been placed together above the executable statements of the program. A primary reason for this is so that the flow of program execution can be easily followed without the interference of nonexecutable statements, such as FORMAT statements. Below the program listing in the figure is sample output for three sets of data values. The data values used are:

```
.......................................
        4.5          6.87
       6.87          4.5
        3.2          3.2
.......................................
```

Figure 4.12 FORTRAN Program for Flowchart of Figure 4.11

```
C     ***** PROGRAM FOR ALGORITHM OF FIGURE 4.9M ***************************
      REAL V1,V2,LARGE
  501 FORMAT(2E12.5)
  502 FORMAT(/,1X,'V1=',E12.5,'   V2=',E12.5)
  503 FORMAT(1X,'LARGEST VALUE=',E12.5)
    1 READ(5,501,END=999) V1,V2
      WRITE(6,502) V1,V2
      IF(V1.GT.V2) GO TO 10
      LARGE=V2
      GO TO 15
   10 LARGE=V1
   15 WRITE(6,503) LARGE
      GO TO 1
  999 STOP
      END
```

```
V1= 0.45000E 01   V2= 0.68700E 01
LARGEST VALUE= 0.68700E 01

V1= 0.68700E 01   V2= 0.45000E 01
LARGEST VALUE= 0.68700E 01

V1= 0.32000E 01   V2= 0.32000E 01
LARGEST VALUE= 0.32000E 01
```

Notice that the data values chosen for testing represented every possible combination of relationships between two data values. While using every possible combination of data values in testing a program is desirable, it is only possible with the simplest of problems.

Figure 4.13 Algorithm Flowchart for the Generalized Largest-Value Problem

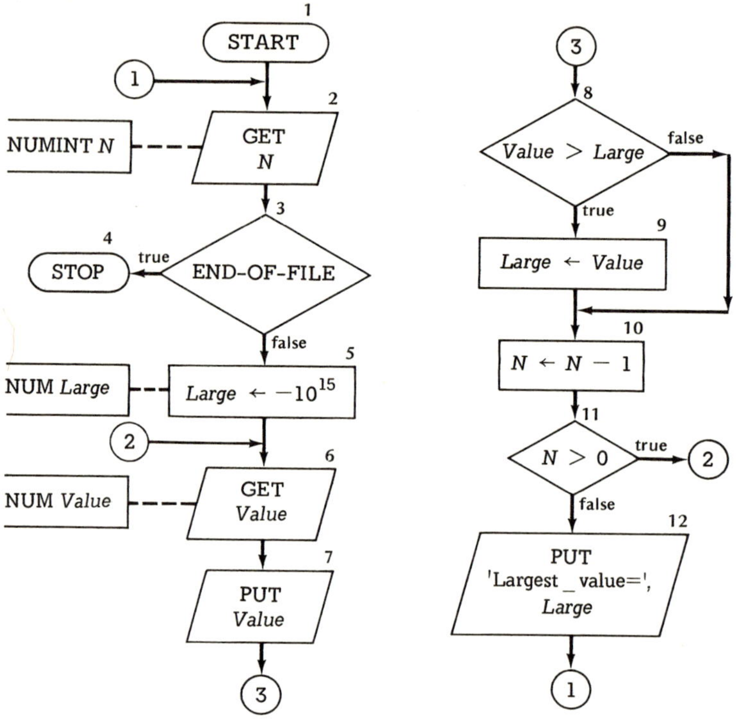

An algorithm flowchart appears in Fig. 4.13* for the generalized problem of finding the largest value in a data set. This algorithm assumes that: (1) the number of values in any data set are known, (2) the data values are greater than -10^{15}, and (3) one or more data sets are to be processed each time the algorithm is executed. The first

*For those using the main text, this flowchart is the same one that appears in Fig. 4.16M.

program statements will be the type statements:

```
REAL LARGE,VALUE
INTEGER N
```

Notice that this program requires an INTEGER type statement in addition to the REAL type statement because the flowchart variable *N* was declared to be NUMINT.

The first executable statement

```
1 READ(5,501,END=999) N
```

corresponds with flowchart boxes 2 and 3. On end-of-file, a branch is taken to the statement labeled 999. If our dialect of FORTRAN does not allow the END= option, then we will have to test for end-of-file using an IF statement just as we did in the previous example. In this case, a good trailer record value would be zero, since only positive values of N would be valid. The FORMAT statement for this READ statement would be:

```
501 FORMAT(I5)
```

Thus, the value of N will be an integer that contains no more than five digits (is less than or equal to 99999). A five-digit field was chosen because we have assumed that we will never use this program to find the largest value of a data set that consists of 100,000 or more numbers.

Flowchart box 5 is implemented in FORTRAN using the statement:

```
LARGE=-1.0E15
```

Notice that we would have written the constant to the right of the assignment operator as -10.0**15 rather than as -1.0E15. However, -10.0**15 is not really a constant; instead it is two arithmetic operations. First, it is an order to multiply 10.0 times itself fourteen times (which is 10.0**15). Second, this result is to have its sign changed. Since these operations require computer processing time, we prefer simply writing the constant -1.0E15, which requires no arithmetic operations.

The next statement in the program is

```
WRITE(6,502)
```

which is executed using the FORMAT statement

```
502 FORMAT('1DATA VALUES',/,' -----------')
```

to produce the output heading:

```
DATA VALUES
-----------
```

This heading is output at the top of a new page because the 1 in the first string constant in the format list occurs in output position one on the line. Since position one of a line is used for carriage control and 1 indicates top of a new page, the heading is output at the top of a new page. Notice that the underline was produced by printing a string constant that consists of a series of hyphens. Finally, note that this output statement does not correspond with any of the flowchart steps. This is because details, such as the output of headings, are not necessary to establish algorithm logic, which is the primary purpose of a flowchart. On the other hand, the headings are convenient in computer output because they are used to describe output produced by executing the program. Therefore, we will include WRITE statements that output headings in our programs even though no corresponding PUT boxes exist in our flowcharts.

Flowchart boxes 6 and 7 are coded as

```
2 READ(5,503) VALUE
  WRITE(6,504) VALUE
```

where the related FORMAT statements are:

```
503 FORMAT(E12.5)
504 FORMAT(1X,E12.5)
```

The reason for selecting E12.5 as the format specification is the same as in the previous example--to allow for a wide range of input values. Notice the 1X format code included in the second FORMAT statement for carriage control. Also observe that the END= option was not included in the READ statement because the corresponding GET box in the flowchart was not followed by an end-of-file condition.

The next three program statements correspond with flowchart boxes 8 through 11. They are:

```
IF(VALUE.GT.LARGE) LARGE=VALUE
N=N-1
IF(N.GT.0) GO TO 2
```

The first of these statements corresponds with flowchart boxes 8 and 9. That is, when the condition VALUE.GT.LARGE is true, then the assignment statement LARGE=VALUE is executed. However, when the condition is false the statement is ignored. In either case, the statement N=N-1 will be executed next. Finally, the last IF statement is used to branch back to statement 2 for the case in which N is positive. When N is not greater than zero, the statement following the IF statement will be executed.

The last four program statements are:

```
    WRITE(6,505) LARGE
    GO TO 1
999 STOP
    END
```

The WRITE statement uses the FORMAT statement

```
505 FORMAT(/,' LARGEST VALUE=',E12.5)
```

to output a string constant and the largest value, in agreement with flowchart box 12. The statement GO TO 1 represents the out-connector following flowchart box 12. The STOP statement corresponds with flowchart box 4, while the END statement tells FORTRAN that there are no more statements in the main program segment. A listing of the complete program appears in Fig. 4.14. The FORMAT

Figure 4.14 FORTRAN Program for Flowchart of Figure 4.13

```
C   ***** PROGRAM FOR ALGORITHM OF FIGURE 4.16M ***************************
      REAL LARGE,VALUE
      INTEGER N
  501 FORMAT(I5)
  502 FORMAT('1DATA VALUES',/,' ------------')
  503 FORMAT(E12.5)
  504 FORMAT(1X,E12.5)
  505 FORMAT(/,' LARGEST VALUE=',E12.5)
    1 READ(5,501,END=999) N
      LARGE=-1.0E15
      WRITE(6,502)
    2 READ(5,503) VALUE
      WRITE(6,504) VALUE
      IF(VALUE.GT.LARGE) LARGE=VALUE
      N=N-1
      IF(N.GT.0) GO TO 2
      WRITE(6,505) LARGE
      GO TO 1
  999 STOP
      END
```

```
DATA VALUES
------------
 0.20000E 01
 0.30000E 01
 0.40000E 01
 0.25000E 01
 0.15000E 01

LARGEST VALUE= 0.40000E 01
```

statements are again grouped together near the top of the program. Below the program listing is sample output produced by executing the program using one data set. A listing of the input data values used is:

```
......................................
    5
         2.0
         3.0
         4.0
         2.5
         1.5
......................................
```

4.6.2 The Depreciation Program

A common problem in business is that of depreciating an asset (for example, a building or a truck) to reflect the fact that it is wearing out as it is being used. An algorithm flowchart for this problem appears in Fig. 4.15.* Instead of developing the program on a statement by statement basis, we have simply shown the listing of the finished program in Fig. 4.16. The REAL and INTEGER type statements appear first in the program. As in the earlier example, the type of the program variables depends on how they were declared in the flowchart. In general, any variable that can assume a fractional value is declared to be real, while any variable that will assume only integer values is declared to be of type integer.

The first executable statement in the program is the READ statement labeled 1, which corresponds with flowchart boxes 2 and 3. Notice that FORMAT statement 501 indicates that the asset cost is

---

*For those using the main text, this flowchart is the same one that appears in Fig. 4.19M.

Figure 4.15 Algorithm Flowchart for the Depreciation Problem

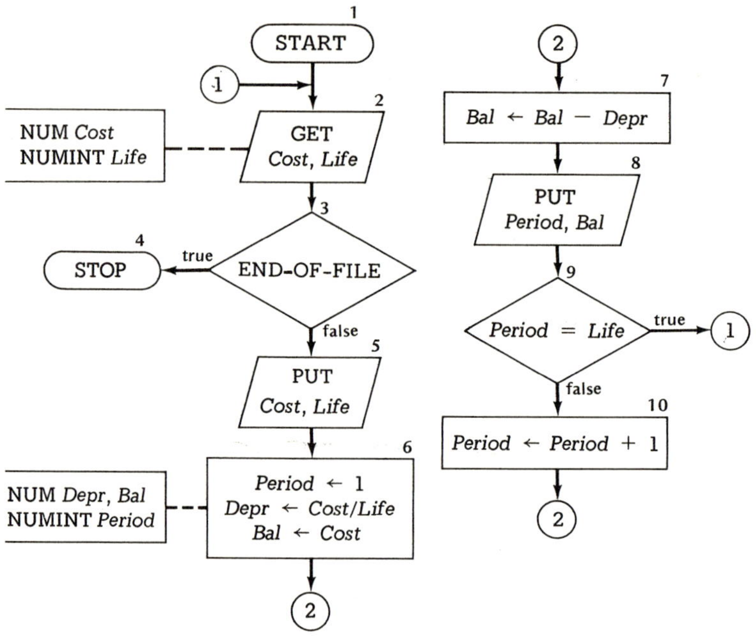

input under an F10.2 format code. The reason for two implied decimal places is that cost is always in dollars and cents. A ten position field was allowed because this permits assets worth up to $99,999,999.99 to be processed by this program. The format code I2 was chosen for N in that the useful life of an asset generally will not exceed 99 accounting periods. If it could, then the field should be increased to three or four digits in width.

Flowchart box 5 is coded in the WRITE statement that follows the READ statement. Observe that FORMAT statement 502 includes headings that did not appear in the flowchart PUT box. Since these headers are useful in describing the various values output, they

Figure 4.16 FORTRAN Program for Flowchart of Figure 4.15

```
C    ***** PROGRAM FOR ALGORITHM OF FIGURE 4.19M *************************
      REAL COST,DEPR,BAL
      INTEGER LIFE,PERIOD
  501 FORMAT(F10.2,I2)
  502 FORMAT('1', 3X,'DEPRECIATION TABLE',/, 5X,'COST=$',F10.2,/,4X,
     * 'LIFE(IN YEARS)=',I3,//,3X,'PERIOD',5X,'BALANCE',/,3X,6('-'),2X,
     * 12('-'))
  503 FORMAT(1X,I6,4X,'$',F10.2)
    1 READ(5,501,END=999) COST,LIFE
      WRITE(6,502) COST,LIFE
      PERIOD=1
      DEPR=COST/FLOAT(LIFE)
      BAL=COST
    2 BAL=BAL-DEPR
      WRITE(6,503) PERIOD,BAL
      IF(PERIOD.EQ.LIFE) GO TO 1
      PERIOD=PERIOD+1
      GO TO 2
  999 STOP
      END
```

```
   DEPRECIATION TABLE
     COST=$    1000.00
    LIFE(IN YEARS)=  5

   PERIOD     BALANCE
   ------   ------------
        1    $    800.00
        2    $    600.00
        3    $    400.00
        4    $    200.00
        5    $      0.00
```

have been included in this output statement. The next three statements in the program are coded from the three assignment statements that appear in flowchart box 6. Notice that the functional operator

FLOAT had to be used in the second statement in order to avoid mixing real and integer variables in an expression. The reason FLOAT was used is that LIFE was declared to be an integer but in this expression it was used to divide the real variable COST. Thus, conversion of the value of LIFE to a real value was necessary.

The statement in flowchart box 7 is coded in FORTRAN as the statement labeled 2. The next three statements in the program correspond with boxes 8, 9, and 10 in the flowchart. The statement GO TO 2 is the result of coding the out-connector that follows flowchart box 10. Finally, the STOP statement is the result of coding flowchart box 4.

Below the program listed in Fig. 4.16 is a listing of sample output for the set of data values:

```
.........................................
    100000 5
.........................................
```

Notice how output tables can be designed by the use of FORMAT statements.

4.6.3 The Vowel-Counting Program

An interesting task involved in the study of writing styles is to determine how many occurrences there are in a manuscript of each of the vowels. That is, the number of times the letter A appears in the manuscript, the number of times the letter E appears, and so on for the letters I, O, and U all are to be counted. We will make the simplifying assumption that all letters in a manuscript are uppercase. Thus, no lowercase letters are permitted. The algorithm flowchart for the solution to this problem appears in Fig. 4.17.*

---

*For those using the main text, this flowchart is the same one that appears in Fig. 4.22M.

Figure 4.17 Algorithm Flowchart for the Vowel-Counting Problem

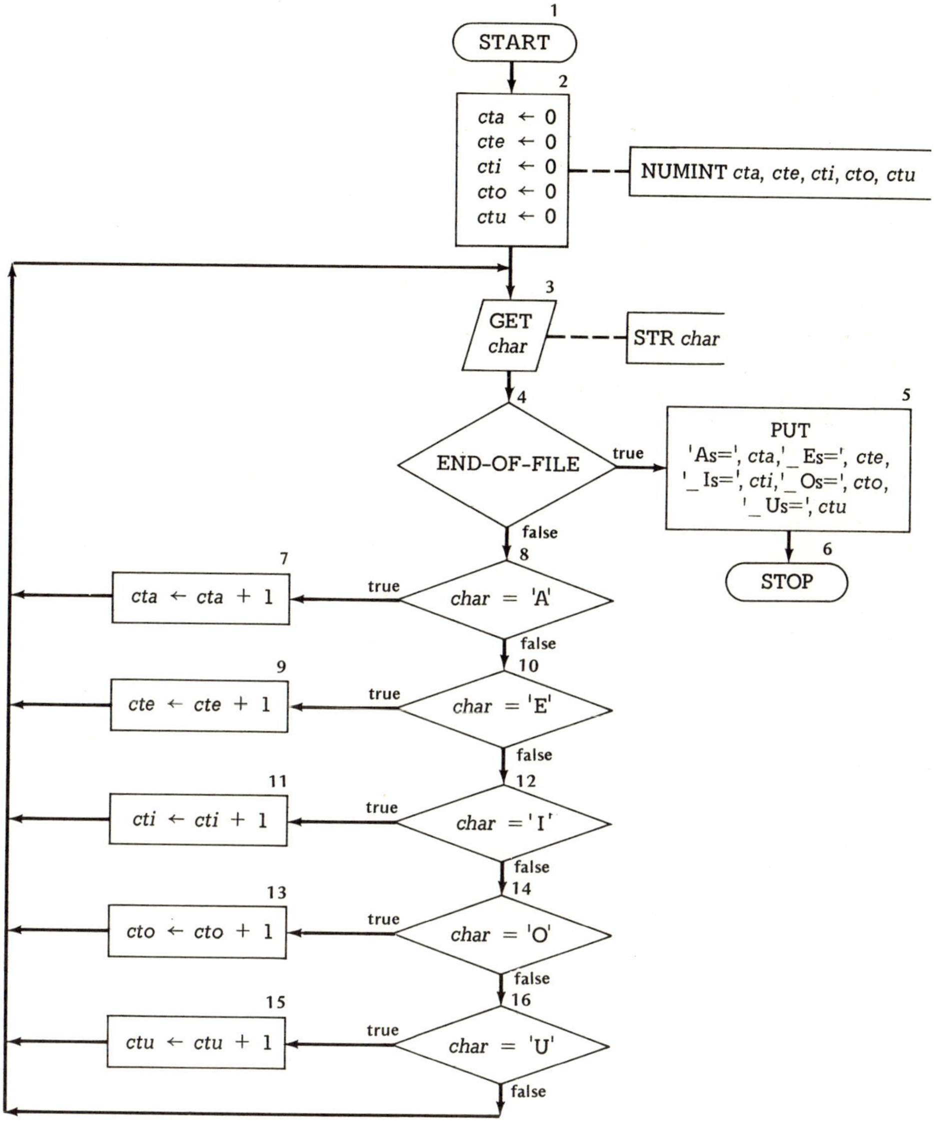

Figure 4.18 FORTRAN Program for Flowchart of Figure 4.17

```
C   ***** PROGRAM FOR ALGORITHM OF FIGURE 4.22M *************************
      INTEGER CTA,CTE,CTI,CTO,CTU,CHAR,A,E,I,O,U
      DATA A,E,I,O,U/'A','E','I','O','U'/
  501 FORMAT(A1)
  502 FORMAT('1',11X,'VOWEL COUNT RESULTS',/,1X,40('-'),/,'    A=',I3,
     *'    E=',I3,'    I=',I3,'    O=',I3,'    U=',I3)
      CTA=0
      CTE=0
      CTI=0
      CTO=0
      CTU=0
   10 READ(5,501,END=40) CHAR
      IF(CHAR.EQ.A) GO TO 15
      IF(CHAR.EQ.E) GO TO 20
      IF(CHAR.EQ.I) GO TO 25
      IF(CHAR.EQ.O) GO TO 30
      IF(CHAR.EQ.U) GO TO 35
      GO TO 10
   15 CTA=CTA+1
      GO TO 10
   20 CTE=CTE+1
      GO TO 10
   25 CTI=CTI+1
      GO TO 10
   30 CTO=CTO+1
      GO TO 10
   35 CTU=CTU+1
      GO TO 10
   40 WRITE(6,502) CTA,CTE,CTI,CTO,CTU
      STOP
      END
```

```
           VOWEL COUNT RESULTS
 ----------------------------------------
    A=  0    E=  3    I=  2    O=  1    U=  2
```

The program listing that appears in Fig. 4.18 is for the FORTRAN program that corresponds with this flowchart. Notice that only integer variables are used in this program. In general, the program is fairly straightforward and easy to understand when compared with the flowchart. An exception to this statement is the handling of the string constants for the five vowels. Since string constants cannot appear in FORTRAN expressions, the string constants needed in flowchart boxes 8, 10, 12, 14, and 16 must be assigned to variables using a DATA statement. Thus, in the DATA statement of the program, the variables A, E, I, O, and U have been initialized with the appropriate string constants. Then in the IF statements that follow statement 10, the variables that have the string constants for the five vowels as values are used in place of the respective string constants. This technique will be used throughout this book to represent and process string constants. Furthermore, the variables used to represent string constants will almost always be chosen as integer variables because in most dialects this produces a more efficient program. Finally, note that each character is input in statement 10 under an A1 format code. This means that the manuscript is being input one-character-per-input-record, with each character being in column 1. While this is a very inefficient approach, it is not until arrays are introduced in Ch. 5 that a more efficient method can be developed. The data values shown in the listing of input records in Fig. 4.19 are the ones used to generate the output shown at the bottom of Fig. 4.18. Again notice that only one letter of the manuscript is contained in each input record.

Figure 4.19 Listing of Data Values Used to Produce the Output in Fig. 4.18

```
.........................................
C
O
M
P
U
T
E
R
S
C
I
E
N
C
E
I
S
F
U
N
.........................................
```

4.7 FINDING AND CORRECTING PROGRAM ERRORS

After a program has been written, it is ready to be run on a computer. At this point, a process called *program testing* begins. This testing represents a systematic attempt to find and correct any errors that might cause the program not to provide correct answers to the problem that it is designed to solve. In a way, testing might be thought of as a *game* in which the object is to discover errors in the program. As in any game, program testing requires experience to learn the techniques required to "win". In the case of program testing, the game is won when all errors in the program have been discovered and corrected. As you will learn, the program-testing game is a very difficult game to win because many program errors are very subtle and thus difficult to discover.

Testing is begun by constructing data sets that represent data that could possibly be expected in the normal use of the program. Then testing proceeds by having the computer translate the program into machine language and execute it using as input the sets of test data. We should observe that the sets of test data selected should include test data that is in error. Common *errors* that usually should be included are:

1. Incorrect data values.
2. Missing data values.
3. Repeated data values.
4. Data values out of order.

In the case of *incorrect data* values, this might be a negative data value in a data set that can only include positive values. Or it might be the appearance of a value larger than was expected when the algorithm was designed. *Missing data* values can create serious problems that cause a program to fail because it expected more values than were provided. It also may cause an input value to be taken as the value of one variable when it was actually intended to be the value of a previous input variable. *Repeated data* values have an impact that is similar to missing data values. *Data values* that are *out of order* also can cause variables to assume the wrong constants as input.

In most cases, the program will contain errors when it is first executed. These errors may cause:

1. The failure of the phase in which the FORTRAN source program is translated into machine language. This failure is usually

caused by one or more syntax errors.

2. The appearance of execution-time errors that are caused by an attempt to perform illegal operations during program execution.
3. The output of incorrect answers for the test data used when the program is executed.
4. No answers to be output when the program is executed.

The first type of failure involves syntax errors. In a FORTRAN program, a *syntax error* is caused by not following the rules of the FORTRAN dialect in which the program was written. That is, each FORTRAN compiler defines the rules for writing correct statements and programs to be translated by that compiler. Any violation of these rules results in a syntax error. Fortunately, all FORTRAN compilers are designed to detect syntax errors. Thus syntax errors are easy to correct.

Syntax errors are noted either in the listing of the source program or immediately following the listing of the source program. They are indicated by the output of either an error-diagnostic message or a code that is used to look up an error-diagnostic message that is contained in a table. These error-diagnostic messages are simply an attempt by the FORTRAN compiler to indicate the type and source of the syntax errors that occur in a program. Caution must be exercised in interpreting error diagnostics, however, because even though FORTRAN compilers always recognize syntax errors they can often be confused about their cause. Thus, we will always know the statement in which a syntax error occurs because an error-diagnostic will be output. However, that error-diagnostic may not always correctly identify the cause of the syntax error.

In Fig. 4.20 we have a listing of a modified version of the program that appeared earlier in Fig. 4.12. The modifications that were made to the program are all ones designed to produce syntax errors. The errors are indicated by the output of error-diagnostic codes. Notice that most of these codes appear following the

Figure 4.20 FORTRAN Program of Fig. 4.12 with Syntax Errors

```
        C   ***** PROGRAM FOR ALGORITHM OF FIGURE 4.9M WITH SYNTAX ERRORS
     1            REAL V1,V2,LARGE
     2            FORMAT(2E12,5)
**WARNING**        FM-2
***ERROR***        FT-2  12,5)
     3        502 FORMAT(/,1X,'V1=',E12.5,'   V2= ,E12.5)
***ERROR***        FT-6
     4        503 FORMET(1X,'LARGEST VALUE=',E12.5)
***ERROR***        ST-5  INVALID FORMET
     5          1 READ(5,501,END=999) V1,V2,
***ERROR***        ID-J  INVALID END-OF-STATEMENT
     6            WRITE(6,502) V1,V2
     7            IF(V1.GT.V2  GO TO 10
***ERROR***        PC-0
***ERROR***        ST-5  INVALID IF
     8            LARGE=V2
     9            GO TO 15
    10         10 6ARGE=V1
***ERROR***        CC-7
***ERROR***        SX-0
    11            WRITE(6,504) LARGE
    12            GO TO 1
    13            STOP
**WARNING**        ST-4
    14            END
        $IBSYS
***ERROR***        JB-1  UNEXPECTED $
***ERROR***        ST-A      501 USED IN LINE       5
***ERROR***        ST-0      999 USED IN LINE       5
***ERROR***        ST-0       15 USED IN LINE       9
***ERROR***        ST-A      504 USED IN LINE      11
```

statement in which the syntax error occurred. The FORTRAN compiler that produced these codes while attempting to compile the program is the popular WATFOR compiler. The error-diagnostic messages for the codes produced by the WATFOR compiler are given in Appendix E, while those for the codes output by the WATFIV compiler appear in Appendix F. Let us now examine the error-diagnostic messages that are associated with the listing in Fig. 4.20.

The first error message code, FM-2, follows the second statement in the program. Looking for the code FM-2 in Appendix E, we discover that the error-diagnostic message is 'NO STATEMENT NUMBER ON A FORMAT STATEMENT'. The reason this error occurred is that the statement label 501 had been omitted from this statement. Since every FORMAT statement must be referenced by a READ or WRITE statement, a FORMAT statement must have a label. In this example, the WATFOR compiler discovered that we had left the label off this FORMAT statement. A second error code, FT-2, also refers to this FORMAT statement. From the table, we learn that the error-diagnostic message for this error code is 'INVALID FORM FOLLOWING A SPECIFICATION'. Since the format code is of the form E*w*.*d*, we notice that the period separating the *w* from the *d* has been incorrectly input as a comma.

The next error detected by the compiler refers to FORMAT statement 502. The error-diagnostic message for the error code FT-6 is 'NO CLOSING QUOTE IN A HOLLERITH FIELD'. At first this message may seem cryptic. However, once it is learned that a Hollerith field is simply a name sometimes used for a string constant we immediately notice that the righthand apostrophe was omitted from the string constant ' V2='. The next statement also contains a syntax error. This time the error is caused by an incorrect spelling of the word FORMAT. Notice that the error code ST-5 that was output means 'UNDECODEABLE STATEMENT'. What WATFOR was trying to say in this case is that it is totally confused with respect to the kind of statement this is intended to be. Therefore, all it can tell you is that some unidentified error exists in the statement. This result is not uncommon when FORTRAN keywords are spelled incorrectly. The next error (IO-J) refers to the fact that a comma appeared following the variable V2 in the READ statement variable list. Since commas are used to separate items in a variable list, the appearance of a comma following a variable infers that another variable follows this variable. When WATFOR cannot locate the next variable, it decides this must be an error and outputs the appropriate error code.

The error code PC-0 that follows the IF statement translates to the error-diagnostic message 'UNMATCHED PARENTHESES'. This error is a result of a missing right parenthesis following the logical expression in the IF statement. The next error code (ST-5) results since WATFOR is not sure whether the GO TO 10 statement is a part of the logical expression of the IF statement or the statement that is to be executed when the logical expression evaluates to a value of true. The error code CC-7 that appears following statement 10 translates to the error-diagnostic message 'FIRST CHARACTER OF STATEMENT NOT ALPHABETIC'. This error probably occurred because the numeric key was depressed when striking the "L" key, thus producing a "6" instead of the desired "L". The error-diagnostic 'MISSING OPERATOR', which is associated with the next error code (SX-0), does not seem to make sense in the context of this statement. In fact, it results because the first error caused the WATFOR compiler to be confused about this statement. This confusion as to the nature of a statement and errors associated with a statement often occurs when syntax errors are present in a program.

The next error code (ST-4) is warning the programmer that there is not a statement number on the statement that follows a GO TO statement. Since the only way to reach a statement following a GO TO is to branch to it, this STOP statement cannot be reached because it does not have a label. The next error code results because WATFOR expects a $ENTRY card rather than a $IBSYS card following the program END statement. The final four error codes are included because there were four statement labels used in program that did not appear on statements in the program. Thus the statements being referenced in these cases are undefined. Hopefully tracing through this example has developed an understanding of what syntax errors are and how FORTRAN compilers identify them. In addition, the fact that syntax errors are easy to detect and correct should now be well understood.

The next topic to be explored is execution-time errors. *Execution-time errors* are the result of attempting to perform operations that are illegal. These execution-time errors are usually more difficult to correct than syntax errors because the cause is often found in results produced by an operation that occurs elsewhere in the program. However, execution-time errors are easy to detect because most FORTRAN compilers produce error messages when they occur. In WATFOR and WATFIV, error codes are produced for execution-time errors just as they were for syntax errors. The meaning of these error codes can be determined by looking up the related error diagnostic message in either Appendix E or Appendix F.

A small program to introduce one example of an execution-time error appears in Fig. 4.21. Notice that the error code was output after the $ENTRY statement, thus indicating that this is an execution-time error. Looking up FM-5 in Appendix E, we learn

Figure 4.21 FORTRAN Program with Execution-Time Error

```
          C  ***** EXECUTION TIME ERRORS -- EXAMPLE 1 *****************************
    1           REAL X
    2        501 FORMAT(I10)
    3           X=10.0
    4           WRITE(6,501) X
    5           STOP
    6           END

          $ENTRY
 ***ERROR***       FM-5

        PROGRAMME WAS EXECUTING LINE      4 IN ROUTINE #MAIN# WHEN TERMINATION OCCURRED
```

that the 'FORMAT SPECIFICATION AND DATA TYPE DO NOT MATCH'. Furthermore the message is output that the error occurred during execution of the statement in line 4 in the main program segment and that program execution was terminated because of the error. Upon examining line 4 and its associated FORMAT statement, we discover that the error is that we were attempting to output the value of the real variable X using the integer format code I10. Since only F*w*.*d* and E*w*.*d* format codes can be used to output real values, this was clearly an error.

Figure 4.22 contains a second program designed to illustrate execution-time errors. The error message in this case (KO-3) indicates that 'TOO MANY EXPONENT OVERFLOWS' have occurred. Again, execution of the program was halted when the error occurred, this time in line 3 of the program. In this example, the cause of the error is easy to detect. This is because in the immediately preceding program statement we see that the variable X has been assigned the value 1.0E40. Since the product of 1.0E40 and 1.0E40 is 1.0E80 and the largest real value that most computers permit is about 1.0E75, we can see that the error occurred in evaluating the expression in the statement in line 3. Had the value of X been computed in a

Figure 4.22 FORTRAN Program with Execution-Time Error

```
       C  ***** EXECUTION TIME ERRORS -- EXAMPLE 2 ****************************
    1        REAL X
    2        X=1.0E40
    3        X=X*X
    4        STOP
    5        END

       $ENTRY
 ***ERROR***      KO-3

      PROGRAMME WAS EXECUTING LINE      3 IN ROUTINE #MAIN# WHEN TERMINATION OCCURRED
```

statement in another part of the program or had it been input, discovering the source of the error would have been much more difficult.

For a third example, we have the program listed in Fig. 4.23. This time the error code of KO-2 refers to 'FLOATING-POINT DIVISION BY ZERO'. The error occurred during the execution of the statement in line 2 and again caused program execution to halt. The cause of the error in this example is obvious. However, in most situations the cause of such an error may be quite difficult to trace down.

Another example of a program that has caused an execution-time error appears in Fig. 4.24. The error diagnostic message for the error code UN-0 is:

'CONTROL CARD ENCOUNTERED ON UNIT 5 DURING EXECUTION'

PROBABLE CAUSE - MISSING DATA OR IMPROPER FORMAT STATEMENTS

In this example, the error was caused by missing data because an input record was not provided following the $ENTRY control statement. Thus, an end-of-file was encountered with no provision made for handling it. In such a case, the computer signals that an error has occurred.

Figure 4.23 FORTRAN Program with Execution-Time Error

```
        C  ***** EXECUTION TIME ERRORS -- EXAMPLE 3 *****************************
    1          REAL X
    2          X=52.0/0.0
    3          STOP
    4          END

        $ENTRY
 ***ERROR***       KO-2

      PROGRAMME WAS EXECUTING LINE      2 IN ROUTINE #MAIN# WHEN TERMINATION OCCURRED
```

Figure 4.24 FORTRAN Program with Execution-Time Error

```
      C   ***** EXECUTION TIME ERRORS -- EXAMPLE 4 *****************************
            REAL X
        501 FORMAT(F12.3)
            READ(5,501) X
            STOP
            END

      $ENTRY
***ERROR***      UN-0

       PROGRAMME WAS EXECUTING LINE      3 IN ROUTINE #MAIN# WHEN TERMINATION OCCURRED
```

As a final example of an execution-time error, we have the program listed in Fig. 4.25. This program was included to illustrate the result of attempting to halt program execution with the END statement instead of with a STOP statement. In closing our discussion of execution time errors, we must note that not all FORTRAN dialects cause program execution to halt for the occurrence of every execution-time error. Instead some dialects will allow up to so many of certain kinds of execution-time errors before program execution is stopped. However, error diagnostics will be output

Figure 4.25 FORTRAN Program with Execution-Time Error

```
      C   ***** EXECUTION TIME ERRORS -- EXAMPLE 5 ****************************
            REAL X
            X=5.2
            END

      $ENTRY
***ERROR***      EN-1

       PROGRAMME WAS EXECUTING LINE      3 IN ROUTINE #MAIN# WHEN TERMINATION OCCURRED
```

for each such execution-time error that occurs.

The third and fourth types of error--the output of incorrect answers or no answers are output--are the most difficult to locate and correct. Such errors are difficult to correct because they can occur for several reasons; these reasons are:

1. A semantical error has been made.
2. A logical error exists in the algorithm.
3. The problem was not correctly defined.

A *semantical error* results when a programmer does not understand the result of executing a particular statement. For example, a programmer might think that the statement in a logical IF statement is executed when the logical expression is false and is skipped when it is true. In this case, the programmer would code the flowchart decision

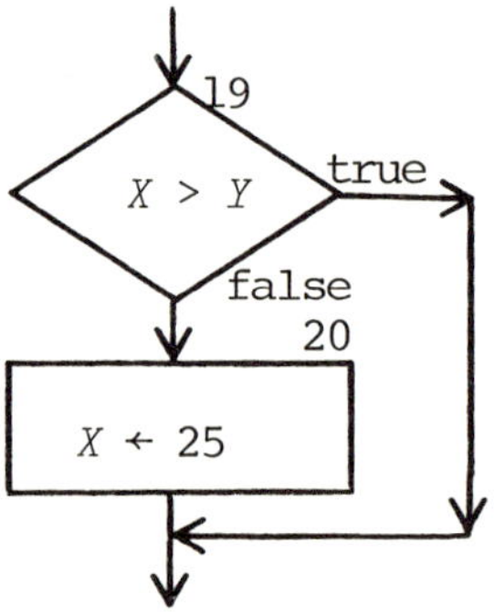

incorrectly as:

```
IF(X.GT.Y) X=25
```

Note that this error is simply a result of the programmer not understanding the semantics of the IF statement. The cause of semantical errors is very difficult to discover because they generally appear as incorrect answers for the set of test data used. Only occasionally do they turn up as execution-time errors. Generally the only way to locate semantical errors is to compare the flowchart steps with the program statements, referring to the manual for the

FORTRAN dialect being used whenever any questions on semantics occur.

Logical errors exist in a program because the flowchart from which the program was coded contains design errors. A similar statement holds true for incorrect results that occur because a problem was not defined correctly. As we stated earlier, these logical and definitional errors usually appear as incorrect results. However, if we are not careful about constructing our test data sets, these errors may not occur at all during testing of the program. In such a case, the program will be considered to be complete and capable of producing correct results for all input data, when in fact is is not.

Locating the cause of semantical and logical errors is usually done by using some kind of trace technique.* These trace techniques involve the placement of WRITE statements at various points in the program. These WRITE statements are designed to provide either a logical trace or a variable trace. In a *logical trace*, the primary objective is to learn the branches taken during program execution. For the case of a program that has not produced any output, the objective is to determine how far execution had gone before program execution halted. A *variable trace* is designed to output the values of program variables at various points during the execution of the program. In this way, we can learn at which point in the program a variable has acquired an incorrect value.

A logical trace is performed by inserting WRITE statements at various points in the program. The variable lists of these WRITE statements will usually be empty and the FORMAT statement will contain a string constant that is used to identify the point of execution. A variable trace is similar to a logical trace, except that the values

---

*For those using the main text, recall the use of trace tables to verify the correctness of the logic of an algorithm flowchart.

of variables are being output. Thus, the WRITE statements will have the variable names in their variable lists. In addition, the FORMAT statements should include string constants that identify which variables are associated with the values output.

The concepts of logical and variable tracing are illustrated in Fig. 4.26. There are three variable trace statements and two WRITE statements that are providing a logical trace of program execution. Looking at the output produced by the execution of this program, we notice that the logical trace message

```
**** LOGICAL TRACE POINT 1 ****
```

was output five times. This indicates that the IF statement that tests the condition CHAR.EQ.O is executed five times. A few moments thought will explain this in that there were four vowels found in the preceding IF statements. Since the test data contained a total of nine characters, this means that there were five characters that were not equal to A, E, or I. Similarly, the logical trace message

```
**** LOGICAL TRACE POINT 2 ****
```

was output three times because there were three characters input that were not vowels.

The variable trace message that is used to output the values input to CHAR is output nine times. Each time it is output the value of CHAR just input is displayed. The variable trace message that outputs the value of the counter variable CTA is shown two times. Each time it is output it shows the value just assigned to that variable. A similar comment applies to the variable trace message for the variable CTI.

This example should illustrate the importance of logical and variable trace statements for locating the cause of execution-time and logical errors. Of course, when all errors in a program have been corrected, the logical and variable trace statements should be

Figure 4.26 FORTRAN Program of Figure 4.18 with Logical and Variable Trace Statements

```
C   ***** PROGRAM FOR ALGORITHM OF FIGURE 4.22M WITH TRACE STATEMENTS ***
      INTEGER CTA,CTE,CTI,CTO,CTU,CHAR,A,E,I,O,U
      DATA A,E,I,O,U/'A','E','I','O','U'/
  501 FORMAT(A1)
  502 FORMAT('1',11X,'VOWEL COUNT RESULTS',/,1X,40('-'),/,'    A=',I3,
     * '    E=',I3,'    I=',I3,'    O=',I3,'    U=',I3)
      CTA=0
      CTE=0
      CTI=0
      CTO=0
      CTU=0
   10 READ(5,501,END=40) CHAR
      WRITE(6,20001) CHAR
20001 FORMAT(1X,'**** VARIABLE TRACE: CHAR= ',A1)
      IF(CHAR.EQ.A) GO TO 15
      IF(CHAR.EQ.E) GO TO 20
      IF(CHAR.EQ.I) GO TO 25
      WRITE(6,10001)
10001 FORMAT(1X,'**** LOGICAL TRACE POINT 1 ****')
      IF(CHAR.EQ.O) GO TO 30
      IF(CHAR.EQ.U) GO TO 35
      WRITE(6,10002)
10002 FORMAT(1X,'**** LOGICAL TRACE POINT 2 ****')
      GO TO 10
   15 CTA=CTA+1
      WRITE(6,20002) CTA
20002 FORMAT(1X,'**** VARIABLE TRACE: CTA= ',I3)
      GO TO 10
   20 CTE=CTE+1
      GO TO 10
   25 CTI=CTI+1
      WRITE(6,20003) CTI
20003 FORMAT(1X,'**** VARIABLE TRACE: CTI= ',I3)
      GO TO 10
   30 CTO=CTO+1
      GO TO 10
   35 CTU=CTU+1
      GO TO 10
   40 WRITE(6,502) CTA,CTE,CTI,CTO,CTU
      STOP
      END
```

Figure 4.26 (continued)

```
**** VARIABLE TRACE: CHAR= L
**** LOGICAL TRACE POINT 1 ****
**** LOGICAL TRACE POINT 2 ****
**** VARIABLE TRACE: CHAR= O
**** LOGICAL TRACE POINT 1 ****
**** VARIABLE TRACE: CHAR= U
**** LOGICAL TRACE POINT 1 ****
**** VARIABLE TRACE: CHAR= I
**** VARIABLE TRACE: CTI=    1
**** VARIABLE TRACE: CHAR= S
**** LOGICAL TRACE POINT 1 ****
**** LOGICAL TRACE POINT 2 ****
**** VARIABLE TRACE: CHAR= I
**** VARIABLE TRACE: CTI=    2
**** VARIABLE TRACE: CHAR= A
**** VARIABLE TRACE: CTA=    1
**** VARIABLE TRACE: CHAR= N
**** LOGICAL TRACE POINT 1 ****
**** LOGICAL TRACE POINT 2 ****
**** VARIABLE TRACE: CHAR= A
**** VARIABLE TRACE: CTA=    2


                  VOWEL COUNT RESULTS
-------------------------------------------------
   A=  2     E=  0     I=  2     O=  1     U=  1
```

removed. That is the reason for using such large numbers on the FORMAT statements associated with the trace statements--so they can be easily identified when it comes time for them to be removed. Another good practice to follow is to not change any statement in the program when inserting either logical or variable trace statements. This is particularly true when the changes involve statement numbers. The reason for this is that, no matter how careful you are in changing statements, the danger exists that the changes will alter program logic or will not be changed back to their original status when removing the trace statements.

One final point is that caution must be exercised in using trace statements. The reason is that a small number of trace statements can produce *large* volumes of output when portions of a program are executed many times. Therefore, be careful when tracing so that you do not become buried in output and, in the process, have your computer center people get mad at you for wasting paper and computer time. To protect against program errors or trace requests that require too much output or computer time, most installations place limits on the amount of output pages and computer time permitted to most users.

PROBLEMS

Problem 12 relates to an algorithm flowchart in the main text. For those not using the main text, this problem should be ignored.

12. Write the FORTRAN program that corresponds with the algorithm flowchart of Fig. 4.11M. Use as test data the values:

    4,5,6, 6,5,4, 5,6,4, 4,6,5

For Problems 13 through 34: (1) develop an algorithm flowchart, (2) write a corresponding FORTRAN program, and (3) test the program using the test data provided. All of these problems correspond with problems in Ch. 4 of the main text (the corresponding main-text problem numbers are given in parentheses). Therefore, those using the main text should already have completed the algorithm development phase.

13. (Prob. 15) The problem is that of finding the largest of four numeric input values using logic that represents an extension of that used in the algorithm flowchart of Fig. 4.11. Use as test data:

    4,6,8,10, 10,4,6,8, 8,6,10,4

14. (Prob. 16) The problem is that of finding the smallest value in a set of numbers. Assume that the number of values in each data set is known. The output for each data set should consist of the input values and the smallest number found in the data set.

Include string constants in the output to identify the different values. Use as test data the values used to test the program in Fig. 4.14.

15. (Prob. 17) A teacher wants to let the computer find the area of a triangle given the length of the base and the height (or altitude) of the triangle. The area is calculated simply as the product of the base and height divided by 2. The algorithm should be designed to accept the base and height measures for a series of triangles and compute the area of each. Output should consist of the input values and their respective areas. Use as test data the values:

    10,5, 12,3, 8,9

16. (Prob. 18) A bank has the problem of converting U.S. dollars into foreign currency and foreign currency into U. S. dollars. To convert from U. S. dollars to foreign currency, it is necessary to multiply the number of dollars by the current exchange rate between dollars and that currency. Conversion from the foreign currency is accomplished by dividing the number of units of foreign currency by the same exchange rate. In developing your conversion algorithm, assume that the input for each conversion is the number of units of currency to be converted, the current exchange rate between dollars and that currency, and either a 1 or 2, where 1 indicates the currency to be converted is dollars and a 2 indicates that it is a foreign currency that is to be converted. Output should include: (1) a string constant that states whether the currency converted is 'U.S.' or 'FOREIGN', (2) the amount converted, (3) the current exchange rate, and (4) the amount of converted currency. Use as test data the values:

    1000,2.20,1, 1000,2.20,2

17. (Prob. 19) Modify the algorithm flowchart of Fig. 4.13 so that the value of *N* is not modified while inputting and processing the data set values. This will require the use of a counter variable that keeps track of how many values have been processed. Use as test data the values used to test the program of Fig. 4.14.

18. (Prob. 20) Modify the algorithm flowchart of Fig. 4.13 so that the variable *Large* is initialized with the first data value of each data set. Is this algorithm more or less efficient than the original version? Use as test data the values used to test the program of Fig. 4.14.

19. (Prob. 21) Modify the algorithm flowchart of Fig. 4.13 so that a count is kept of how many data sets have been processed. Before each data set is input, a heading should be output which states

that 'DATA_SET_NUMBER_'*n*'_FOLLOWS', where *n* is the number of that data set. Use as test data the values used to test the program of Fig. 4.14.

20. (Prob. 22) A teacher wants to let the computer assign course grades, where the grading system used is:

0-59	F
60-69	D
70-79	C
80-89	B
90-100	A

Assume that the input is a student's name followed by his or her course average, where the average is given as an integer number. Output should consist of the student's name, course average, and course letter grade. Use as test data the values:

TIM,75, MARY,58, BABS,96, CAL,82

21. (Prob. 23) An accountant wants to use the computer to compute social security tax. The tax is calculated by taking 6 percent of the person's gross pay up to $13,200 per year. That is, social security tax is only charged on the first $13,200 of a person's income for each year. Your algorithm inputs should be a person's: (1) name, (2) accumulated earnings for the year, and (3) salary for this pay period. Output should include the input values and the social security tax. Use as test data the values:

TIM,13400,245, MARY,13130,220, BABS,8500,150

22. (Prob. 24) Modify the algorithm flowchart of Fig. 4.13 for the case in which the number of values in each data set is not known. To accomplish this, assume that the last data value in each data set is followed by a dummy value that is equal to 10^{15}. In addition, assume that all legitimate data values must be less than that value. Use as test data the values used to test the program in Fig. 4.14.

23. (Prob. 25) An engineer wants to have the computer find the area of a triangle given the length of the three sides. The area is defined to be

$$area = \sqrt{T\cdot(T - X)\cdot(T - Y)\cdot(T - Z)}$$

where X, Y, and Z are the lengths of the respective sides of the triangle, and T is equal to the sum of the lengths of the three sides divided by 2. The algorithm should be designed to accept the lengths of the three sides for a series of triangles and compute the area of each. Output should consist of the input values and their respective areas. Use as test data the values:

10,5,5, 5,5,5, 10,3,9

24. (Prob. 26) A stockbroker wants the computer to add up dollar stock sales for each day. The algorithm for this problem should be developed assuming that the number of stock transactions is known. Assume that input will be the values of these transactions, while output will consist of the values and their sum. You should assume that the algorithm is capable of performing this task for more than one day's stock sales each time that it is used. Use as test data the values:

    4,10200,24000,22600,18320, 3,6200,4800,9270

25. (Prob. 27) Solve Problem 24 assuming that the number of stock transactions is not known in advance. Assume for this problem that each stock sale does not exceed $1,000,000,000. Use as test data the values:

    $10200,24000,22600,18320,10^{10},\ 6200,4800,9270,10^{10}$

26. (Prob. 28) A system of two simultaneous linear equations of the form

$$a \cdot x + b \cdot y = e$$
$$c \cdot x + d \cdot y = f$$

can be solved using the equations

$$x = (e \cdot d - b \cdot f)/(a \cdot d - b \cdot c)$$
$$y = (a \cdot f - e \cdot c)/(a \cdot d - b \cdot c)$$

for the case in which $a \cdot d \neq b \cdot c$. An error message can be output should $a \cdot d = b \cdot c$. The input in this problem will be values for the variables a, b, c, d, e, and f. The output should consist of the input values and the two values that represent the solutions for the inputs. Use as test data the values:

    1,2,3,1,3,2, 1,2,1,2,3,1, 1,2,1,2,1,1

27. (Prob. 29) A mathematician thinks that he has discovered an important fact and wants to use the computer to help verify that it is correct. He has discovered that for any positive integer, N, the square of that integer (N^2) is equal to the sum of the first N odd integers. For example, $4^2 = 16$ is equal to $1 + 3 + 5 + 7 = 16$. The input to your algorithm should be values of N and the output should be N, N^2, and the sum of the first N odd integers. Use as test data the values:

    2,6,13,0,4,-5,8

28. (Prob. 30) Depreciation methods other than straight line are often used in depreciating an asset. One of these methods is the sum-of-the-years-digits method. In this method, a denominator d is formed using the formula $d = Y \cdot (Y + 1)/2$, where Y is the life of the asset. Then the depreciation is computed by

multiplying the original cost of the asset by the number of periods of asset life remaining at the beginning of that period and then dividing this product by the denominator. Your algorithm inputs should be original asset cost and life in periods. Output should be the input values and a table that shows depreciation of the asset. Use as test data the values used to test the program of Fig. 4.16.

29. (Prob. 31) Depreciation methods other than straight line are often used in depreciating an asset. One of these methods is the declining balance method. In this method a constant factor is multiplied times the remaining asset value to obtain each year's depreciation amount. This constant factor is calculated by dividing a depreciation multiplier by the life of the asset. Thus in the first year the constant factor is multiplied times the original cost value of the asset to obtain the first year's depreciation. In the second year the constant factor is multiplied times the original asset cost less first year's depreciation to arrive at second-year depreciation. And so the process continues for future years until the useful life of the asset is over. Your algorithm inputs should be original asset cost, asset life, and the depreciation multiplier (which must be greater than 1). Output should include input values and a table that shows the depreciation of the asset. Use as test data the values:

    1000,5,2, 4000,10,1.5

30. (Prob. 32) Modify the algorithm flowchart of Fig. 4.15 so that the variable *Bal* is eliminated. This change must be made in a way that does not change the results produced by the algorithm. Is the resulting algorithm more or less efficient than the unmodified version? Use as test data the values used to test the program of Fig. 4.16.

31. (Prob. 33) Modify the algorithm flowchart of Fig. 4.15 so that the condition in box 9 does not involve either the variable *Period* or *Life*. This change must be made in a way that does not change the results produced by the algorithm. Use as test data the values used to test the program of Fig. 4.16.

32. (Prob. 34) A mathematician needs to solve some quadratic equations of the form

$$a \cdot x^2 + b \cdot x + c = 0$$

using the quadratic formula

$$x = \frac{-b \pm \sqrt{b^2 - 4 \cdot a \cdot c}}{2 \cdot a}$$

The inputs for this algorithm will be the coefficient values *a*, *b*, and *c*, while the output should consist of these input values together with the two values (the two roots) of *x*. The message that imaginary roots have occurred should be output instead of the results in the case where $b^2 < 4 \cdot a \cdot c$. Use as test data the values:

4,7,2, 2,6,3, 4,2,3, 3,9,6

33. (Prob. 35) An English professor wants to use the computer to help him count the number of words in a manuscript. This can be accomplished by counting the number of blank spaces since words are separated from each other by a blank space (we will assume that there is never more than one space between words in the manuscript). Assume that the manuscript is input one character at a time and that output is to consist of the number of words preceded by a string constant that describes this value. Use as test data the string:

    THIS IS A VERY SHORT MANUSCRIPT.

34. (Prob. 36) An executive prefers that his employees use two consecutive hyphens instead of semicolons in their correspondence. Since all letters for this company are computer-edited anyway, the executive wants the computer department to write an algorithm through which all letters are processed to change all occurrences of semicolons to two hyphens. Assume that all such letters are input to the algorithm one character at a time. Output should consist of the edited letter. Use as test data the string:

    STOCK PRICES ARE HIGH; HOWEVER, HOGS ARE LOW. BUT, INFLATION IS HERE; SO IT DOES NOT MATTER.

SUMMARY

1. There are a number of versions of the FORTRAN programming language. Each of these versions is called a FORTRAN dialect.
2. The symbols in the alphabet of the FORTRAN programming language are:
    a. The alphabetic symbols, which consist of the 26 uppercase letters of the English alphabet.
    b. The numeric symbols, which consist of the ten decimal digits.
    c. The special symbols, which are

       + - * / = .) , ($ *blank* ' ;

3. FORTRAN has two classes of symbol combinations that are used to replace position or single symbols in the flowchart language. These are:
   a. The exponentiation operator, in which the symbol combination ** indicates the arithmetic operation of exponentiation.
   b. Keywords, which are certain strings of alphabetic characters that define operations in the language.

4. The words in FORTRAN consist of: (a) constants, (b) variables, and (c) keywords.

5. The four basic types of FORTRAN statements are:
   a. Processing statements.
   b. Control statements.
   c. Declarative statements.
   d. Input/Output statements.

6. There are two types of constants in FORTRAN. They are:
   a. Numeric constants.
   b. String constants.

   The numeric constants are of two types: (a) integer constants and (b) real constants.

7. All FORTRAN variable names are declared to be numeric, even though FORTRAN numeric variables can be used to store values that are string constants. The two types of FORTRAN numeric variables are: (a) integer variables and (b) real variables.

8. A variable is a name that refers to a place in computer main memory where a constant is stored.

9. Variable names are declared as to the type of numeric values they may have using the INTEGER and REAL type statements, both of which are declarative statements that are nonexecutable.

10. The FORTRAN assignment statement is of the form

    variable = expression

    where the symbol = is an assignment operator and not an equal sign.

11. Conversion between integer and real constants can cause problems in a program. Thus integer and real values must not be combined in an arithmetic expression without explicitly indicating the conversion that is to take place.

12. Evaluation of an expression is the process of successively reducing subexpressions to constant values until the entire expression is reduced to a single constant value.

13. Evaluation of a FORTRAN arithmetic expression is done using the precedence rules of Fig. 2.3, with the possible exception of the exponentiation operation.

14. Strings are difficult to process in FORTRAN. This is because:
    a. String constants cannot appear in assignment statements or the logical expression of an IF statement.
    b. Only a limited number of characters may appear in a string constant assigned to a variable.

    The first problem can be overcome by using DATA statements or READ statements to assign string constants as the values of variables.

15. A READ statement contains a list of variable names that are assigned values obtained from input records. The layout of the values on the input records is defined using a FORMAT statement.

16. A WRITE statement contains a list of variables the values of which are displayed as output records. The layout of these output records is defined using a FORMAT statement.

17. The FORTRAN unconditional branching statement is the GO TO statement.

18. The conditional branching statement in FORTRAN is the IF statement, which has the form:

    IF(*logical expression*) *statement*

    The action of the IF statement is to execute *statement* if *logical expression* evaluates to true and ignore it if *logical expression* evaluates to false.

19. Program testing represents a systematic attempt to find and correct any errors that might cause the program to not provide correct answers to the problem that it is designed to solve.

20. Some of the common types of errors are: (a) syntax errors, which occur at compile time, (b) execution-time errors, (c) semantical errors, and (d) logical errors.

21. Locating the cause of logical and semantical errors is usually done by using program tracing techniques. The two kinds of traces are: (a) the logical trace, in which program execution flow is being monitored and (b) the variable trace, which traces the values of selected variables during program execution.

CHAPTER 5

PROGRAM DESIGN II: LOOPING AND ITERATIVE PROGRAMS

In Chapters 2 and 4 we learned about the basic aspects of problem analysis, algorithm design, and FORTRAN programming. In this chapter we are going to study some additional concepts of algorithm design and FORTRAN programming.

5.1 LOOPING

In almost every algorithm and program we have developed thus far in the text, one or more steps have been executed more than once. In fact, virtually all algorithms ever designed for execution using a computer have in common that they contain one or more steps that will be executed more than once. The steps that are executed over and over again in an algorithm or program make up what is called a loop. That is, a loop is a series of algorithm or program steps that is executed repetitively.

Because of the importance of loops, FORTRAN includes a statement that provides a built-in looping facility. This built-in looping facility is provided by the DO statement. Its general form is

DO *label* *v*=*s*,*u*,*i*

where: (1) *label* is a statement label on an executable statement that physically follows the DO statement, (2) *v* is a scalar integer variable, (3) *s*, *u*, and *i* (called the *loop parameters*) are either unsigned positive integer constants or scalar integer variables, and (4) *i* is optional. The label given in the DO statement defines the range of the loop, since all statements from the DO statement through the statement labeled with the value of *label* are included in the loop. The variable *v* is called the *index* of the DO-loop and is assigned the value of *s*, the starting value, when the loop is being entered. The body of the DO-loop is then executed, with the value of *i* being added to the value of *v* after each execution. This process is repeated until the value of *v* is greater than the value of the upper limit *u*, at which point control is passed to the first executable statement following the DO-loop. When *i* is omitted, the increment is assumed to be 1. In addition, the value of *s* must not be greater than the value of *u*. A flowchart that provides the effect of a DO-loop is given in Fig. 5.1 to aid in understanding the action of the DO statement.

Figure 5.1 Flowchart Equivalent of a FORTRAN DO Statement

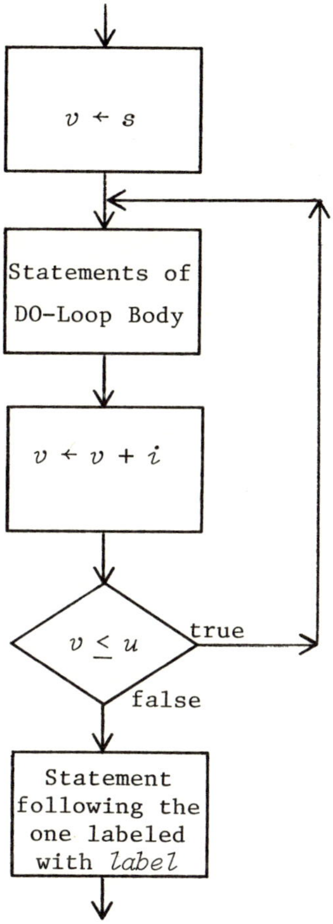

As an example, the DO-loop

```
      DO 10 I=1,8,2
        READ(5,502) X
10      SUM=SUM+X
20
```

is equivalent to the sequence

```
      I=1
 5      READ(5,502) X
10      SUM=SUM+X
      I=I+2
      IF(I.LE.8) GO TO 5
20
```

where statement 20 is any executable FORTRAN statement. For a second example, the DO-loop

```
      DO 50 J=L,M
        READ(5,502) A,R
        PROD=A*R
50      WRITE(6,503) A,R,PROD
60
```

is equivalent to the sequence

```
      J=L
30      READ(5,502) A,R
        PROD=A*R
50      WRITE(6,503) A,R,PROD
      J=J+1
      IF(J.LE.M) GO TO 30
60
```

where statement 60 is any executable statement. Notice in this example that the value 1 is used as an increment since the value of i is omitted. Also, observe that any or all of the loop parameters may be scalar integer variables. However, they may not be expressions. In these two examples, note that one DO statement replaces two assignment statements and one IF statement.

There are four rules relating to DO-loops that must be observed in most dialects. These are:

1. The index *v* and loop parameters *s*, *u*, and *i* may not have their values changed within the range of a DO-loop.
2. A DO-loop may be placed inside of another DO-loop only as long as the inner loop is completely contained within the outer loop.
3. A DO-loop must be entered by first executing the DO statement. That is, it is illegal to branch to a statement inside of a DO-loop from a statement outside of the loop.
4. The last statement in a DO-loop must not be a GO TO, STOP, RETURN, or DO statement, nor can it be any nonexecutable statement.*

The first rule means that the loop index and loop parameters cannot appear to the left of an assignment operator or in a READ statement that is in the range of the loop. The second rule means that the sequence

```
      DO 70 J=1,5
        DO 80 I=1,10
80
70
```

is a legal nesting of DO-loops since the inner loop is completely contained within the outer loop. On the other hand, the sequence

---

*In addition, it may not be either an arithmetic IF or a CALL EXIT statement (two statements we have not discussed in this book).

```
      DO 70 J=1,5
        DO 80 I=1,10
70
80
```

is an illegal nesting of DO-loops since the end of the inner loop falls after the end of the outer loop.

The third rule is required to ensure that the loop index *v* is properly initialized. Note that this rule does not mean that branches out of a loop or branches within a loop are illegal. For example, the sequence

```
      DO 15 I=1,1000
        READ(5,504) X
        IF(I.GT.25) GO TO 10
 5      IF(X.GT.0) GO TO 20
10
15
20
```

is perfectly legal. This sequence simply causes statement 5 to be skipped whenever the loop index, I, is greater than 25, and causes a branch out of the loop whenever it is determined in statement 5 that a value of X just input is greater than zero.

The fourth rule would pose a problem in certain situations, if it were not for the executable dummy statement CONTINUE. This statement is used as the terminal statement of a DO-loop whenever it is desired that the looping process be continued. For example, algorithm logic may require values to be input until a negative value is read, at which time the value will be output and a branch taken out of the loop. This can be accomplished by the statements

```
      DO 15 K=1,1000
        READ(5,515) A
        IF(A.GE.0.0) GO TO 15
        WRITE(6,516) A
        GO TO 20
15      CONTINUE
20
```

Without the CONTINUE statement, the loop would have to end with a GO TO statement. But, since this is illegal, the dummy statement CONTINUE can be used, which simply causes no action to be taken other than to continue with the looping process. The moment the negative value is input, the IF statement will cause the value of A to be output and a branch to statement 20, which is outside of the loop.

As a final point, the loop index v is generally not defined outside of the range of the DO-loop for which it is the index. An exception to this rule exists when a branch is taken outside of the loop. In that case the loop index will retain the value it had when the branch out of the loop was made. Thus, in the most recent example, K would have a value whenever the GO TO statement causes a branch to statement 20. However, if statement 20 is reached because the value of the loop index K exceeds 1000, then the variable K will not be defined when statement 20 is executed.

5.2 SUBSCRIPTED VARIABLES

Recall from algebra that we often have a variable name that has a group (or array) of values associated with it. In such a case we place a subscript on the variable to indicate to which value of the variable we are referring. Similarly, we have a need for subscripted variables in flowcharts and in FORTRAN programs.

Declarative statements must be used in both flowcharts and FORTRAN programs to indicate the number of elements in the set of values associated with a subscripted variable. In flowcharts, a subscripted variable for a one-dimensional array is declared by simply placing an integer constant enclosed in parentheses following the variable name in the NUM, NUMINT, or STR declaration. For example, the annotation box

NUM *X*(100)

declares *X* to be a one-dimensional array that consists of 100 numeric values. Similarly, in a FORTRAN program a one-dimensional array variable is declared by placing an integer constant enclosed in parentheses following the variable name in an INTEGER or REAL type statement. Thus, the FORTRAN program declaration for the above flowchart example would be:

```
REAL X(100)
```

In both flowcharts and FORTRAN, subscripts are assumed to be the set of consecutive unsigned positive integers that begin at 1 and progress through the limit given by the declaration. Note that the maximum subscript value given in the declaration must be a constant; it may not be a variable.

In flowcharts a subscript may be any expression that evaluates to a positive integer value. This subscript expression must be enclosed in parentheses following the array variable name. In a FORTRAN program, subscripts may be: (1) an unsigned positive integer constant, (2) an integer variable with a value that is a positive integer, or (3) an expression that takes one of the forms

$$v \pm c$$
$$c * v$$
$$c * v \pm c$$

where *v* is any integer variable and *c* is any unsigned positive integer constant. Note that in the case of the subscript expression *c*v±c*, the two constants may have different values.

For both flowcharts and FORTRAN programs, a subscript value may never be greater than the maximum subscript value given in the declaration for that array variable. In addition, a subscript may never have a value that is less than or equal to zero. Examples of valid subscripts and subscript expressions are contained in the FORTRAN statement:

```
A(2)=B(J)+C(I-5)*V(4*I-3)
```

In this example, the array elements being referenced are, in left-to-right order: (1) the second element in the one-dimensional array A, (2) the Jth element in the one-dimensional array B, (3) the (I-5)th element in the one-dimensional array C, and (4) the (4*I-3)th element in the one-dimensional array V. Thus, if I and J are equal to 6 and 12, respectively, when this statement is executed, then the elements being referenced would be A(2), B(12), C(1), and V(21). Of course, the variables I and J must be declared to be of type integer and must be assigned values before this statement is first executed. In addition, the variables A, B, C, and V must be declared in a REAL or an INTEGER type statement to be one-dimensional array variables.

In both a flowchart and a FORTRAN program, an array name may appear without a subscript only in:

1. A GET box or READ statement.
2. A PUT box or WRITE statement.
3. A DATA statement in a FORTRAN program.
4. A statement used to communicate with a subalgorithm or subprogram (these will be discussed in Ch. 9).

When an array name appears without a subscript, a reference to all of the array elements is assumed. Thus, the flowchart step

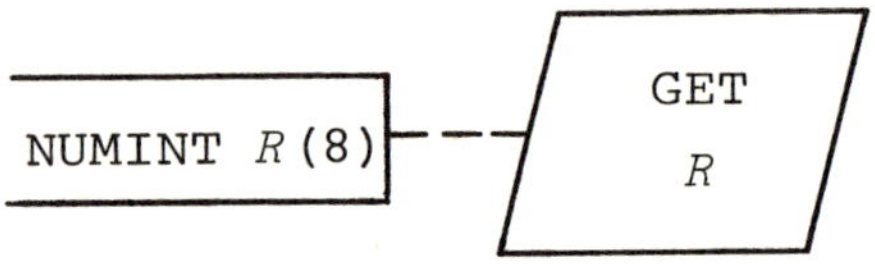

and equivalent FORTRAN program declaration and input statement

```
INTEGER  R(8)
READ(5,505) R
```

cause eight integer constants to be input.

Let us now consider an example that uses subscripted variables. Suppose that we have the problem of computing class exam-score averages for each student and for the class in total. Assume that each student has five test scores entering into his or her average and that each score is to be equally weighted. Furthermore, we will assume that the number of students in the class for which averages are to be computed is known.

For each student in the class, we will input to our algorithm the student's name and five test scores. The output from the algorithm for each student will be the student's name and test average. We will assume that all test scores are integers on the interval 0 to 100, inclusive. Following the output of the last student's name and test average, the class average is to be output.

The algorithm flowchart for this problem appears in Fig. 5.2.* Notice the use of the one-dimensional array, *grade*, which is used to store the five test grades for a student. In Fig. 5.3 is a FORTRAN program that corresponds with this flowchart. Below the program

---

*For those using the main text, this flowchart is the same one that appears in Fig. 5.3M.

Figure 5.2 Algorithm Flowchart for Student-Test-Score-Averaging Problem

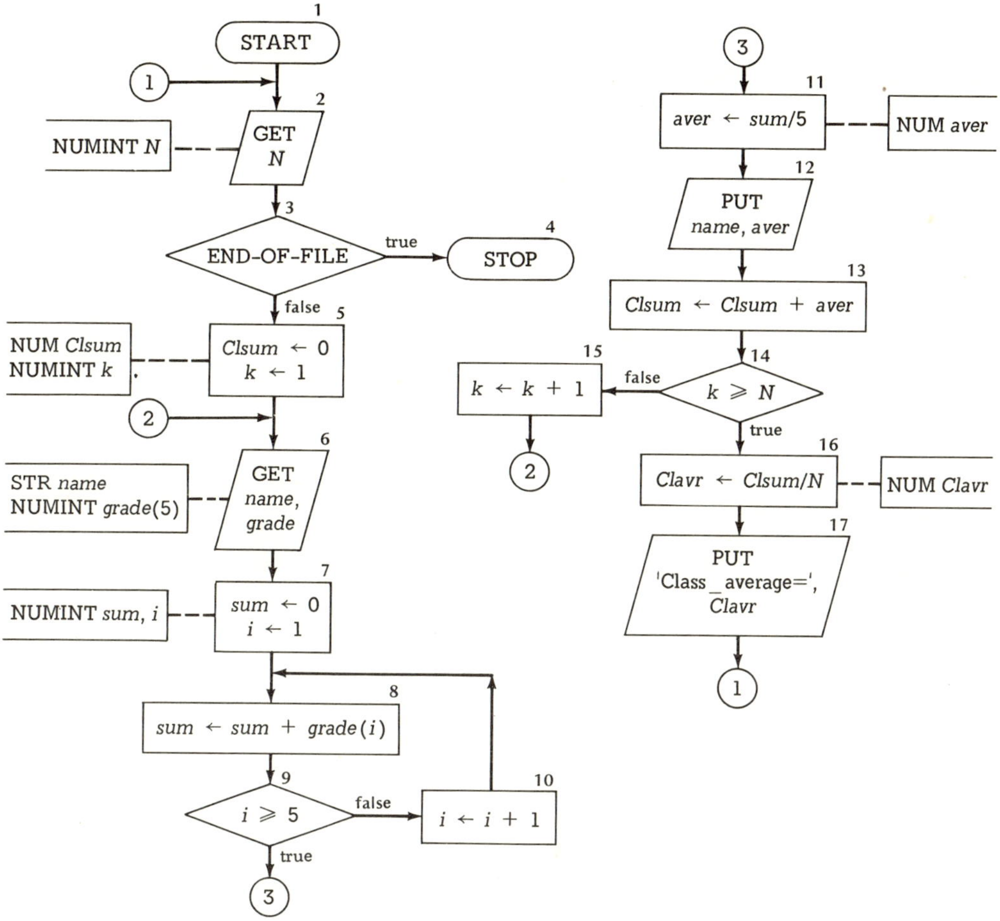

listing in this figure is the output that resulted from executing the program using the following input data records:

Figure 5.3 FORTRAN Program for Flowchart of Figure 5.2

```
C   ***** PROGRAM FOR ALGORITHM OF FIGURE 5.3M ****************************
      REAL CLSUM,NAME(5),AVER,CLAVR
      INTEGER N,K,GRADE(5),SUM,I
  501 FORMAT(I5)
  502 FORMAT('1',5X,'STUDENT GRADE AVERAGES',/,1X,34('-'))
  503 FORMAT(5A4,5I3)
  504 FORMAT(1X,5A4,' AVERAGE=',F5.1)
  505 FORMAT(//,5X,'CLASS AVERAGE=',F5.1)
    1 READ(5,501,END=999) N
      WRITE(6,502)
      CLSUM=0.0
      DO 15 K=1,N
        READ(5,503) NAME,GRADE
        SUM=0
        DO 10 I=1,5
   10     SUM=SUM+GRADE(I)
        AVER=FLOAT(SUM)/5.0
        WRITE(6,504) NAME,AVER
   15   CLSUM=CLSUM+AVER
      CLAVR=CLSUM/FLOAT(N)
      WRITE(6,505) CLAVR
      GO TO 1
  999 STOP
      END
```

```
     STUDENT GRADE AVERAGES
 ----------------------------------
 JIMMY ADAMS          AVERAGE= 70.0
 JERRY JEROME         AVERAGE= 97.2
 ALICE LEWIS          AVERAGE= 85.4
 MARY PARRY           AVERAGE= 80.8
 TOM SMITH            AVERAGE= 88.2


     CLASS AVERAGE= 84.3
```

```
.......................................
    5
JIMMY ADAMS             50 60 70 80 90
JERRY JEROME            95 98 97 96100
ALICE LEWIS             82 86 87 87 85
MARY PARRY              75 80 82 83 84
TOM SMITH               96 75 82 95 93
.......................................
```

Observe in the program that NAME is declared to be an array variable consisting of five elements, which differs from its declaration in the flowchart. The reason NAME is declared as an array is that in most FORTRAN dialects a real variable may not represent string constants with more than four characters. Thus, by declaring NAME as a five-element array, we can store a twenty-character name as five four-character string constants. NAME is declared to be a real variable because: (1) the name is used only for input and output, not for any other purpose, and (2) in some dialects integer variables can hold only two characters per array location.

The variables CLSUM, AVER, and CLAVR are declared to be real variables because they are used in computing averages, which may contain fractional values. In addition, notice that GRADE is declared to be an array consisting of five elements, which is used to store a student's grades. Since all student grades will be integer values, GRADE is declared as an integer array. Because SUM is the variable used in forming the sum of these grades, it is declared to be an integer variable. The variables K and I are both used as counters; therefore they are declared to be integer variables. In general, counters should always be declared as integers. Because the value of N is a count of the number of students, it is also declared to be an integer variable.

The first statement executed in the program of Fig. 5.3 causes a count of the number of students to be input from the first five columns of the next input record. Notice that should an end-of-file condition occur when executing this statement, then a branch is taken to statement 999, which is a STOP statement. Thus, the END=999 portion of this READ statement corresponds with flowchart boxes 3 and 4 of Fig. 5.2. The WRITE statement that follows statement 1 does not have a corresponding step in the flowchart. However, it is included in the program to output an underlined heading. In the next statement, the variable CLSUM is initialized to a value of zero. Notice that the real constant 0.0 is used instead of the integer constant 0 because CLSUM is declared to be a real variable.

The loop that begins with the second statement in flowchart box 5 and continues through flowchart box 15 is given in the program by the statement that begins with DO 15 and ends with statement 15. Notice that the statements that make up the body of this DO-loop are indented two spaces. While this is not a requirement in FORTRAN, we will adopt the convention of indenting the body of DO-loops two spaces to make programs more readable. In the first statement of the loop, the student's: (1) name is input into the five positions of the array NAME, each under an A4 format code, and (2) five grades are input into the elements of the integer array GRADE using I3 format codes. The choice of A4 format codes was explained above, while I3 was selected because test grades are integers between 0 and 100. The next statement initializes the integer variable SUM. Notice that the integer constant 0 is used rather than the real constant 0.0 since SUM is declared to be an integer variable. The DO-loop that follows is the program equivalent of the loop that begins with the second statement of flowchart box 7 and continues through box 10. Again, notice that the one statement that makes up the body of this DO-loop is indented two spaces so that it stands out.

In the line following statement 10, observe that the FLOAT numeric functional operator is used to convert the integer value of the variable SUM to a real value. Then division by the real constant 5.0 is performed, with the quotient being assigned to the real variable AVER. Next the student's name and grade average is output and the average is added to the variable CLSUM. When execution of the DO-loop ending with statement 15 has been completed, the value of CLAVR is computed. Notice that the integer variable N had to have its value converted to a real constant before division of the real value CLSUM took place. The class average is output next and a branch is then taken back to statement 1. This corresponds with the out-connector that follows flowchart box 17 in Fig. 5.2.

Arrays with more than one-dimension occur in many problems. Therefore, both the flowchart language and FORTRAN permit arrays with two or three dimensions. Such arrays are declared in a flowchart annotation box and the FORTRAN program REAL and INTEGER type statements by stating the maximum subscript value for each dimension, with each of these values being separated by a comma. For example, the annotation box

NUM *X*(10,3),*Y*(5,4,2)
NUMINT *ALK*(2,3,7)

and the equivalent FORTRAN type statements

```
REAL  X(10,3),Y(5,4,2)
INTEGER  ALK(2,3,7)
```

declare: (1) X to be a two-dimensional real array with ten rows and three columns; (2) Y to be a three-dimensional real array with five rows, four columns, and two pages; and (3) ALK to be a three-dimensional integer array with two rows, three columns, and seven pages. As in the case of one-dimensional arrays, the subscripts for two- and three-dimensional arrays are assumed to include every positive integer from 1 through the maximum declared for that dimension. Unlike one-dimensional arrays, however, two- and three-dimensional arrays may not appear in an input (GET or READ) or output (PUT or WRITE) statement without subscripts. However, two- or three-dimensional array variables may appear without subscripts in DATA statements and as subalgorithm parameters. These topics will be covered in Chs. 9 and 10.

One final topic needs to be covered under looping--the *implied* DO-loop. In most FORTRAN dialects, the implied DO-loop is used exclusively in READ and WRITE statements. The purpose of the implied DO-loop is to input or output arrays. It consists simply of: (1) a list of one or more variables (where the list is followed by a comma), (2) a loop index *v* followed by an assignment operator and a set of loop parameters *s*, *u*, and *i*, as defined above for the DO statement, and (3) a set of parentheses to enclose the variable list, comma, loop index, assignment operator, and loop parameters. As an example, the statements

```
    READ(5,520) (A(I),I=1,12)
520 FORMAT(12I5)
```

cause twelve integer constants to be read from one input record into the first twelve locations of the one-dimensional array A. Notice that the implied DO-loop in this example is not equivalent to the sequence:

```
   DO 10 I=1,12
10   READ(5,520) A(I)
```

The reason is that each time execution of a READ statement is begun, a new input record is begun. Therefore, the example using the DO statement would cause twelve integer constants to be input from twelve input records. Thus, the implied DO-loop has definite advantages over a regular DO-loop when inputting and outputting arrays.

As another example, the statements

```
      READ(5,525) N,(B(J),J=1,N)
  525 FORMAT(I5,/,(8F10.2))
```

show that the value for an implied DO-loop parameter can be input in the statement in which it is used. Of course, the value must be input before it is needed. The format list in this example also illustrates how a sequence of format codes can be enclosed in parentheses at the extreme right side of a format list when an unknown number of data items are to be input or output. In this example, the value of N will be input from a field consisting of the first five columns of an input record. The slash then causes the remainder of that card to be skipped. Finally, the N values of the one-dimensional array B would be input, eight values per card, into the first N locations of the array B. Recall from Sec. 4.4 that when a format list is exhausted before all of the variable list values have been processed, the scan of the format list resumes with the *rightmost* left parenthesis. In addition, a new input or output record is always begun when returning to the rightmost left parenthesis.

Finally, implied DO-loops can be nested for purposes of inputting or outputting arrays of two or more dimensions. For example, the statements

```
      WRITE(6,530) ((I,J,Z(I,J),J=1,5,2),I=3,4)
  530 FORMAT(2(3(2I4,F8.2),/))
```

cause six values of the two-dimensional array Z to be output, three per output record, where each value is preceded by the values of its two subscripts. The values of Z output will be, in order, Z(3,1), Z(3,3), Z(3,5), Z(4,1), Z(4,3), and Z(4,5). Therefore, the output would appear as

```
3   1  -12.47   3   3  845.67   3   5 -985.69
4   1    8.52   4   3   -7.01   4   5  -19.88
```

This example shows that, by using implied DO-loops, two-dimensional arrays can be input and output in any desired order.

PROBLEMS

1. Give the number of elements for each of the variables declared in the following statements.
   a. `REAL A(5),B,IKL,R(42),Z(113)`
   b. `INTEGER D(4),FOX(4,3),G,S,TOM(7,10)`
   c. `REAL Q(8,5),ZT(70),V,W(5,4)`
   d. `INTEGER P(4,2,3),RV(7,2),TR(2,3,5)`
2. Assuming the declarations

   ```
   REAL   I,J
   INTEGER  K,L
   ```

   determine which of the following FORTRAN subscript expressions are in error and suggest how each may be corrected.

a. 5	d. I+K	g. K+L
b. I+3	e. 2*K-3	h. J*I-1.0
c. K+2	f. L*K+1	

3. Assuming the declarations

   ```
   INTEGER  K,L,M,N
   ```

   write FORTRAN statements that create DO-loops for the following cases.
   a. Iterate a loop forty times, with the loop index K assuming the values: 7, 8, 9, ..., 46.
   b. Iterate a loop, with the loop index L assuming all odd values between 2 and 20.
   c. Iterate a loop, with the loop index M assuming the values 2, 5, 8, ..., 101.
   d. Iterate a loop N times, with the loop index L beginning with a value of K.

4. Assuming the declarations

```
REAL X(1000),Y(8,10)
INTEGER I,J,K,N,A(40)
```

write the FORTRAN input/output statements for the following cases.

a. Input twenty-five integer constants (appearing in two input records using I5 format codes) into the array elements A(6), A(7), A(8), ..., A(30).

b. Input the value of N and N real constants (appearing in (N+4)/5 input records using E16.5 format codes) into the array elements X(1), X(2), X(3), ..., X(N).

c. Input twenty string constants (appearing in one input record using A4 format codes) into the array elements Y(1,1), Y(1,2), Y(1,3), ..., Y(1,10), Y(2,1), ..., Y(2,9), Y(2,10).

d. Output the values of the array elements X(8), X(10), X(12), ..., X(N), five values per output record, using E15.6 format codes.

e. Output the values of the array elements Y(2,5), Y(2,7), Y(2,9), Y(5,5), Y(5,7), Y(5,9), two values per line, using F10.2 format codes and preceding each element with its two subscript values using I3 format codes.

f. Output the values of the array elements A(1), X(1), A(2), X(3), A(3), X(5), ..., A(40), X(79), six values per line, alternating between I5 and E12.4 format codes.

5. Rewrite the program of Fig. 4.14 using DO-loops wherever possible.

6. Rewrite the program of Fig. 4.14 so that all of the data values of one data set are stored in an array before searching for the largest value. Assume that none of the data sets to be processed will have more than 1,000 values.

7. Rewrite the program of Fig. 4.16 so that the depreciation table values are stored in an array as they are computed. Then the table should be output using one WRITE statement that contains an implied DO-loop. Assume that the maximum life of an asset is 100 accounting periods.

8. Rewrite the program of Fig. 4.18 so that the text is input six characters at a time into a one-dimensional array. Then each of these six characters will be processed using a DO-loop and the next six characters of text input. This process will continue until an end-of-file condition occurs.

9. Rewrite the program of Fig. 4.18 so that: (1) the five vowels are stored in a one-dimensional array that is initialized using a DATA statement and (2) the vowel counters are represented as a five-element one-dimensional array.

5.3 THREE EXACT ITERATIVE PROGRAMS

In this section we will give flowcharts and programs for three iterative algorithms that provide what are essentially exact results. By *iterative algorithm*, we mean an algorithm that solves a problem by repeating certain steps one or more times. The notion of algorithms that produce exact results will be more meaningful after the study, in Section 5.4, of algorithms that produce approximate results. In fact, all of the algorithms that have been given up to now in this book have produced what are basically exact results. The only thing that may have been inexact about the results produced by these algorithms would be caused by the finite nature of numbers as represented in a digital computer.

5.3.1 THE SEQUENCING PROGRAM

One of the most frequently performed tasks for which a computer is used involves the resequencing of the records of a file. The process of putting the records of a file into some particular order is called *sorting*. The order into which the records of a file are sequenced is usually dependent on an item within each record called the sort item or sort field.

In this section we will present a flowchart and program for an algorithm for sorting a file that is stored in main memory as a one-dimensional array. That is, the file to be sorted consists of records that consist of only one item or field. Furthermore, we will assume that this field can contain a numeric value that is not greater than 10^{15} in value. The algorithm flowchart for the sequencing problem is given in Fig. 5.4,* while a listing of the program appears in

*For those using the main text, this flowchart is the same one that appears in Fig. 5.7M.

Figure 5.4 Algorithm Flowchart for the Sequencing Problem

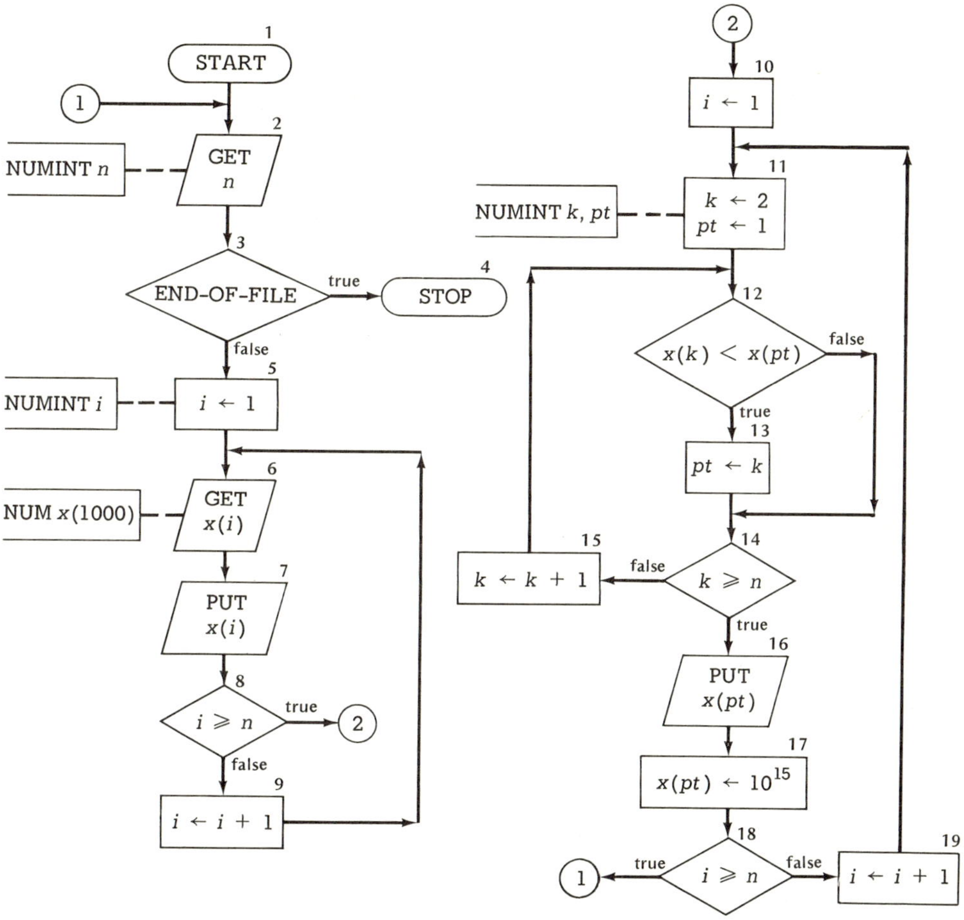

Fig. 5.5. Notice how the indenting of the statements of the bodies of the DO-loops makes the structure of the program easier to determine. Since the program follows the logic of the flowchart, it will not be explained. However, you should study it carefully to be certain that

Figure 5.5 FORTRAN Program for Flowchart of Figure 5.4

```
C    ***** PROGRAM FOR ALGORITHM OF FIGURE 5.7M ***************************
      REAL X(1000)
      INTEGER N,I,K,PT
  501 FORMAT(I4)
  502 FORMAT('1 INPUT ARRAY',/,1X,13('-'),/,4X,'N=',I4,/,1X,13('-'))
  503 FORMAT(E13.5)
  504 FORMAT(//,' SORTED ARRAY',/,1X,13('='))
    1 READ(5,501,END=999) N
      WRITE(6,502) N
      DO 10 I=1,N
        READ(5,503) X(I)
   10   WRITE(6,503) X(I)
    2 WRITE(6,504)
      DO 20 I=1,N
        PT=1
        DO 15 K=2,N
   15     IF(X(K).LT.X(PT)) PT=K
        WRITE(6,503) X(PT)
   20   X(PT)=1.0E15
      GO TO 1
  999 STOP
      END
```

```
 INPUT ARRAY
-------------
   N=    4
-------------
  0.62700E 02
  0.35900E 02
 -0.82600E 02
  0.12700E 02


 SORTED ARRAY
=============
 -0.82600E 02
  0.12700E 02
  0.35900E 02
  0.62700E 02
```

you understand the purpose of each statement and the overall sequencing of steps. The input records used to produce the sample output shown in Fig. 5.5 are not listed since the program outputs all input values. Notice the use of WRITE statements to produce descriptive headings on the output.

5.3.2 The Table-Lookup Programs

A task that must be done in almost any field of study and, in fact, in everyday living involves looking something up in a table. For example, in mathematics there are tables of logarithms, tables of trigonometric functions, and so forth. In English and other natural languages, we have dictionaries which contain the definitions for the words that make up that language. In chemistry there are tables of the basic elements and their symbols, while in accounting there are income tax tables. This list could go on and on.

We can identify three basic elements when looking something up in a table. First, there is the *search argument*, which is the key to be used in searching the table. The table that is being searched for a value usually consists of two sets of elements:

1. A set of list arguments.
2. A set of function values.

The *list arguments* are the pieces of information that are used to access the proper function information in the table. That is, table lookup involves finding a list argument in the table that matches the search argument you have and then outputting the *function value* that corresponds with that list argument.

A flowchart and FORTRAN program listing for the table lookup problem appear in Figs. 5.6* and 5.7, respectively. Notice the use

---

*For those using the main text, this flowchart is the same one that appears in Fig. 5.11M.

Figure 5.6 Algorithm Flowchart for the Table-Lookup Problem

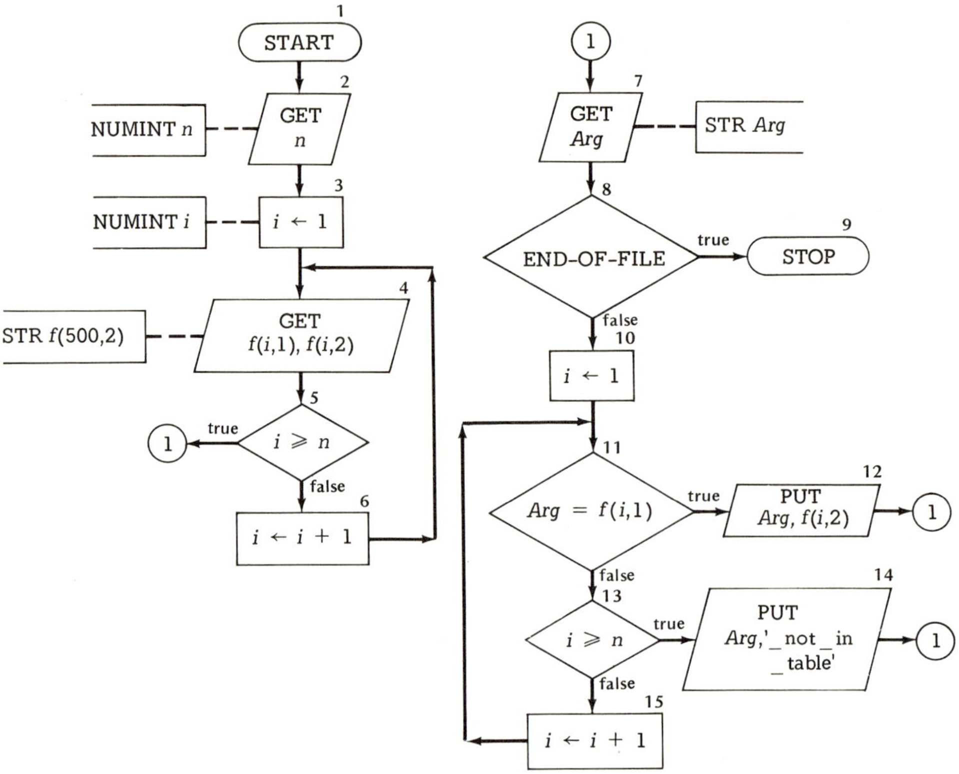

of a nested implied DO-loop in the second READ statement of the program. Execution of this single statement accomplishes the input of the table to be searched, which is the equivalent of boxes 3 through 6 of the flowchart in Fig. 5.6. The input records used to generate

Figure 5.7 FORTRAN Program for Flowchart of Figure 5.6

```
C    ***** PROGRAM FOR ALGORITHM OF FIGURE 5.11M *************************
      REAL F(500,2),ARG
      INTEGER N,I,J
  501 FORMAT('1TABLE LOOKUP RESULTS',/,1X,21('-'),/,2X,'SEARCH    FUNC',
     * 'TION',/,1X,'ARGUMENT    VALUE',/,1X,8('-'),1X,12('-'))
  502 FORMAT(I4)
  503 FORMAT(20A4)
  504 FORMAT(3X,A4,'   NOT IN TABLE')
  505 FORMAT(3X,A4,6X,A4)
      WRITE(6,501)
      READ(5,502) N
      READ(5,503) ((F(I,J),J=1,2),I=1,N)
    1 READ(5,503,END=999) ARG
      DO 15 I=1,N
   15   IF(ARG.EQ.F(I,1)) GO TO 20
      WRITE(6,504) ARG
      GO TO 1
   20 WRITE(6,505) ARG,F(I,2)
      GO TO 1
  999 STOP
      END
```

```
TABLE LOOKUP RESULTS
---------------------
 SEARCH    FUNCTION
ARGUMENT    VALUE
-------- ------------
   FRED      ANNE
   JACK   NOT IN TABLE
   DICK      SARA
   TOM    NOT IN TABLE
   MACK      FERN
```

the sample output shown in Fig. 5.7 are:

```
••••••••••••••••••••••••••••••••••••••••
    5
JOHNMARYJAKESUE MACKFERNDICKSARAFREDANNE
FRED
JACK
DICK
TOM
MACK
••••••••••••••••••••••••••••••••••••••••
```

Observe that the use of implied DO-loops for input allowed the five sets of table values to be input from one input record rather than from five input records. However, the search argument values had to be handled one per input record because they are processed one at a time.

Notice that the search argument and function values in this example each contain only four characters. The reason is that most FORTRAN dialects will allow only four-character string constants to be stored in the locations associated with a REAL variable. Therefore, a revised version of the program appears in Fig. 5.8, together with some sample output. This revision of the program is designed to process a table in which list argument and function fields contain twenty-character string constants. Thus, it is a more generalized version of the program of Fig. 5.7. The four character limitation is overcome in the revision by the use of a three-dimensional array for the table, F, and a one-dimensional array for holding the search argument, ARG.

Since five real-variable locations are required to hold twenty characters, a third dimension of length five has been added to F, and ARG has been made a one-dimensional array of length five. These changes are reflected in the REAL type statement. The READ statement used for input of the table values now consists of three implied DO-loops nested within each other. Notice that the variable K varies

Figure 5.8 Revision of Program of Figure 5.7

```
C   ***** PROGRAM FOR ALGORITHM OF FIGURE 5.11M *************************
C   *****                REVISION                *************************
      REAL F(500,2,5),ARG(5)
      INTEGER N,I,J,K
  501 FORMAT('1',12X,'TABLE LOOKUP RESULTS',/,1X,45('-'),/,3X,'SEARCH ',
     * 'ARGUMENT',11X,'FUNCTION VALUE',/,1X,2(20('-'),5X))
  502 FORMAT(I4)
  503 FORMAT(20A4)
  504 FORMAT(1X,5A4,5X,5A4)
  505 FORMAT(1X,5A4,5X,'NOT IN TABLE')
      WRITE(6,501)
      READ(5,502) N
      READ(5,503) (((F(I,J,K),K=1,5),J=1,2),I=1,N)
    1 READ(5,503,END=999) ARG
      DO 20 I=1,N
        DO 15 K=1,5
   15     IF(ARG(K).NE.F(I,1,K)) GO TO 20
        WRITE(6,504) ARG,(F(I,2,K),K=1,5)
        GO TO 1
   20   CONTINUE
      WRITE(6,505) ARG
      GO TO 1
  999 STOP
      END
```

```
            TABLE LOOKUP RESULTS
 ---------------------------------------------
   SEARCH ARGUMENT           FUNCTION VALUE
 --------------------     --------------------
 CASH                     MONEY
 BRUSH                    NOT IN TABLE
```

most rapidly because all five words associated with a list argument or function should be input before going on to the next table entry. Because each table entry now consists of twenty characters, only two lines of the table F can be placed on each input record.

Observe that while statement 1 is unchanged from the first version, ARG is now a one-dimensional array. Therefore, execution of statement 1 causes five string constants (representing one search argument) to be input. The final change required in this revised program is the necessity of a second DO-loop in the table lookup routine. This DO-loop (the one terminated by statement 15) simply compares all five locations of the search argument with the five locations of the different list arguments. Only in the case where all five locations contain equal string constants will a natural exit be made out of this inner DO-loop. When the first search argument location is found that is not equal to the corresponding list argument location for a table entry, then a branch is taken to statement 20, where the loop index I is incremented to move to the next list argument in the table. The input records used to generate this sample output follow:

```
..........................................................................
   8
A                   FIRST LETTER ENG ALPABOUND                TO BE IN GREAT PLNTY
CASH                MONEY               DISCOURAGE            TO DISSUADE
PEAK                THE TOP OF A MOUNTAISTRIP                 TO DEPRIVE OF CVRING
UPSET               TO OVERTURN         ZOO                   A ZOOLOGICAL GARDEN
CASH
BRUSH
..........................................................................
```

5.3.3 THE PRIME-NUMBER PROGRAM

In elementary mathematics, a student is often asked whether or not a given number is a prime number. Recall that for any positive integer $n>1$, we say that n is a prime number if and only if n cannot be factored into the product of any two positive integers that are greater than 1. Conversely, if n can be factored into the product of two positive integers that are greater than 1, then by definition n is not a prime number.

A flowchart and a FORTRAN program for an algorithm that determines whether or not a number is a prime number appear in Figs. 5.9* and 5.10, respectively. The input data records used to produce the sample output shown in Fig. 5.10 are not listed since input values are output by the program. Notice that the numeric functional operator *trun* that is used in flowchart boxes 8 and 11 was not implemented in the program. The reason is that in FORTRAN an integer quotient is truncated automatically. Also notice in statement 3 that the value of N had to be converted to a real constant by using the FLOAT functional operator. The reason this is done is that the SQRT functional operator is defined only for real arguments. Finally observe that a DO-loop is used for the looping process of the algorithm. Furthermore, the DO statement has an increment of 2.

---

*For those using the main text, this flowchart is the same one that appears in Fig. 5.16M.

Figure 5.9 Algorithm Flowchart for the Prime Number Problem

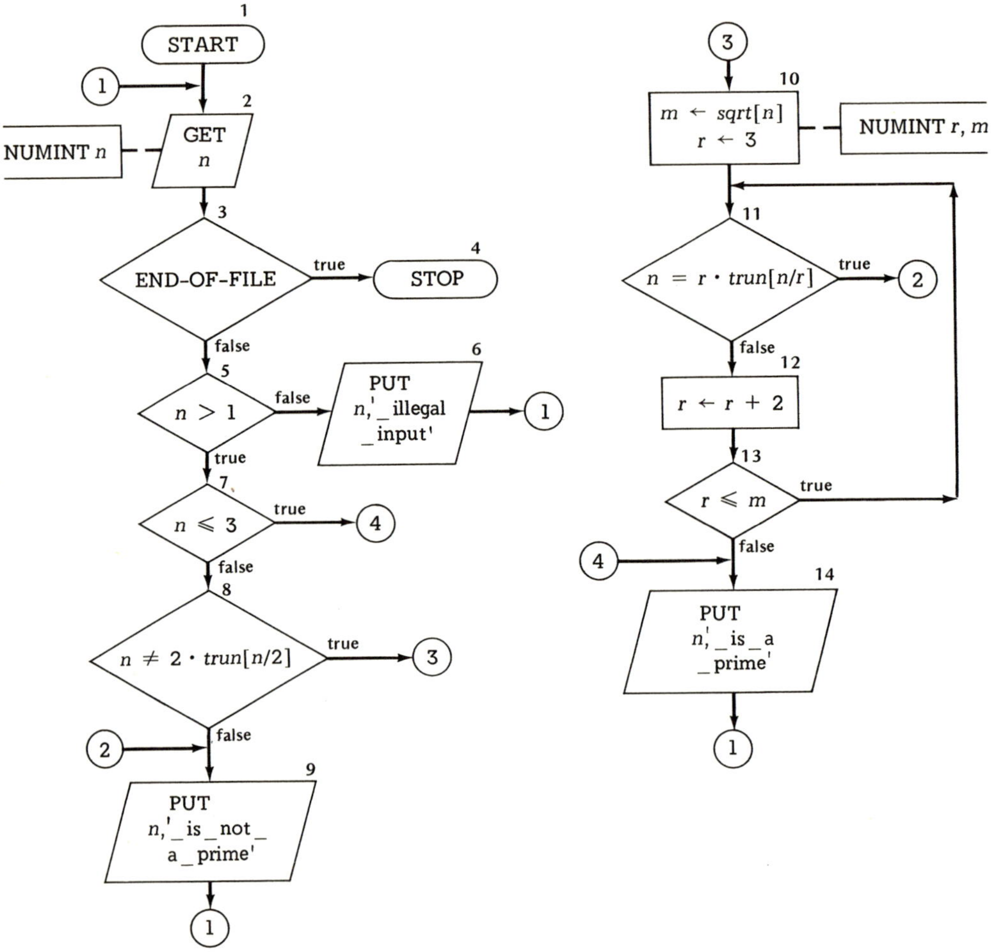

Figure 5.10 FORTRAN Program for Flowchart of Figure 5.9

```
C   ***** PROGRAM FOR ALGORITHM OF FIGURE 5.16M *************************
      INTEGER N,R,M
  501 FORMAT('1',5X,'PRIME NUMBER RESULTS',/,1X,31('-'))
  502 FORMAT(I10)
  503 FORMAT(I10,' ILLEGAL INPUT')
  504 FORMAT(I10,' IS NOT A PRIME')
  505 FORMAT(I10,' IS A PRIME')
      WRITE(6,501)
    1 READ(5,502,END=999) N
      IF(N.GT.1) GO TO 10
      WRITE(6,503) N
      GO TO 1
   10 IF(N.LE.3) GO TO 4
      IF(N.NE.2*(N/2)) GO TO 3
    2 WRITE(6,504) N
      GO TO 1
    3 M=IFIX(SQRT(FLOAT(N)))
      DO 15 R=3,M,2
   15   IF(N.EQ.R*(N/R)) GO TO 2
    4 WRITE(6,505) N
      GO TO 1
  999 STOP
      END
```

```
      PRIME NUMBER RESULTS
 -------------------------------
          1 ILLEGAL INPUT
          3 IS A PRIME
       8677 IS A PRIME
       8676 IS NOT A PRIME
         33 IS NOT A PRIME
          5 IS A PRIME
```

PROBLEMS

Problem 10 relates to an algorithm flowchart in the main text. For those not using the main text, this problem should be ignored.

10. Write the FORTRAN program that corresponds with the algorithm flowchart of Fig. 5.14M. Use the input records from Fig. 5.10 as test data.

For problems 11 through 20: (1) develop an algorithm flowchart, (2) write a corresponding FORTRAN program, and (3) test the program using the test data provided. All of these problems correspond with problems in Ch. 5 of the main text (the corresponding main-text problem numbers are given in parentheses). Therefore, those using the main text should already have completed the algorithm flowchart development phase.

11. (Prob. 9) A mathematics teacher wants the computer to produce a multiplication table that has ten rows and ten columns. The entries in the table should be the products of the successive integers given in a row at the top of the columns and the successive integers given in a column at the left of the respective rows. Input to the algorithm should be the value of the leftmost integer in the column-heading row and the value of the topmost integer in the row-heading column. The rows and columns of integers and their products should all be stored in a single two-dimensional array that consists of eleven rows and eleven columns. Algorithm output should consist of all elements of this array except for the element in the first row of the first column. Use as test data: 1,1.

12. (Prob. 10) A mathematician wants to use the computer to develop and output a table that contains the first n terms of the Fibonacci sequence. The first several terms in the sequence are

    0,1,1,2,3,5,8,13,21,...

    and each subsequent term in the sequence is computed using the equation

$$F_{i+2} = F_{i+1} + F_i$$

    where $i \geq 0$, $F_0 = 0$, and F_i=1. Use 15 as your test data value.

13. (Prob. 11) To operate on strings of characters, an English professor needs an algorithm that will concatenate (join together) two strings of characters. The input to this algorithm should be: (a) two integers that provide the number of characters in each input string, and (b) two strings of characters that are each to be stored in separate one-dimensional arrays with one character per array element. The output should include both

input strings as well as the concatenated string, which is to be in a third one-dimensional array. Use as test data:

7,23,'THIS_IS','_A_CONCATENATED_STRING.'.

14. (Prob. 12) A mathematics teacher wants the computer to factor any positive integer into its prime factors. Recall from algebra that the prime factors of a positive integer are those prime numbers that when multiplied together give the number for which they are the prime factors. The number and its prime factors should be output by the algorithm. Use as test data: 11, 15, 16.

15. (Prob. 13) A physicist wants the computer to perform table lookups on some numeric values that are in tabular form. However, the search arguments may not be equal to a list argument value but instead may fall between two list argument values. Should the search argument lie between the ith and $(i + 1)$th list argument values, then the function value output should be calculated using

$$f(i,2) + [f(i+1,2) - f(i,2)] \cdot \frac{Arg - f(i,1)}{f(i+1,1) - f(i,1)}$$

where f is a two-dimensional table of list argument and function values and Arg contains the search argument value. The assumption is made that the values in the table are sequenced so that the list argument values are in ascending order. Use as test data: 5,1,20,2,30,3,40,4,50,5,60, 4,3.5,1.3,6,0,2.4,5.

16. (Prob. 14) To perform some linguistics research, a professor needs an algorithm that will extract a substring from a string of characters. The input to the algorithm should be: (a) an integer value that gives the number of characters in the input string, (b) an input string of characters that is to be stored in a one-dimensional array with one character per array element, (c) an integer value that gives the length of the substring to be extracted, and (d) an integer value that specifies the symbol position in the input string (counting from the left) that marks the beginning of the substring to be extracted. Output should consist of all of the input values and the array that contains the substring. Use as test data:

31,'SALLY_LOVES_SOUTHWEST_LOUISIANA',6,7.

17. (Prob. 15) A statistician wants the computer to be able to calculate the permutation of x objects taken from n objects. The definition of a permutation is

$${}_nP_x = n!/(n-x)!$$

where $n!=n\cdot(n-1)\cdot(n-2)\cdot\ldots\cdot3\cdot2\cdot1$. The input to the algorithm should be values for n and x, where $1000>n\geq0$ and $n\geq x\geq0$. Use as test data: 10,5, 5,0, 5,5, 50,2, 50,48, -5,3, 5,7.

18. (Prob. 16) The statistician of Problem 17 wants the computer to output a table of permutations for a given value of n and a set of consecutive values of x. That is, the algorithm is to input an integer value for n and a pair of integer values x_{high} and x_{low} for the upper and lower bounds for x. Then develop a table of ${}_nP_x$ for all values of x between x_{low} and x_{high}. Include the value of n and the values taken on by x in the output. Also include a test to be certain that $x_{high} \leq n$ and $x_{low} \geq 0$. Use as test data: 10,10,0, 10,10,11, 20,17,14, 1040,12,10.

19. (Prob. 17) A mathematician wants to use the computer to develop tables of prime numbers. A method that can be used to generate such a table involves sifting a list that consists of all odd integer numbers greater than 2 and less than or equal to n arranged in ascending order. The sifting procedure involves the deletion of every kth number in the list subsequent to the value of k. That is, delete: (a) every third element after 3, (b) every fifth element after 5, (c) every seventh element after 7, and so forth. The algorithm developed should output a table containing all of the prime numbers up through n. Assume that n is always less than 100,000. Use 2,000 as a test data value.

20. (Prob. 18) An English professor wants to use the computer to search for substrings in strings of characters. That is, given two input arrays that contain character strings, an algorithm is needed that determines whether or not the second string is contained in the first string. An integer pointing to the position that contains the leftmost character of the substring in the string should be output along with the two input strings. In the case in which the second string is not contained in the first string, the output pointer value should be zero. Use as test data: 16,'TEST_DATA_STRING', 2,'ST', 3,'_ST', 5,'DATUM'.

5.4 PROGRAMS THAT YIELD APPROXIMATIONS

All of the algorithms and programs that we have constructed thus far have provided what are essentially exact results. By *exact results* we mean that the technique or method used in the algorithm was designed to provide an answer that is completely correct. If there was any error in the answer, the error was not caused by the computational technique. Rather, the error was introduced because in a computer we attempt to represent real numbers by a finite number of digits. For example, in many modern computers only the seven most significant digits of a number will fit into one memory location. Thus, inputting the real number 1234567890123 would result instead in the storage of the value 1234567000000. Another kind of error creeps in during computations as a result of having to represent real numbers using a fixed finite number of digits. This kind of error is called computational error and results, for example, because the fourteen-digit product of two seven-digit numbers must be reduced to a seven-digit result.

In general, algorithms for solving other than mathematical types of problems are designed to provide exact solutions. In many problems in mathematics, however, we choose methods of solution that are designed to provide *approximations* to the exact solutions. The reason for this choice is that in many cases the algorithms which produce exact solutions: (1) are not known, (2) are inefficient, or (3) are difficult to implement on a computer. Therefore, algorithms are designed in some cases which give only approximations to the true solutions. A basic characteristic of algorithms which generate approximations to the true solutions is that they are iterative. That is, they arrive at solutions by using a looping process. There is a basic distinction, however, between the looping procedures of approximate algorithms and exact algorithms. In an approximate algorithm the number of times a loop must be repeated in order to get a satisfactory solution cannot be determined analytically before a solution is computed. On the other hand, in the case of an exact algorithm, we can determine analytically the maximum number of times a loop must be repeated to yield a solution before the algorithm has been executed.

5.4.1 THE SQUARE-ROOT PROGRAM

An algorithm flowchart for a crude method for approximating the square root of a positive number appears in Fig. 5.11.* A listing of a FORTRAN program for this flowchart, together with sample output, are given in Fig. 5.12. The input records used to generate the sample output are not shown because the input values are listed by the program. Notice that this algorithm only produces two decimal places of accuracy, which means that it has only limited application.

PROBLEMS

Problem 21 relates to an algorithm flowchart in the main text. For those not using the main text, this problem should be ignored.

21. Write the FORTRAN program that corresponds with the algorithm flowchart of Fig. 5.22M. Use the input data values of Fig. 5.23M as test data.

For problems 22 through 28: (1) develop an algorithm flowchart, (2) write a corresponding FORTRAN program, and (3) test the program using the test data provided. All of these problems correspond with problems in Ch. 5 of the main text (the corresponding main-text problem numbers are given in parentheses). Therefore, those using the main text should already have completed the algorithm flowchart development phase.

---

*For those using the main text, this flowchart is the same one that appears in Fig. 5.19M.

Figure 5.11 Algorithm Flowchart for the Square-Root Problem

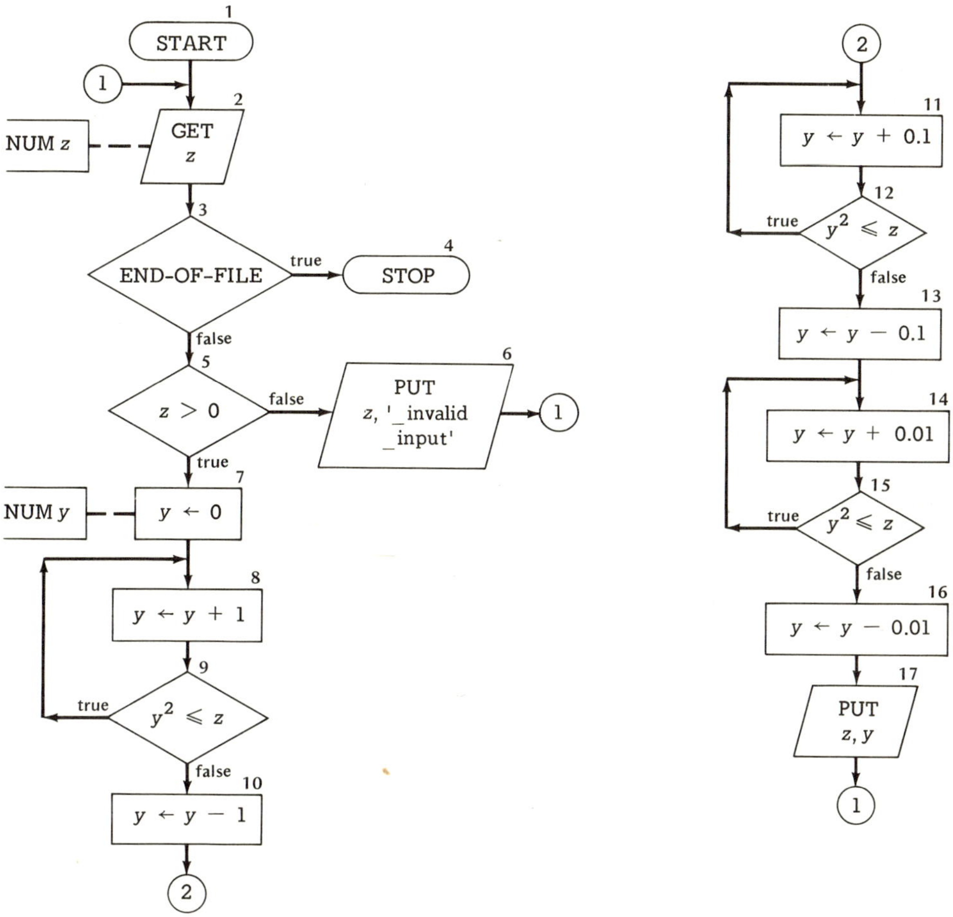

Figure 5.12 FORTRAN Program for Flowchart of Figure 5.11

```
C   ***** PROGRAM FOR ALGORITHM OF FIGURE 5.19M ***************************
      REAL Z,Y
  501 FORMAT('1SQUARE ROOT APPROXIMATIONS',/,1X,26('-'),/,4X,'NUMBER',
     * 5X,'SQUARE ROOT',/,1X,12('-'),1X,13('-'))
  502 FORMAT(2E13.5)
  503 FORMAT(E13.5,' INVALID INPUT')
      WRITE(6,501)
    1 READ(5,502,END=999) Z
      IF(Z.GT.0.0) GO TO 10
      WRITE(6,503) Z
      GO TO 1
   10 Y=0.0
   15 Y=Y+1.0
      IF(Y**2.LE.Z) GO TO 15
      Y=Y-1.0
    2 Y=Y+0.1
      IF(Y**2.LE.Z) GO TO 2
      Y=Y-0.1
   20 Y=Y+0.01
      IF(Y**2.LE.Z) GO TO 20
      Y=Y-0.01
      WRITE(6,502) Z,Y
      GO TO 1
  999 STOP
      END
```

```
SQUARE ROOT APPROXIMATIONS
--------------------------
   NUMBER      SQUARE ROOT
------------ -------------
 0.50000E 01  0.22300E 01
 0.50000E 00  0.70000E 00
 0.50000E-01  0.22000E 00
-0.50000E 01 INVALID INPUT
 0.91847E 05  0.30306E 03
```

22. (Prob. 21) A certain mathematician thought that the algorithm flowchart of Fig. 5.11 was rather interesting but thought that it would be improved by making the number of fractional digits of accuracy a variable. Develop such an algorithm, where the number of significant fractional digits is an input value. Use as test data: 5,2, 5,3, 15,6, (the second number in each input pair represents the number of decimal digits desired).

23. (Prob. 23) A mathematician decided that the algorithm flowchart of Fig. 5.11 could be improved by beginning with 100 instead of 1 as the initial trial value for the square root. Develop such an algorithm that begins with hundreds, then works through the tens position, and so forth. Use the data of Fig. 5.12 to test your program.

24. (Prob. 24) A mathematician wants to generate an approximation to the mathematical constant π. This is accomplished by summing as many terms of the infinite series

$$\pi = 4 - \frac{4}{3} + \frac{4}{5} - \frac{4}{7} + \frac{4}{9} - \frac{4}{11} + \cdots$$

as might be necessary to achieve the desired degree of accuracy. Use the formula

$$error = \frac{|approx - 3.14159|}{3.14159}$$

to measure error. Design your algorithm so that as many terms are included in computing the approximation as are needed to make *error* less than some critical difference that is an input value. Also included as an input value should be a number that gives the maximum number of terms of the series to be included in computing the approximation. Output should consist of every 100th value of the approximation, as well as the final value. Use as test data: 0.01,2000, 0.001,300, 0.00001,1500, 0.001,1900.

25. (Prob. 25) The mathematician in Problem 24 discovered an infinite product that can be used to generate an approximation to π. This product is

$$\pi = 4 \cdot \frac{2}{3} \cdot \frac{4}{3} \cdot \frac{4}{5} \cdot \frac{6}{5} \cdot \frac{6}{7} \cdot \frac{8}{7} \cdot \frac{8}{9} \cdot \cdots$$

Use this infinite product to develop an algorithm similar to the one in Problem 24, using the test data of that problem to test your program.

26. (Prob. 27) A mathematician wants to use the technique of Fig. 5.11 to develop an algorithm that finds the cube root of a number. Develop an algorithm flowchart similar to the one in that figure to compute cube roots, using the data of Fig. 5.12 to test your program.

27. (Prob. 28) An engineer wants to use a computer to calculate the cube root of a number. An iterative formula that can be used to calculate an approximation to the cube root is:

$$x_{i+1} = (2 \cdot x_i + z/x_i^2)/3$$

Develop your algorithm using the formula

$$|x_i - x_{i+1}| \;/\; (|x_i| + |x_{i+1}|)$$

to compute the error term. Output should consist of the input values (the number and the maximum absolute relative error) and the final value of the approximation. Use as test data: 10,0.001, 27,0.0001, 9,0.0001.

28. (Prob. 29) A statistician needs to compute the mathematical constant e, which is equal to 2.71828 accurate to six significant digits. The infinite series that can be used to compute an approximation to e is

$$e = 1 + \frac{1}{1!} + \frac{1}{2!} + \frac{1}{3!} + \frac{1}{4!} + \cdots$$

Use this series to develop an algorithm similar to the one in Problem 24, using the data of that problem to test your program.

SUMMARY

1. A loop is a sequence of program steps (which are called the loop body) that may be executed more than once.
2. The steps of a program are repeated more than once because:
   a. The program performs the same operations on different data items.
   b. The results of the program are obtained by performing operations over and over again beginning with a given set of data
3. The FORTRAN language provides the DO statement to facilitate the programming of loops. The general form of the DO statement is

   DO *label v=s,u,i*

   where *label*, *v*, *s*, *u*, and *i* are defined in Section 5.1.
4. Nested DO-loops are permitted in which one DO-loop resides inside of another DO-loop.

5. Subscripted variables must be declared in both flowcharts and FORTRAN programs. The reason is that the maximum values of subscripts must be known in order to allocate memory to the arrays.
6. Subscripted variables are referenced in FORTRAN by enclosing the subscripts in parentheses. Subscripts may be: (a) integer constants, (b) integer variables, or (c) limited forms of integer arithmetic expressions.
7. When a subscripted variable appears without a subscript, this will be a reference to the entire array associated with that variable.
8. Algorithms can be classified as exact algorithms or as approximate algorithms.
9. An exact algorithm is an algorithm that is designed to provide an exact answer to a problem.
10. In an exact algorithm, it is possible, before the algorithm has been executed, to determine analytically the maximum number of times that a loop must be repeated to yield a solution.
11. An approximate algorithm is an algorithm that is designed to provide only an approximation to an exact answer.
12. In an approximate algorithm, the number of times that a loop must be repeated to get a satisfactory solution cannot be determined analytically before a solution is computed.
13. Approximate algorithms rather than exact algorithms are used to solve some problems because in many cases exact algorithms:
    a. Are not known.
    b. Are inefficient.
    c. Are difficult to implement on a computer.

CHAPTER 6

FORTRAN PROGRAMMING IN BUSINESS AND PUBLIC ADMINISTRATION

The largest use of computers for solving problems is in the area of business and government. However, very few of the applications in these areas are programmed using FORTRAN. Instead, such languages as COBOL and PL/I are used for programming applications in business and government data processing. However, in this chapter we will present FORTRAN programs for the solutions to two common data processing problems in order to give some idea of the types of problems found in these areas. Recall that we have already solved two business-type problems in Chs. 4 and 5. One of these was the depreciation problem (Ch. 4) and the other was the sequenceing problem (Ch. 5).

6.1 THE AMORTIZATION-TABLE PROGRAM

A typical problem found in business and personal finance is the problem of developing an amortization table. An amortization table is simply a list that tells what the balance on a loan is on a period-by-period basis. It is developed given that a certain amount of each fixed payment is being repaid on the loan and another portion of the payment goes for interest on the outstanding balance.

In Fig. 6.1* we have an algorithm flowchart for the amortization table problem. The FORTRAN program for this flowchart is given in Fig. 6.2. The input data record used to produce the sample output is

```
..................................................
     1000.00          .06       300.0012 574
..................................................
```

*For those using the main text, this flowchart is the same one that appears in Fig. 6.5M.

Figure 6.1 Algorithm Flowchart for the Amortization Table Problem

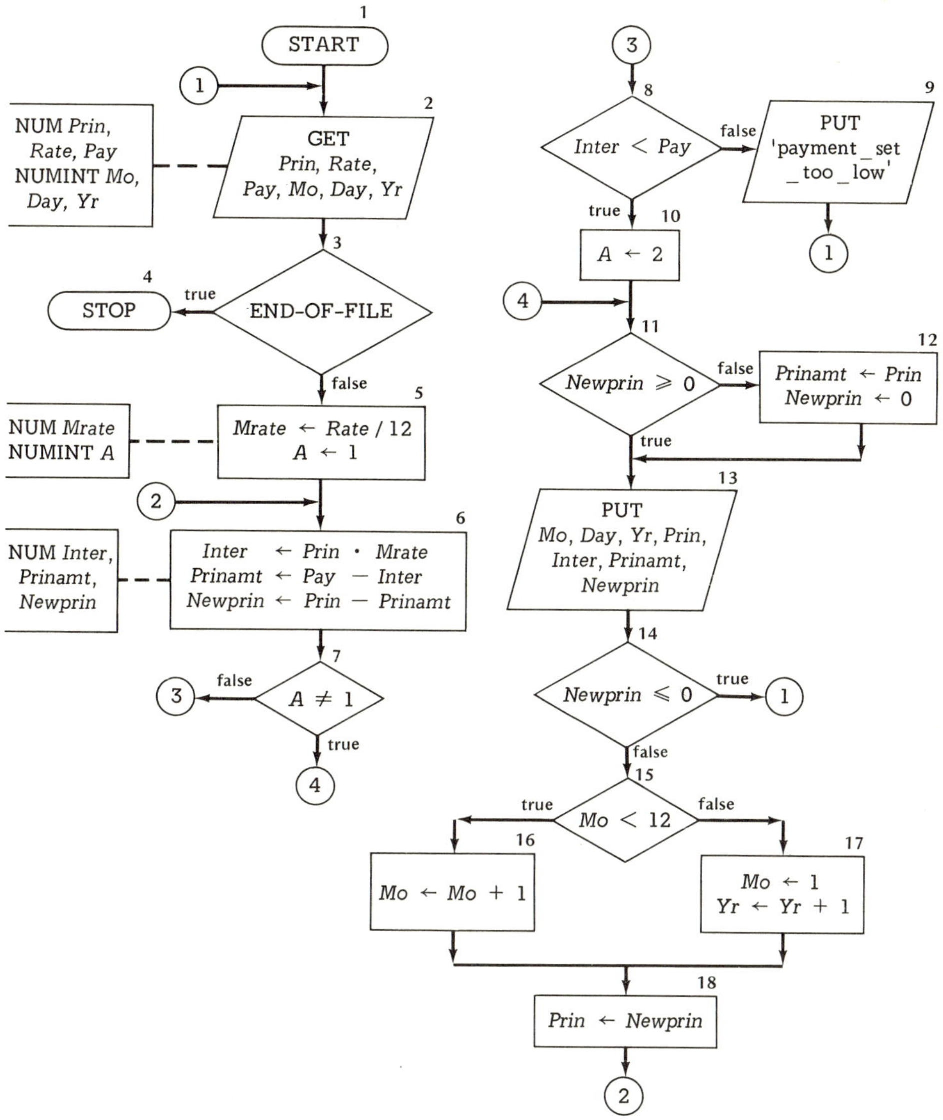

Figure 6.2 FORTRAN Program for Flowchart of Figure 6.1

```
C   ***** PROGRAM FOR ALGORITHM OF FIGURE 6.5M ************************
      REAL PRIN,RATE,PAY,MRATE,INTER,PRINAM,NEWPRI
      INTEGER MO,DAY,YR,A
  501 FORMAT(3F12.2,3I2)
  502 FORMAT('1',15X,'AMORTIZATION TABLE',/,2X,49('-'),/,4X,'DUE',5X,
     * 'BEGINNING',2X,'INTEREST',2X,'PRINCIPAL',2X,'ENDING',/,4X,'DATE
     * 5X,'BALANCE',3X,'PAYMENT',4X,'PAYMENT',3X,'BALANCE',/,2X,
     * 2(8('-'),2X,9('-'),2X),7('-'))
  503 FORMAT(' *** PAYMENT SET TOO LOW ***')
  504 FORMAT(I4,2('/',I2),3F10.2,F11.2)
    1 READ(5,501,END=999) PRIN,RATE,PAY,MO,DAY,YR
      WRITE(6,502)
      MRATE=RATE/12.0
      A=1
    2 INTER=PRIN*MRATE
      PRINAM=PAY-INTER
      NEWPRI=PRIN-PRINAM
      IF(A.NE.1) GO TO 4
      IF(INTER.LT.PAY) GO TO 10
      WRITE(6,503)
      GO TO 1
   10 A=2
    4 IF(NEWPRI.GE.0.0) GO TO 15
      PRINAM=PRIN
      NEWPRI=0.0
   15 WRITE(6,504) MO,DAY,YR,PRIN,INTER,PRINAM,NEWPRI
      IF(NEWPRI.LE.0.0) GO TO 1
      IF(MO.LT.12) GO TO 20
      MO=1
      YR=YR+1
      GO TO 25
   20 MO=MO+1
   25 PRIN=NEWPRI
      GO TO 2
  999 STOP
      END
```

Figure 6.2 (Continued)

AMORTIZATION TABLE

DUE DATE	BEGINNING BALANCE	INTEREST PAYMENT	PRINCIPAL PAYMENT	ENDING BALANCE
12/ 5/74	1000.00	5.00	295.00	705.00
1/ 5/75	705.00	3.52	296.47	408.53
2/ 5/75	408.53	2.04	297.96	110.57
3/ 5/75	110.57	0.55	110.57	0.00

Notice that the FORTRAN DO-loop was not used in this program because it is not well suited to the looping process of this algorithm.

PROBLEMS

For problems 1 through 3: (1) develop an algorithm flowchart, (2) write a corresponding FORTRAN program, and (3) test the program using test data that you create. All of these problems correspond with problems in Ch. 6 of the main text (the corresponding main-text problem numbers are given in parentheses). Therefore, those using the main text should already have completed the algorithm flowchart development phase.

1. (Prob. 2) Modify the amortization-table algorithm of Fig. 6.1 so that the payment periods may be more than one month in length. This change will require the input of an additional value which gives the number of months in a payment period. For example, the input value would be 3 if payments are made every three months. Assume that the number of months in a period is always an integer value.

2. (Prob. 4) An investor wants the computer to produce tables of the value of a fixed investment at each time period, where the investment accrues interest that is compounded at a fixed rate. The value of the compounded investment at the end of the *i*th period can be computed as $(1 + r) \cdot I_{t-1}$, where r is the interest rate per period and I_{t-1} (for $t=1,2,3,\ldots,n$) is the investment value at the end of the previous period. The value of I_0 is equal to the initial investment. The algorithm inputs should consist of the initial investment, the constant interest rate, and the number of time periods for which the investment has been made.

3. (Prob. 5) A loan manager wants the computer to be able to generate an amortization table for the case in which the amount of the periodic payment is not given. That is, algorithm input will be the annual interest rate, the initial principal amount, the due date of the first payment, the number of periods over which the loan is to be repaid, and the number of months in each payment period. The amount of each payment can be calculated using the formula

$$payment = \frac{Prin \cdot Mrate \cdot (1 + Mrate)^n}{(1 + Mrate)^n - 1}$$

where *Prin* is the principal amount, *Mrate* is the interest rate for one period, and n is the number of periods over which the loan is to be repaid.

6.2 THE CREDIT-CARD BILLING PROGRAM

File maintenance and processing are a very important part of business data processing. File maintenance and processing often involve adding records to or deleting records from a file, changing the values in certain fields of certain records in the file, and printing reports based on current information in the file. A file that contains permanent information is called the *master file*. A *transactions file* consists of records that contain information used to update or revise the records of the master file.

A typical problem is that of maintaining the credit-card master file for an oil company. A flowchart for this problem appears in Fig. 6.3.* The variables associated with the old master file and their meanings are:

1. *mact* -- customer account number.
2. *mname* -- customer name.
3. *maddr* -- customer address.
4. *mcity* -- customer city, state, and zip code.
5. *mpbal* -- previous month's balance.
6. *mchge* -- current charges for this month.
7. *mdate* -- billing date.

The new master file produced by this algorithm uses variable names that are identical to these, with the exception that the prefix *m* is replaced by the letter *n*. The transactions file variables and their meanings are:

1. *tact* -- customer account number.

---

*For those using the main text, this flowchart is the same one that appears in Fig. 6.10M.

Figure 6.3 Algorithm Flowchart for the Credit-Card Billing Problem

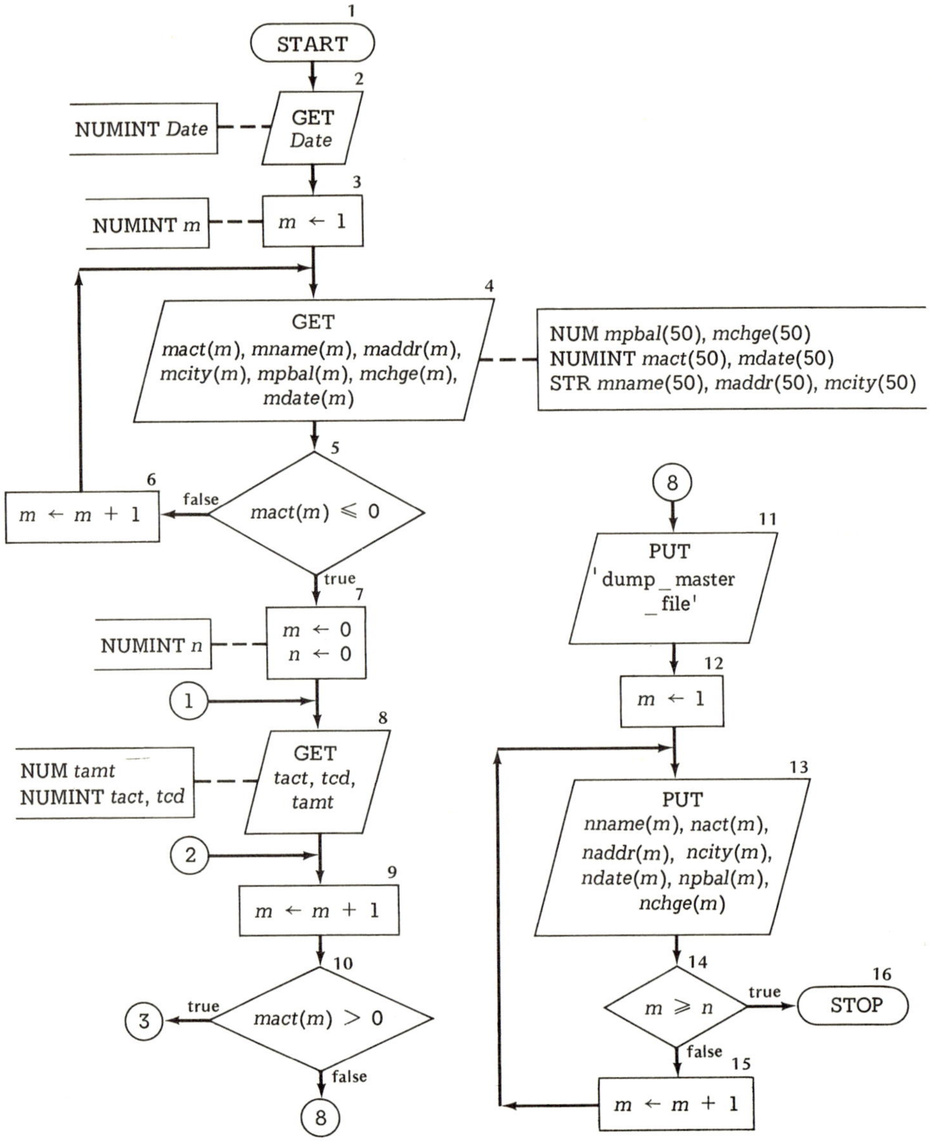

Figure 6.3 (Continued)

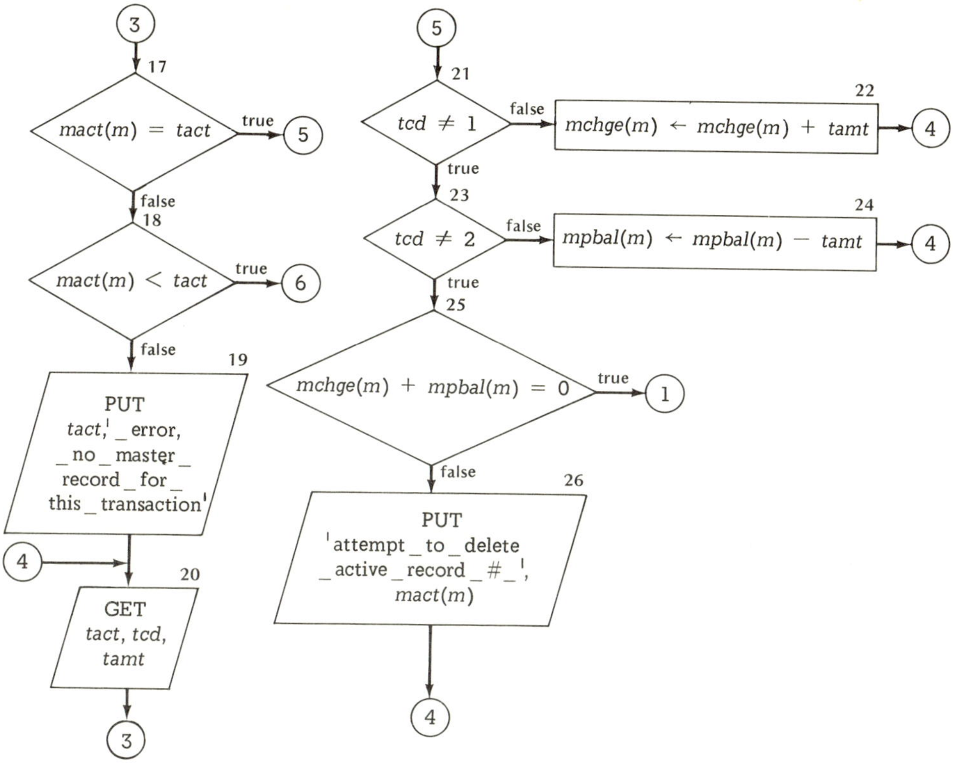

2. *tcd* -- transaction code:
   a. A value of 1 indicates a charge sale.
   b. A value of 2 indicates a payment on account.
   c. A value of 3 indicates that the account has been closed.
3. *tamt* -- transactions amount.

Finally, the variable *Date* gives the current date or day of the month.

Figure 6.3 (Continued)

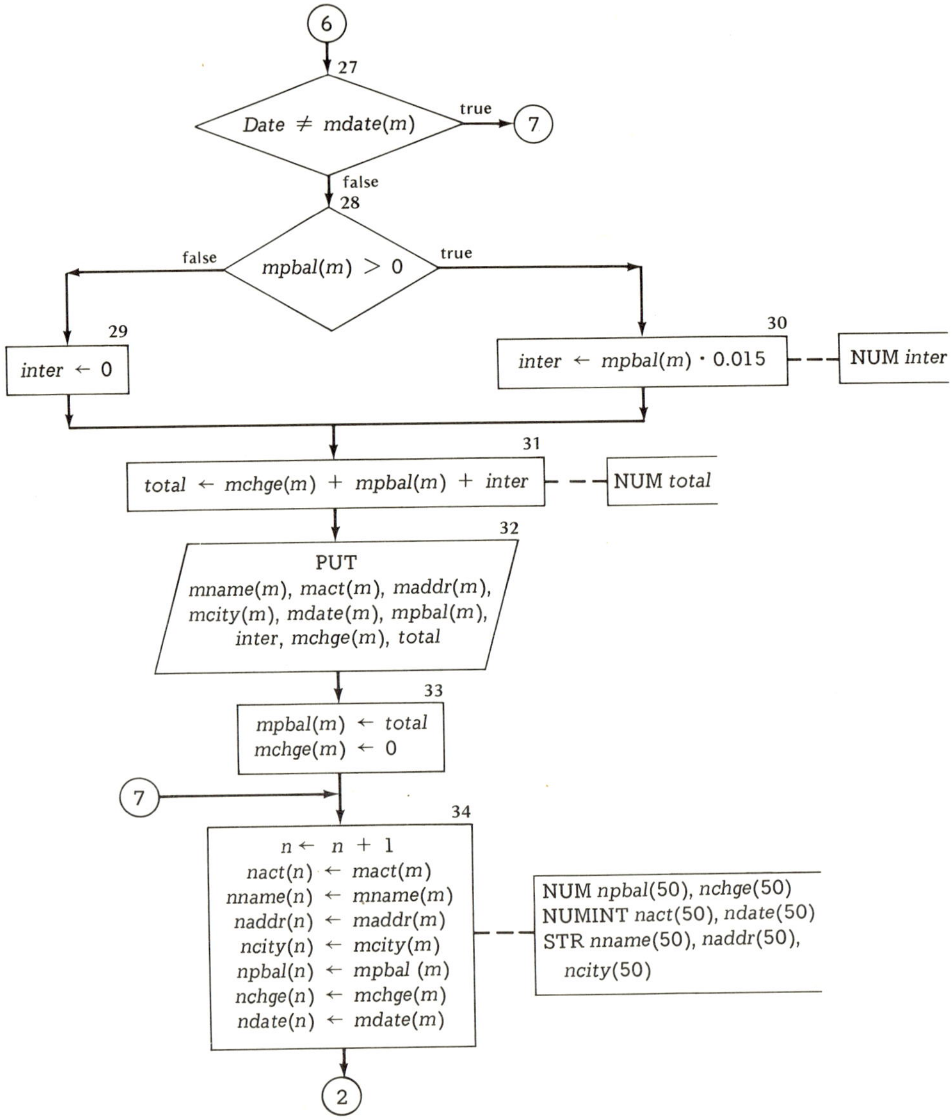

Figure 6.4 FORTRAN Program for Flowchart of Figure 6.3

```
C   ***** PROGRAM FOR ALGORITHM OF FIGURE 6.10M *************************
      REAL MPBAL(50),MCHGE(50),MNAME(50,5),MADDR(50,5),MCITY(50,5),TAMT,
     * INTER,TOTAL,NPBAL(50),NCHGE(50),NNAME(50,5),NADDR(50,5),
     * NCITY(50,5)
      INTEGER DATE,M,MACT(50),MDATE(50),N,TACT,TCD,NACT(50),NDATE(50),I
  501 FORMAT(I2)
  502 FORMAT(I9,15A4,/,2F10.2,I2)
  503 FORMAT(I9,I1,F10.2)
  504 FORMAT('1',4X,'DUMP OF NEW MASTER FILE',/,1X,31('-'))
  505 FORMAT(/,1X,5A4,I9,/,1X,5A4,/,1X,5A4,/,' DATE:',I3,2X,
     * 'BALANCE: $',F11.2,/,7X,'CUR. CHGES.: $',F11.2)
  506 FORMAT(//,I5,' ERROR, NO MASTER RECORD FOR THIS TRANSACTION')
  507 FORMAT(//,5X,'ATTEMPT TO DELETE ACTIVE RECORD # ',I9)
  508 FORMAT(//,15X,'GREASY OIL COMPANY',/,1X,50('-'),//,12X,5A4,I10,
     * 2(/,12X,5A4),//,1X,'BILLING DATE:',I4,3X,'PREVIOUS BALANCE: $',
     * F11.2,/,1X,'INTEREST: $',F6.2,3X,'CURRENT CHARGES: $',F12.2,/,
     * 20X,'TOTAL AMOUNT DUE: $',F12.2,/,1X,50('-'))
      READ(5,501) DATE
      DO 10 M=1,50
        READ(5,502) MACT(M),(MNAME(M,I),I=1,5),(MADDR(M,I),I=1,5),
     *   (MCITY(M,I),I=1,5),MPBAL(M),MCHGE(M),MDATE(M)
   10   IF(MACT(M).LE.0) GO TO 15
   15 M=0
      N=0
    1 READ(5,503) TACT,TCD,TAMT
    2 M=M+1
      IF(MACT(M).GT.0) GO TO 3
      WRITE(6,504)
      WRITE(6,505) ((NNAME(M,I),I=1,5),NACT(M),(NADDR(M,I),I=1,5),
     * (NCITY(M,I),I=1,5),NDATE(M),NPBAL(M),NCHGE(M),M=1,N)
      STOP
```

The program for this flowchart is given in Fig. 6.4. The input data records used to generate the sample output are shown in Fig. 6.5. Notice in the program that the flowchart string variables had to be set up as arrays because of the four-character limitation that exists in FORTRAN.

Figure 6.4 (Continued)

```
    3 IF(MACT(M).EQ.TACT) GO TO 5
      IF(MACT(M).LT.TACT) GO TO 6
      WRITE(6,506) TACT
    4 READ(5,503) TACT,TCD,TAMT
      GO TO 3
    5 IF(TCD.NE.1) GO TO 20
      MCHGE(M)=MCHGE(M)+TAMT
      GO TO 4
   20 IF(TCD.NE.2) GO TO 25
      MPBAL(M)=MPBAL(M)-TAMT
      GO TO 4
   25 IF(MCHGE(M)+MPBAL(M).EQ.0.0) GO TO 1
      WRITE(6,507) MACT(M)
      GO TO 4
    6 IF(DATE.NE.MDATE(M)) GO TO 7
      IF(MPBAL(M).GT.0.0) GO TO 30
      INTER=0.0
      GO TO 35
   30 INTER=MPBAL(M)*0.015
   35 TOTAL=MCHGE(M)+MPBAL(M)+INTER
      WRITE(6,508) (MNAME(M,I),I=1,5),MACT(M),(MADDR(M,I),I=1,5),
     * (MCITY(M,I),I=1,5),MDATE(M),MPBAL(M),INTER,MCHGE(M),TOTAL
      MPBAL(M)=TOTAL
      MCHGE(M)=0.0
    7 N=N+1
      NACT(N)=MACT(M)
      DO 40 I=1,5
         NNAME(N,I)=MNAME(M,I)
         NADDR(N,I)=MADDR(M,I)
   40    NCITY(N,I)=MCITY(M,I)
      NPBAL(N)=MPBAL(M)
      NCHGE(N)=MCHGE(M)
      NDATE(N)=MDATE(M)
      GO TO 2
      END
```

```
                    GREASY OIL COMPANY
------------------------------------------------------------

              J. JONES                          10
              2 ELM
              CITY              70501

BILLING DATE:   30    PREVIOUS BALANCE: $          8.03
INTEREST: $   0.12    CURRENT CHARGES: $          17.10
                     TOTAL AMOUNT DUE: $          25.25
------------------------------------------------------------
```

Figure 6.4 (Continued)

```
 11 ERROR, NO MASTER RECORD FOR THIS TRANSACTION

   ATTEMPT TO DELETE ACTIVE RECORD #          12

                GREASY OIL COMPANY
------------------------------------------------------

           S. LAMP                         56
           8 OAK
           CITY              70043

BILLING DATE:  30   PREVIOUS BALANCE: $        0.00
INTEREST: $  0.00   CURRENT CHARGES: $         2.75
                   TOTAL AMOUNT DUE: $         2.75
------------------------------------------------------


     DUMP OF NEW MASTER FILE
----------------------------------

J. JONES                    10
2 ELM
CITY              70501
DATE: 30  BALANCE: $      25.25
      CUR. CHGES.: $       0.00

T. ZOE                      12
4 ASH
CITY              72603
DATE:  5  BALANCE: $     -17.00
      CUR. CHGES.: $      25.27

S. LAMP                     56
8 OAK
CITY              70043
DATE: 30  BALANCE: $       2.75
      CUR. CHGES.: $       0.00
```

Figure 6.5 Input Data Records for Output of Figure 6.4

```
30
       10J. JONES            2 ELM               CITY          70501
       803      123530
       12T. ZOE              4 ASH               CITY          72603
       475        467 5
       47A. CAR              4 TOP               CITY          71032
         0      189420
       56S. LAMP             8 OAK               CITY          70043
      1408         030
        0
         0         0 0
       101       475
       112       563
       121      1635
       121       425
       122      2175
       123         0
       472      1894
       473         0
       561       275
       562      1408
99999999
```

PROBLEMS

Problem 4 relates to an algorithm flowchart in the main text. For those not using the main text, this problem should be ignored.

4. Write the FORTRAN program that corresponds with the algorithm flowchart of Fig. 6.8M. Use the input data records from Section 5.3.1 as test data.

For problems 5 through 7: (1) develop an algorithm flowchart, (2) write a corresponding FORTRAN program, and (3) test the program using test data that you create. All of these problems correspond with problems in Ch. 6 of the main text (the corresponding main-text problem numbers are given in parentheses). Therefore, those using the main text should already have completed the algorithm flowchart development phase.

5. (Prob. 8) Another sorting strategy that can be used involves scanning the file and comparing the sort fields in consecutive record pairs. During the scan, records would be exchanged in any pair when the sort-field values in those records were not in the desired order. After completing one scan of the list, the record with the largest sort-field value will be the bottom record in the list. Another scan of the list is then performed, this time excluding the last list element. This procedure is repeated, with one element being dropped off of the list on each successive scan, until the scan includes only the first two elements of the array. This sort method is called an *exchange sort*.

6. (Prob. 11) Design an algorithm for processing the payroll of the Sunshine Shrimp Co. Assume that each master file record contains in order an employee's: (1) social security number, (2) name, (3) home address, (4) pay rate, (5) number of dependents, (6) union dues amount, (7) year-to-date social security tax withheld, and (8) year-to-date federal income tax withheld. In addition, each transactions record contains an employee's: (1) social security number, and (2) hours worked for this pay period. Both the transactions file and master file should be assumed to be stored on separate magnetic tapes as sequentially organized files. In addition, both the transactions and master file records are in ascending order by social security number. Gross pay is calculated by multiplying the first forty hours worked times employee pay rate, and everything over forty hours worked by one-and-one-half times the pay rate. Social security tax is calculated at 6.0 percent of the gross salary on the first $13,200 earnings per year. Income tax withholding is computed by taking the gross pay less ten dollars for each dependent

claimed times 20 percent. Net pay is calculated by deducting from gross pay: (1) union dues, (2) social security tax, and (3) income tax. The updated master file records should be output to magnetic tape after each transactions file record is processed. An employee's paycheck should be output to the printer. Each paycheck should consist of the current date, the employee's name and home address, gross pay, itemized deductions, and net pay.

7. (Prob. 12) Develop an algorithm for processing student records at Dixie University. Assume that each master file record contains in order a student's: (1) student number, (2) name, (3) campus address, (4) major, (5) a list that will hold up to sixty four-digit course numbers and their respective grades, (6) total credit hours passed, and (7) cumulative grade-point average. The first two items in a transactions record are a student number and a transactions code. The three possible transactions codes mean to input and process: (1) 1—a change in name, address, or major; (2) 2—a new-student master file record; or (3) 3—a list of courses and respective grades. When a transactions code of 1 or 2 is processed, name, address, and major data fields must be input. If any one or two of these fields contains all blanks, that item in the record should not be altered on a code of 1. When the transactions code is 3, course numbers and grades must be input. A course number of 0000 indicates that no more course numbers and grades remain to be processed for this student. Note that in all three transaction types, the transactions record is variable in length. When the transactions code is 1 or 2, then the appropriate changes should be made in the respective master file record. When the transaction is of type 3, then we want to: (1) enter the course numbers and grades in the master file record; (2) update the total credit hours passed and grade-point average fields; (3) print a grade report that contains the student's name, address, student number, major, courses and grades for the current term, and cumulative grade-point average; and (4) put in a scholastic probation file the name and student number of any student whose cumulative grade-point average is below 2.0. Assume that a new master file record is to be produced for each transaction record and thus there is only one transaction per student. The system used for computing grade-point averages is A=4, B=3, C=2, D=1, and F=0. Only these five grades are possible. Simulated magnetic tapes should be used for the current master file, the transactions file, the new master file, and the scholastic probation file.

CHAPTER 7

FORTRAN PROGRAMMING IN THE SOCIAL SCIENCES AND ARTS

Most of the early uses of computers were in the physical sciences and engineering. Next came the application of computers in the solution of problems in government and business data processing. In recent years the computer has begun to be used to solve problems in the social sciences and arts. The areas in which they have been used range from sociology and psychology to music and the languages. In sociology, computers are used to summarize and analyze data collected about various groups. Meanwhile, computers are used to compose musical scores and to analyze such things as writing style.

Many problems in the social sciences involve the collection and analysis of large amounts of data. The analysis usually involves an area known as *statistics*. An industrial psychologist, for example, might collect data on the responses of the employees of a firm given certain changes in their work environment. The data collected might then be analyzed in an effort to determine which conditions produced the most employee output. A sociologist might collect data on how preschool training affects children from socially deprived homes. An economist may be interested in the effect that money supply has on the rate of inflation. The list of applications in the social sciences can be extended almost without limit. In fact, to date the limit has been the creativity of social scientists in selecting applications for the computer.

In this chapter we are going to examine methods for solving some simple problems from several of the social sciences and arts. There are many more-complicated problem-solving methods available for application to the solution of problems in these areas. However, this chapter will give some notion as to how computers can be applied to solve problems in the social sciences and arts.

7.1 THE STATISTICAL-ANALYSIS-OF-TEXT PROGRAM

A typical problem in the study of languages involves the statistical analysis of textual material. The statistical analysis of text can be performed in many ways. One example would be computing averages, such as the average number of words that appear in a sentence. Another example might be the average number of sentences contained per paragraph. A third example might include the average number of vowels used per word or per sentence. All of these statistics tend to vary from writer to writer and to provide a series of indexes of writing style.

In this section we will give an algorithm and a program that analyzes text in order to determine measures of style. The three things that we will count in our analysis are the total number of sentences, the total number of words, and the total number of characters contained in the text. The output will consist of the total number of sentences contained in the text, the average number of words per sentence, and the average number of characters per word. The algorithm is designed to handle multiple texts. The end of a text is signaled by the appearance of a slash where the first character of a new sentence would begin. A new text is always begun in a new eighty-character input group. Eighty characters are input at a time into a one-dimensional array of one-character strings. After processing this eighty-character group, another group of eighty characters is input. This process continues until the appearance of a slash where a new sentence would begin. The algorithm assumes that only one blank space separates words in the text. In addition, all commas, semicolons, and hyphens are to be ignored. A period, indicating the end of a sentence, always follows a nonblank character. Furthermore, this period is assumed to be followed by two blank spaces.

Figure 7.1 Algorithm Flowchart for the Statistical-Analysis-of-Text Problem

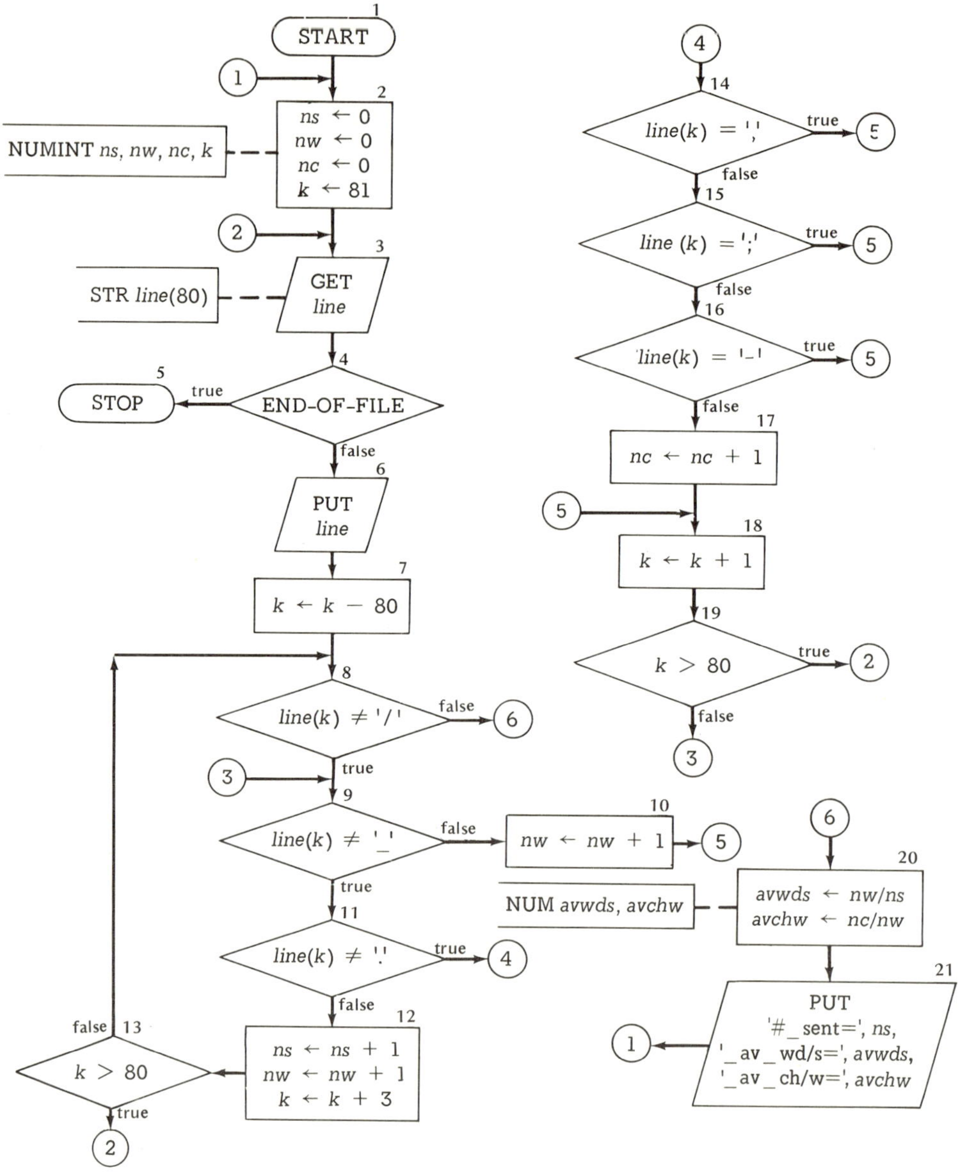

The algorithm flowchart for this problem appears in Fig. 7.1*, while the corresponding FORTRAN program and sample output are listed in Fig. 7.2. The input records used to produce the sample output are listed by the program in the sample output and therefore do not need to be listed separately. Since the program statements closely follow the flowchart steps, little discussion of the program is needed. However, notice the use of the numeric functional operator FLOAT to convert the values of the counter variables from integer to real. This conversion is performed to produce averages that are not truncated values.

PROBLEMS

For problems 1 through 5: (1) develop an algorithm flowchart, (2) write a corresponding FORTRAN program, and (3) test the program using input data records that you create. All of these problems correspond with problems in Ch. 7 of the main text (the corresponding main-text problem numbers are given in parentheses). Therefore, those using the main text should already have completed the algorithm flowchart development phase.

1. (Prob. 2) Develop an algorithm that: (1) inputs a name consisting of a first name, a middle name or initial, and a last name, in that order; (2) forms a string consisting of the last name followed by the first and middle initials, each followed by a period; and (3) outputs both the input and edited names. Assume that: (1) input names appear left-justified in the input stream, (2) one blank separates the first and middle names and one blank separates the middle and last names, and (3) the last name is immediately followed by a comma.

2. (Prob. 3) Develop an algorithm similar to the one described in Problem 1. Assume that the middle name or initial may or may not appear and that there may be more than one middle name or initial.

---

*For those using the main text, this flowchart is the same one that appears in Fig. 7.2M.

Figure 7.2 FORTRAN Program for the Flowchart of Figure 7.1

```
C    ***** PROGRAM FOR ALGORITHM OF FIGURE 7.2M *************************
      REAL AVWDS,AVCHW
      INTEGER NS,NW,NC,K,LINE(80),SLASH,BLANK,PERIOD,COMMA,SCOL,HYPHN
      DATA SLASH,BLANK,PERIOD,COMMA,SCOL,HYPHN/'/',' ','.',',',';','-',
  501 FORMAT('1',30X,'INPUT TEXT ANALYZED',/,1X,80('-'))
  502 FORMAT(80A1)
  503 FORMAT(1X,80A1)
  504 FORMAT(1X,80('-'),/,26X,'NUMBER OF SENTENCES=',I8,/,19X,'AVERAGE'
     * ' NUMBER OF WORDS/SENTENCE=',F8.2,/,20X,'AVERAGE NUMBER OF SYMB'
     * 'OLS/WORD=',F8.2,/,1X,80('-'))
    1 NS=0
      NW=0
      NC=0
      K=81
      WRITE(6,501)
    2 READ(5,502,END=999) LINE
      WRITE(6,503) LINE
      K=K-80
   10 IF(LINE(K).NE.SLASH) GO TO 3
      AVWDS=FLOAT(NW)/FLOAT(NS)
      AVCHW=FLOAT(NC)/FLOAT(NW)
      WRITE(6,504) NS,AVWDS,AVCHW
      GO TO 1
    3 IF(LINE(K).NE.BLANK) GO TO 15
      NW=NW+1
      GO TO 5
   15 IF(LINE(K).NE.PERIOD) GO TO 4
      NS=NS+1
      NW=NW+1
      K=K+3
      IF(K.GT.80) GO TO 2
      GO TO 10
    4 IF(LINE(K).EQ.COMMA) GO TO 5
      IF(LINE(K).EQ.SCOL)  GO TO 5
      IF(LINE(K).EQ.HYPHN) GO TO 5
      NC=NC+1
    5 K=K+1
      IF(K.GT.80) GO TO 2
      GO TO 3
  999 STOP
      END
```

Figure 7.2 (Continued)

```
                              INPUT TEXT ANALYZED
--------------------------------------------------------------------------------
LOUISIANA HAS A LONG COASTLINE ON THE GULF OF MEXICO.  ITS LARGEST CITY IS NEW O
RLEANS.  THE STATE CAPITAL IS IN BATON ROUGE.  MORE NATURAL GAS IS PRODUCED IN L
OUISIANA THAN IN ANY OTHER STATE.  IT IS ALSO AN IMPORTANT SOURCE OF RICE AND SU
GAR CANE.  SOUTHWESTERN LOUISIANA IS THE STATES SECOND LARGEST UNIVERSITY.  BYE.
 /
--------------------------------------------------------------------------------
                         NUMBER OF SENTENCES=       7
                   AVERAGE NUMBER OF WORDS/SENTENCE=     7.86
                    AVERAGE NUMBER OF SYMBOLS/WORD=    4.60
--------------------------------------------------------------------------------
```

Each name will be separated from its successor by one blank and the last name is again followed by a comma. Output for each name should consist of the input name followed by an edited name that consists of last name followed by an initial and a period for the first and each middle name.

3. (Prob. 5) Develop an algorithm similar to the one in Fig. 7.1 for a single text that is divided into paragraphs and chapters. Each paragraph is to be terminated by a period-blank-blank-slash sequence. Similarly, each chapter is terminated by a period-blank-blank-asterisk sequence. The text will be terminated by the end-of-file indicator. The following are to be computed and printed after each respective unit:
   a. For each paragraph: (1) the number of sentences, (2) the average number of words per sentence, and (3) the average number of symbols per word.
   b. For each chapter: (1) the number of paragraphs, (2) the average number of sentences per paragraph, (3) the average number of words per sentence, and (4) the average number of symbols per word.
   c. For the entire book: (1) the number of chapters, (2) the average number of paragraphs per chapter, (3) the average number of sentences per paragraph, and (4) the average number of words per sentence.

4. (Prob. 6) Develop an algorithm similar to the one of Fig. 7.1 in which the occurrences of the words 'AND', 'BUT', and 'OR' are counted. Output should consist of the number of occurrences of each of these words in each text and the average number of times any of these words appears in a sentence.

5. (Prob. 7) An interesting problem involves the justification of type lines. Let us assume that words are not to be divided between lines and that every line is to be both left- and right-justified. Any extra blanks required to achieve left- and right-justification should be distributed evenly between the words of a line. Assume that there are no new paragraphs, pagination is not a concern, and that the number of character positions per line is an input value that does not exceed 80. Develop an algorithm to perform type-line justification as described above. Assume the existence of an input data stream from which one character at a time is to be input and processed.

7.2 THE USE OF STATISTICS TO SUMMARIZE DATA PROGRAM

The first step in social science research usually involves the collection of data concerning the various attributes of the item being studied. This results in the accumulation of a large number of data values that individually do not provide the researcher with much information about the item under study. The reason is that it is difficult for a person to comprehend the meaning of a large mass of data. For example, it is very difficult for a sociologist to draw any conclusion about the educational level of the inmate population of the state prison given the number of years of formal schooling completed by each of the 1,000 inmates at the prison. This is because all that the sociologist sees is 1,000 numbers—more values than an individual can easily comprehend. Thus a need exists to have a means of summarizing collections of raw data.

One method for summarizing raw data involves grouping the data together into classes and then counting the number of values that falls into each class. Such statistical summaries are called frequency distributions. Since the number of classes chosen for a frequency distribution is usually rather small, the researcher is better able to deal with ten or fifteen summary numbers than with the large mass of raw data.

Figure 7.3* contains a flowchart for an algorithm that inputs raw data values and outputs a frequency distribution that contains both raw frequencies and relative frequencies. The FORTRAN program that corresponds with this flowchart appears in Fig. 7.4, together with sample output for one data set. The input data records used to produce the sample output are shown in Fig. 7.5.

Notice that only one data value is input per data card. In addition, note the frequent use of the FLOAT functional operator to avoid mixed-mode expressions. Also note the use in the program of the variable RN, which has no counterpart in the flowchart. This variable simply contains the real representation of the value of N. RN is used to reduce the number of times that the value of the integer variable N would have to be converted to a real constant. Finally, notice that the flowchart functional operators *max* and *min* have as their FORTRAN counterparts the functional operators AMAX1 and AMIN1, respectively.

PROBLEMS

Problems 6 and 7 relate to algorithm flowcharts in the main text. For those not using the main text, these problems should be ignored.

6. Write the FORTRAN program that corresponds with the algorithm flowchart of Fig. 7.8M. Use the values given in Prob. 9 of Ch. 7M as input test data.

7. Write the FORTRAN program that corresponds with the algorithm flowchart of Fig. 7.11M. Use the values given in Prob. 20 of Ch. 7M as input test data.

---

*For those using the main text, this flowchart is the same one that appears in Fig. 7.6M.

Figure 7.3 Algorithm Flowchart for the Frequency Distribution Problem

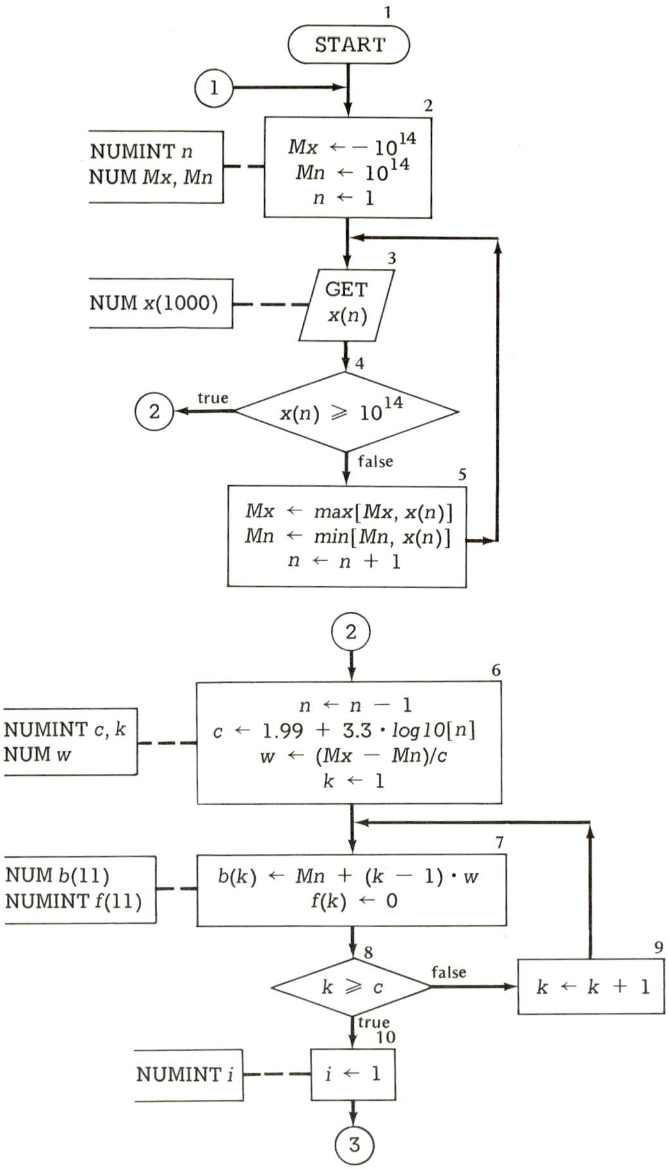

Figure 7.3 (Continued)

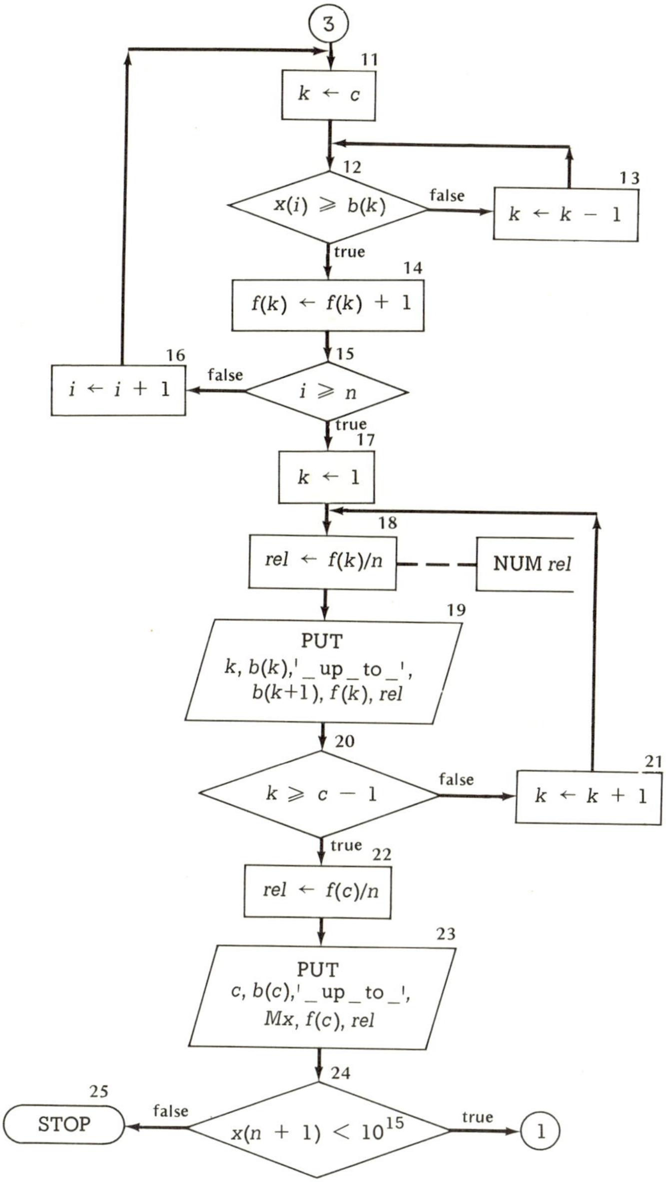

Figure 7.4 FORTRAN Program for the Flowchart of Figure 7.3

```
C   ***** PROGRAM FOR ALGORITHM OF FIGURE 7.6M ***************************
      REAL MX,MN,X(1000),W,B(11),REL,RN
      INTEGER N,C,K,F(11),I
  501 FORMAT(F12.5)
  502 FORMAT('1',15X,'FREQUENCY DISTRIBUTION',/,1X,53('-'),/,' CLASS',
     * 7X,'CLASS BOUNDARIES',8X,'FREQ.',2X,'REL. FREQ.',/,1X,5('-'),2X,
     * 27('-'),'  -----  ',10('-'))
  503 FORMAT(I4,E14.4,' UP TO',E11.4,I5,F11.2)
    1 MX=-1.0E14
      MN=1.0E14
      DO 10 N=1,1000
        READ(5,501) X(N)
C   A VALUE OF X(N) GE 10**14 SIGNALS END OF A DATA SET ****************
        IF(X(N).GE.1.0E14) GO TO 2
        MX=AMAX1(MX,X(N))
   10   MN=AMIN1(MN,X(N))
    2 N=N-1
      RN=FLOAT(N)
      C=IFIX(1.99+3.3*ALOG10(RN))
      W=(MX-MN)/FLOAT(C)
      DO 15 K=1,C
        B(K)=MN+FLOAT(K-1)*W
   15   F(K)=0
      DO 25 I=1,N
        K=C
   20   IF(X(I).GE.B(K)) GO TO 25
        K=K-1
        GO TO 20
   25   F(K)=F(K)+1
      I=C-1
      WRITE(6,502)
      DO 30 K=1,I
        REL=FLOAT(F(K))/RN
   30   WRITE(6,503) K,B(K),B(K+1),F(K),REL
      REL=FLOAT(F(C))/RN
      WRITE(6,503) C,B(C),MX,F(C),REL
C   A VALUE OF X(N+1) GE 10**15 SIGNALS END-OF-FILE *******************
      IF(X(N+1).LT.1.0E15) GO TO 1
      STOP
      END
```

Figure 7.4 (Continued)

FREQUENCY DISTRIBUTION

CLASS	CLASS BOUNDARIES	FREQ.	REL. FREQ.
1	0.6800E 01 UP TO 0.8583E 01	7	0.28
2	0.8583E 01 UP TO 0.1037E 02	5	0.20
3	0.1037E 02 UP TO 0.1215E 02	6	0.24
4	0.1215E 02 UP TO 0.1393E 02	2	0.08
5	0.1393E 02 UP TO 0.1572E 02	3	0.12
6	0.1572E 02 UP TO 0.1750E 02	2	0.08

Figure 7.5 Input Data Records for Output of Figure 7.4

```
..........................................
        6.8
       12.3
        8.9
       14.6
        7.5
       10.2
        9.0
       11.4
        8.5
        8.0
       16.0
       11.4
       15.5
        7.8
       11.0
       12.0
        7.2
       10.4
        8.5
       10.6
        9.9
       17.5
       14.2
        9.4
       13.5
     1.0E16
..........................................
```

For problems 8 through 13: (1) develop an algorithm flowchart, (2) write a corresponding FORTRAN program, and (3) test the program using test data that you create. All of these problems correspond with problems in Ch. 7 of the main text (the corresponding main-text problem numbers are given in parentheses). Therefore, those using the main text should already have completed the algorithm flowchart development phase.

8. (Prob. 12) Develop an algorithm similar to the one in Fig. 7.3 for constructing a frequency and relative frequency distribution. Assume that the class boundaries are to be input rather than generated by the algorithm.

9. (Prob. 13) Develop an algorithm that is designed to develop a frequency and relative frequency distribution for alphabetic data. Assume that all data consist of uppercase alphabetic characters and that class boundaries are to be input. The algorithm should construct the classes using regular alphabetical order.

10. (Prob. 15) Develop an algorithm for computing the arithmetic mean and standard deviation of a set of data values assuming that all of the data values cannot be stored in memory at one time. The formula for computing the standard deviation is

$$std = \sqrt{\Sigma x^2/n - M^2}$$

where M is the arithmetic mean and $\Sigma x^2 = x_1^2 + x_2^2 + \cdots + x_n^2$.

11. (Prob. 17) Two measures of central tendency that are sometimes used are the geometric mean (GM) and the harmonic mean (HM). They are defined as

$$GM = \sqrt[n]{x_1 \cdot x_2 \cdot x_3 \cdot \ldots \cdot x_n}$$

$$HM = n/\Sigma(1/x)$$

where $\Sigma(1/x) = 1/x_1 + 1/x_2 + \cdots + 1/x_n$. Develop an algorithm that can input an unlimited number of data values in each data set and compute their arithmetic, geometric, and harmonic means. Use the sentinel values of Fig. 7.3 to indicate the end of each data set.

12. (Prob. 18) Two measures of dispersion that are sometimes used are the root mean square (RMS) and the mean deviation (MD). They are defined as

$$RMS = \sqrt{\Sigma x^2/n}$$

$$MD = \Sigma|x - M|/n$$

where $\Sigma|x - M| = |x_1 - M| + |x_2 - M| + \cdots + |x_n - M|$. Develop an algorithm that can input, one at a time, data sets consisting of up to 1,000 values and compute the root mean square, mean deviation, and standard deviation for each data set.

13. (Prob. 22) The correlation coefficient r can be used to measure the degree of linear correlation between two sets of variables x and y. The formula for calculating r is:

$$r = \frac{n \cdot \Sigma xy - \Sigma x \cdot \Sigma y}{\sqrt{[n \cdot \Sigma x^2 - (\Sigma x)^2] \cdot [n \cdot \Sigma y^2 - (\Sigma y)^2]}}$$

where (1) n is the number of data pairs; (2) the Σxy, Σx Σy, Σx^2, and Σy^2 are defined as the sum of the respective values; and (3) the value of r always satisfies $-1 \leq r \leq 1$. Develop an algorithm for computing the correlation coefficient; assume that the number of data values in a data set is known prior to processing. That is, you should utilize the sentinal values used in the algorithm of Fig. 7.3 to signal the end of a data set.

CHAPTER 8

FORTRAN PROGRAMMING IN EDUCATION

8.1 COMPUTER-ASSISTED INSTRUCTION PROGRAM PROBLEMS

Education is an area that offers a great deal of opportunity for the use of computers to solve problems. In earlier chapters we have examined some of these problems and their solutions. For example, in Section 5.2 we developed an algorithm for averaging student test grades, which is a very common problem for teachers in all aspects of education. Similarly, in Chapter 6 we examined concepts of file processing, which is important in education because of the need to keep student records. Statistical problems, similar to the ones in Chapter 7, also occur in education. This is because of the need to evaluate student groups, teaching techniques, and other things that involve statistics.

8.1 COMPUTER-ASSISTED INSTRUCTION PROGRAM

Although all of the applications mentioned in the previous paragraph are important in education, they are not a part of the main purpose of education. That is, they do not directly relate to the process of teaching people things they do not already know. In this chapter we will examine an application from the main line of education—computer-assisted instruction. The essence of computer-assisted instruction (abbreviated as CAI) is using the computer to introduce new concepts to a student and to test the student's comprehension of those concepts. Computer-assisted instruction has thus far been applied primarily to rote learning situations, that is, to teaching things that are primarily factual. For example, common applications of computer-assisted instruction have been in teaching arithmetic, remedial grammar, and certain factual aspects of history. Since computer-assisted instruction is still in its infancy, we can expect it to be used to teach more difficult subjects in the future.

When the algorithms have been carefully prepared and tested, computer-assisted instruction has proved to be a popular means of teaching from the student viewpoint. One apparent reason for this is the fascination that people have for machines (particularly computers). Another reason is the fact that a properly developed computer-assisted instruction algorithm will cause the computer to display what seems to be an almost unlimited amount of patience.

An algorithm flowchart for the computer-assisted instruction of addition appears in Fig. 8.1,* while a program and sample output are given in Fig. 8.2. Because most FORTRAN student programs are input using punched cards, that is the medium used for this example. However, computer-assisted instruction is always performed in the real world using an interactive terminal. The reason is that the CAI program and the student must interact during the learning process. In the example output of Fig. 8.2, however, the student responses are not shown because they were input from punched cards. The input records used to generate the responses shown in Fig. 8.2 appear in Fig. 8.3. These data records should be compared with the sample output generated.

PROBLEMS

Problem 1 relates to an algorithm flowchart in the main text. For those not using the main text, this problem should be ignored.

1. Write the FORTRAN program that corresponds with the algorithm flowchart of Fig. 8.8M. Use the input data records of Fig. 8.7 to test the program.

For problems 2 through 4: (1) develop an algorithm flowchart, (2) write a corresponding FORTRAN program, and (3) test the program using test data that you create. All of these problems correspond with problems in Ch. 8 of the main text (the corresponding main-text problem numbers are given in parentheses). Therefore, those using

---

*For those using the main text, this flowchart is the same one that appears in Fig. 8.3M.

Figure 8.1 Algorithm Flowchart for the Computer-Assisted Instruction Problem

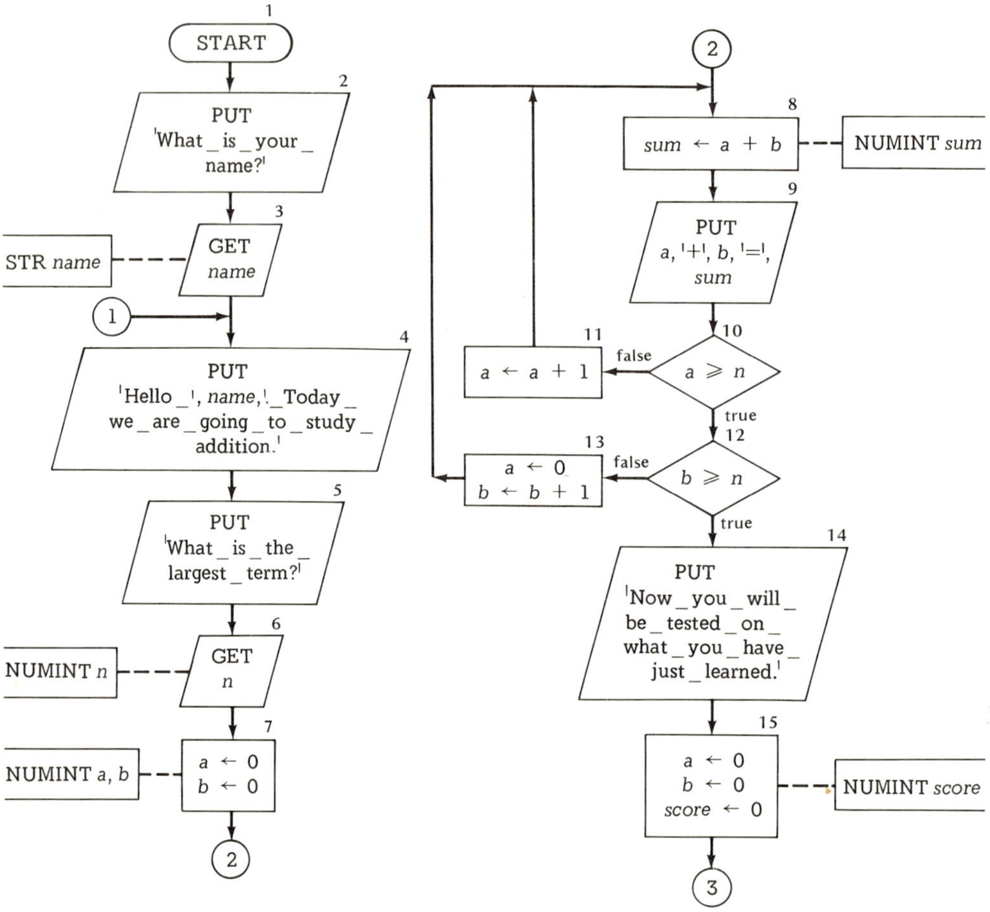

the main text should already have completed the algorithm flowchart development phase.

2. (Prob. 2) Modify the algorithm flowchart of Fig. 8.1 based on the following assumptions: (a) the lower bounds of the addition table (i.e., the initial values given to *a* and *b*) are input by the student rather than fixed at a value of zero, (b) the lower and upper bounds are not necessarily the same on both variables,

Figure 8.1 (Continued)

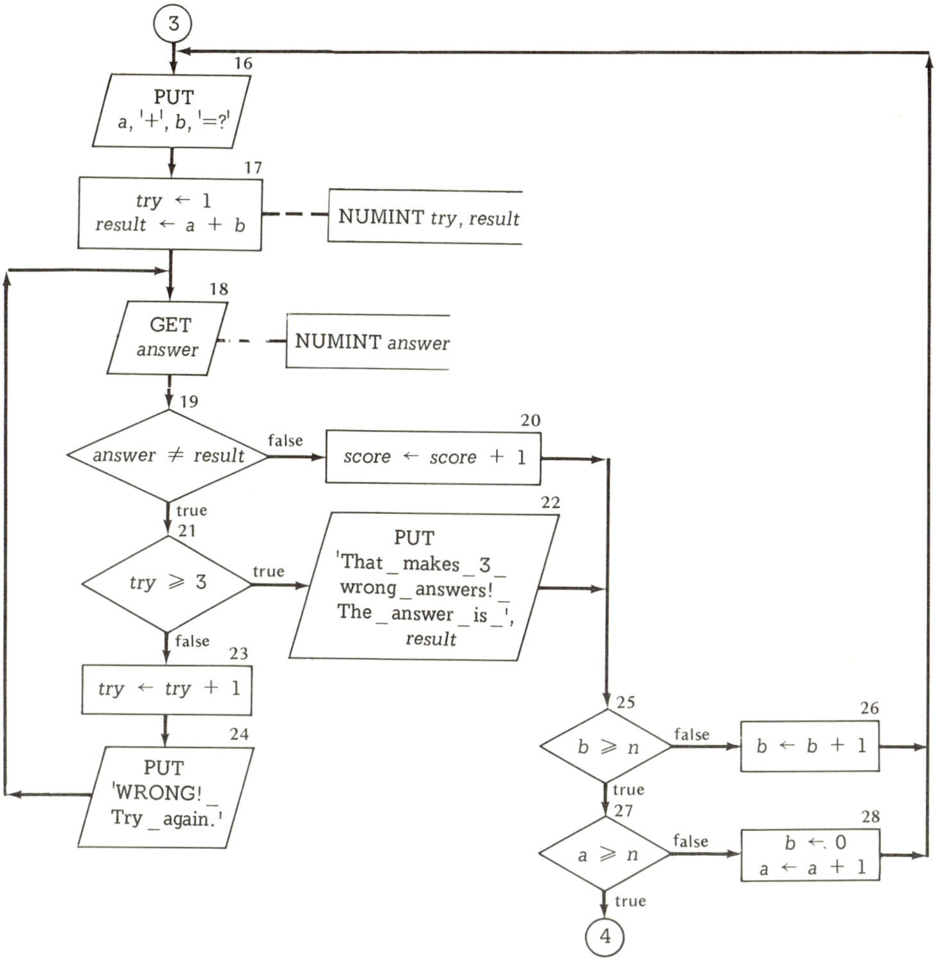

(c) the number of trys allowed per problem is an input variable rather than fixed at 3, and (d) the average is computed as the number of correct answers divided by the number of answers input, with this quotient multiplied by 100.

3. (Prob. 5) A geography teacher needs an algorithm that will allow students to learn about the capital cities of various countries and states. A learning session should begin (after

Figure 8.1 (Continued)

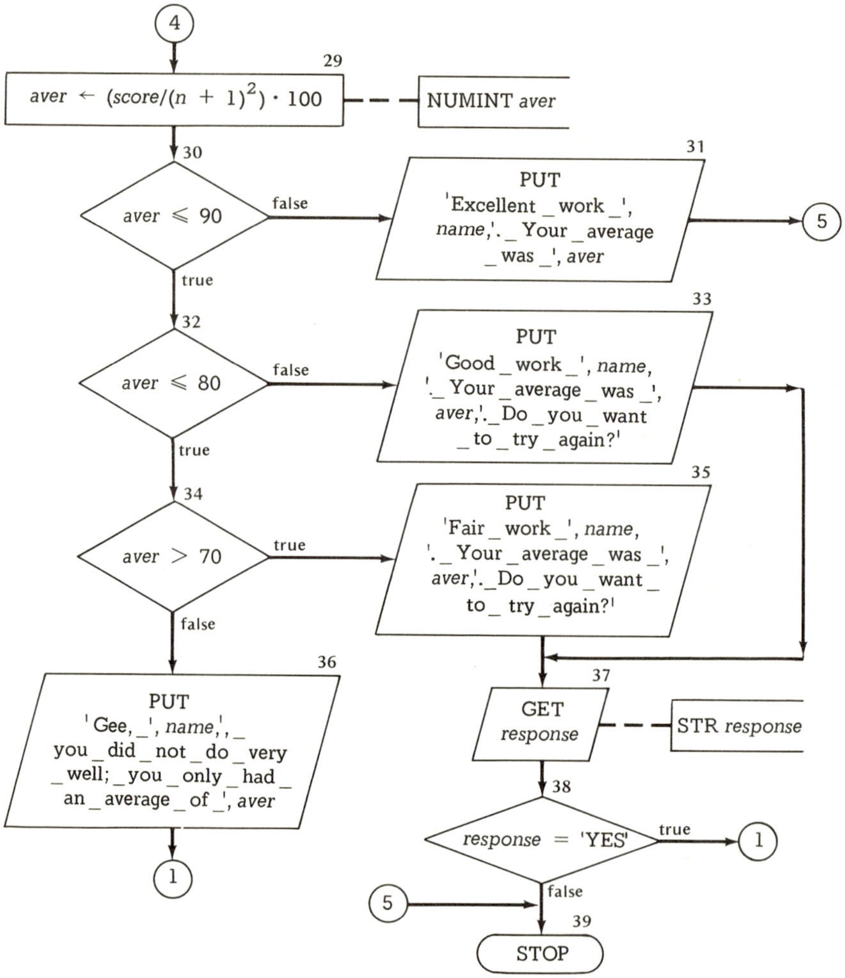

the usual opening formalities, such as learning the student's name) by instructing the student on the capital cities of a group of states. Then the student should be tested on retention of the facts involved by being given the name of a

Figure 8.2 FORTRAN Program for Flowchart of Figure 8.1

```
C   ***** PROGRAM FOR ALGORITHM OF FIGURE 8.3M *************************
      REAL NAME(5),RESPON,YES
      INTEGER N,A,B,SUM,SCORE,TRY,RESULT,ANSWER,AVER
      DATA YES/'YES'/
  501 FORMAT('1WHAT IS YOUR NAME?  ')
  502 FORMAT(5A4)
  503 FORMAT(' HELLO ',5A4,'. TODAY WE ARE GOING TO STUDY ADDITION.')
  504 FORMAT(' WHAT IS THE LARGEST TERM?  ',//)
  505 FORMAT(I3)
  506 FORMAT(I4,'+',I3,'=',I4)
  507 FORMAT(//,' NOW YOU WILL BE TESTED ON WHAT YOU HAVE JUST LEARNED',
     * '.',//)
  508 FORMAT(I4,'+',I3,'=?  ')
  509 FORMAT(I4)
  510 FORMAT(' WRONG! TRY AGAIN.')
  511 FORMAT(' THAT MAKES 3 WRONG ANSWERS! THE ANSWER IS ',I4)
  512 FORMAT(' EXCELLENT WORK ',5A4,'. YOUR AVERAGE WAS ',I2)
  513 FORMAT(' GOOD WORK ',5A4,'. YOUR AVERAGE WAS ',I2,'. DO YOU WANT',
     * ' TO TRY AGAIN?  ')
  514 FORMAT(' GEE, ',5A4,', YOU DID NOT DO VERY WELL; YOU ONLY HAD AN',
     * ' AVERAGE OF ',I2)
  515 FORMAT(' FAIR WORK ',5A4,'. YOUR AVERAGE WAS ',I2,'. DO YOU WANT',
     * ' TO TRY AGAIN?  ')
  516 FORMAT(A3)
      WRITE(6,501)
      READ(5,502) NAME
    1 WRITE(6,503) NAME
      WRITE(6,504)
      READ(5,505) N
      A=0
      B=0
    2 SUM=A+B
      WRITE(6,506) A,B,SUM
      IF(A.GE.N) GO TO 10
      A=A+1
      GO TO 2
   10 IF(B.GE.N) GO TO 15
      A=0
      B=B+1
      GO TO 2
```

Figure 8.2 (Continued)

```
15 WRITE(6,507)
   A=0
   B=0
   SCORE=0
 3 WRITE(6,508) A,B
   TRY=1
   RESULT=A+B
20 READ(5,509) ANSWER
   IF(ANSWER.NE.RESULT) GO TO 25
   SCORE=SCORE+1
   GO TO 35
25 IF(TRY.GE.3) GO TO 30
   TRY=TRY+1
   WRITE(6,510)
   GO TO 20
30 WRITE(6,511) RESULT
35 IF(B.GE.N) GO TO 40
   B=B+1
   GO TO 3
40 IF(A.GE.N) GO TO 4
   B=0
   A=A+1
   GO TO 3
 4 AVER=IFIX((FLOAT(SCORE)/FLOAT(N+1)**2)*100.0)
   IF(AVER.LE.90) GO TO 45
   WRITE(6,512) NAME,AVER
   GO TO 5
45 IF(AVER.LE.80) GO TO 50
   WRITE(6,513) NAME,AVER
   GO TO 60
50 IF(AVER.GT.70) GO TO 55
   WRITE(6,514) NAME,AVER
   GO TO 1
55 WRITE(6,515) NAME,AVER
60 READ(5,516) RESPON
   IF(RESPON.EQ.YES) GO TO 1
 5 STOP
   END
```

Figure 8.2 (Continued)

```
WHAT IS YOUR NAME?
HELLO TERRY WALKER          . TODAY WE ARE GOING TO STUDY ADDITION.
WHAT IS THE LARGEST TERM?


  0+  0=   0
  1+  0=   1
  2+  0=   2
  0+  1=   1
  1+  1=   2
  2+  1=   3
  0+  2=   2
  1+  2=   3
  2+  2=   4


NOW YOU WILL BE TESTED ON WHAT YOU HAVE JUST LEARNED.


  0+  0=?
  0+  1=?
WRONG! TRY AGAIN.
  0+  2=?
  1+  0=?
WRONG! TRY AGAIN.
  1+  1=?
  1+  2=?
  2+  0=?
WRONG! TRY AGAIN.
WRONG! TRY AGAIN.
  2+  1=?
WRONG! TRY AGAIN.
WRONG! TRY AGAIN.
THAT MAKES 3 WRONG ANSWERS! THE ANSWER IS    3
  2+  2=?
GOOD WORK TERRY WALKER          . YOUR AVERAGE WAS 88. DO YOU WANT TO TRY AGAIN
```

state (or country) and having to respond with the name of the capital city. No more than four attempts should be provided to answer any question correctly. Use the criteria of the algorithm of Fig. 8.1 in determining whether or not the lesson for that group of states (or countries) needs to be repeated. Grades

Figure 8.3 Input Records for the Output of Figure 8.2

```
.....................................
TERRY WALKER
 2
  0
  0
  1
  2
  0
  1
  2
  3
  1
  3
  2
  2
  0
  1
  4
 NO
.....................................
```

should be computed as 100 times the ratio of the total number of correct answers and the total number of times the student input an answer. The states and countries should be entirely input prior to the beginning of each student session.

4. (Prob. 6) A computer science professor would like to have an algorithm that drills students on the precedence rules for arithmetic expressions, as discussed in Section 4.3. The algorithm should begin by outputting the precedence rules. Then the student should be tested by the output of various expressions that he or she must evaluate and input an answer. The expressions used for testing should be input, together with the correct answers and the values to be used in evaluating those expressions. Grades should be computed as 100 times the ratio of the total number of correct answers and the total number of times the student input an answer. No more than four attempts should be provided to answer any question correctly. Use the criteria of the algorithm of Fig. 8.1 in determining whether or not the lesson should be repeated.

CHAPTER 9

PROGRAM DESIGN III: SUBPROGRAMS

As we have seen in the three previous chapters, the concepts introduced in Chs. 4 and 5 have given us all of the tools we actually need to write FORTRAN programs. However, one concept still needs to be covered so that our programming task can be made as easy as possible. The concept is the FORTRAN subprogram.

9.1 FUNDAMENTAL SUBPROGRAM CONCEPTS

The term "subalgorithm" is actually a way of saying subordinate algorithm. A *subalgorithm* is therefore simply an algorithm that is subordinate to another algorithm. Since we have defined an algorithm to be a procedure that provides the solution to a class of problems, a subalgorithm must be a procedure that provides a solution to a class of subproblems.

In the flowchart language, we write subalgorithms as algorithm flowcharts that have an annotation box attached to their START box and the word RETURN instead of STOP in their terminal box. The annotation box contains the entry point name of the subalgorithm and a formal parameter list. The *entry point name* is used to refer to a particular subalgorithm while the formal parameter list is simply a group of variable names. The variable names in such a formal parameter list are used to input values to the subalgorithm and output values from the subalgorithm. The algorithm that calls on a subalgorithm is called the *invoking algorithm* while the subalgorithm being used is said to be the *invoked subalgorithm.*

The points in the invoking algorithm where a call is made to a subalgorithm are called *points of invocation.* At each point of invocation an entry point name and an actual parameter list appear. The entry point name is the one associated with the subalgorithm that is to be invoked at that point. The actual parameter list is a group of arithmetic expressions or string constants or variables.

These actual parameters provide the means by which values are output to the invoked subalgorithm and input to the invoking algorithm. The parameters in actual and formal parameter lists are matched one-for-one on a left-to-right basis.

There are two types of subalgorithms, depending on how the subalgorithm is invoked. A *general subalgorithm* is one in which invocation takes place by the appearance in a predefined process box of an entry point name followed by the actual parameter list. In contrast, a *function subalgorithm* is invoked by having the entry point name and actual parameter list appear in an arithmetic expression in the invoking algorithm. For both general and function subalgorithms, any variables in the actual parameter list whose corresponding formal parameters have been assigned values during subalgorithm execution will have new values after invocation. Invocation of a function subalgorithm also causes a value to be returned to the point in the arithmetic expression where invocation took place. The value that is returned is determined by placing an arithmetic expression in between a pair of square brackets following the word RETURN in the subalgorithm.

The subprogram is the FORTRAN equivalent of the subalgorithm flowchart. Just as a subalgorithm is simply an algorithm that is subordinate to another algorithm, a subprogram is a program segment that is subordinate to another program segment. There are two kinds of subprograms just as there are two kinds of subalgorithms. These two kinds of subprograms are: (1) a function subprogram and (2) a subroutine subprogram. A *subroutine subprogram* corresponds with a general subalgorithm.

The first statement of a subprogram provides the *entry point* to that subprogram. For a function subprogram, the first statement must be

type FUNCTION *name* (*formal parameter list*)

where *type* will be either REAL or INTEGER, depending on the type of value that is to be returned by the subprogram to the point of invocation. The first statement of a subroutine subprogram must be:

SUBROUTINE *name* (*formal parameter list*)

For the FUNCTION and SUBROUTINE statements: (1) *name* is formed by using the rules for writing a FORTRAN variable name and represents an entry-point name for that subprogram and (2) *formal parameter list* is optional and corresponds with the formal parameter list of a subalgorithm.

The FUNCTION and SUBROUTINE statements are both nonexecutable. Both function and subroutine subprograms should include type statements which declare every variable used in the subprogram, including variables that are formal parameters. In addition, every subprogram must be terminated with an END statement. The labels and all variables defined in a subprogram are known only in that subprogram, unless they are formal parameters. Thus, the same variable names and labels can be used in several program segments and never be confused with one another. Variables used in a subprogram that do not appear in the formal parameter list are called *local variables*.

A function subprogram is invoked implicitly by the appearance of its entry-point name in an arithmetic expression of the invoking program segment. When the entry point of the invoked subprogram has a formal parameter list, then the name is followed by an actual parameter list enclosed in parentheses. The entry name of a function subprogram must be declared in a type statement in the invoking program segment. The type of the entry name determines the type of value returned to the point of invocation when the subprogram is invoked.

A subroutine subprogram is invoked explicitly by the appearance of its entry name in a CALL statement of the invoking program segment

The general form of the CALL statement is

CALL *name* (*actual parameter list*)

where: (1) *name* is an entry name to a subroutine subprogram, and (2) *actual parameter list*, which may be omitted, corresponds with a flowchart-language actual parameter list.

Execution of a subprogram begins with the first executable statement following the subprogram statement that defines the entry name used for invocation. Upon invocation, the actual parameters are related to the formal parameters in the entry statement. Execution of the subprogram then proceeds until the RETURN statement in the subprogram is executed. When this occurs, a branch is taken back to the point of invocation in the invoking program segment.

A FORTRAN *actual parameter list* may contain only arithmetic expressions.* Since string expressions are not permitted in FORTRAN executable statements, string values are passed to and from subprograms using real or integer arithmetic variables as parameters. Aside from this exception, FORTRAN actual parameter lists are the same as flowchart-language actual parameter lists.

A FORTRAN *formal parameter list* may contain only arithmetic variable names. As with actual parameter lists, string constants are stored in locations associated with arithmetic variable names because string variables are not permitted in FORTRAN. The rules for correspondence of actual and formal parameters are the same in FORTRAN as they are in the flowchart language.

---

*Most dialects of FORTRAN also permit as actual parameters: (1) names of subprogram entry points and (2) labels of statements defined in the invoking program segment. However, we will not use either of these in this text.

9.2 SUBROUTINE SUBPROGRAMS

A FORTRAN subroutine subprogram is one that is invoked explicitly by the use of a CALL statement. The action taken by the invocation of a subroutine is to associate the actual and formal parameters with each other on a one-to-one basis. Then control is transferred to the first executable statement in the subprogram. Execution of the statement in the subroutine then takes place in the same manner in which the statements of any FORTRAN program segment would be executed. Any values of actual parameter variables that are changed through their associated formal parameters in the subprogram will remain changed upon return to the invoking program segment. All variable names used in the subroutine but not appearing in the formal parameter list are known only in the subprogram. Furthermore, only variable names and statement labels appearing in the subprogram are known within the subroutine. Thus values can be passed between the invoking program segment and the subprogram only through the parameter lists. The values of as many variables in the actual parameter list as we desire can be changed in the subprogram.

The flowcharts in Fig. 9.1 through 9.3* are as follows:

1. Figure 9.1 contains an algorithm flowchart for an invoking algorithm to process an organization's payroll.
2. Figure 9.2 contains a general subalgorithm for computing gross pay.
3. Figure 9.3 contains a general subalgorithm for computing payroll tax deductions.

---

*For those using the main text, these flowcharts are the same ones that appear in Figs. 9.4M through 9.6M.

The variables used in the flowchart of Fig. 9.1 have the following meanings:

1. *name* is the employee's name.
2. *rate* is the employee's hourly pay rate.
3. *ytde* is the employee's year-to-date earnings.
4. *hrs* is the number of hours the employee worked this pay period.
5. *dep* is the number of dependents claimed by the employee.

Figure 9.1 Flowchart for the Payroll Problem Invoking Algorithm

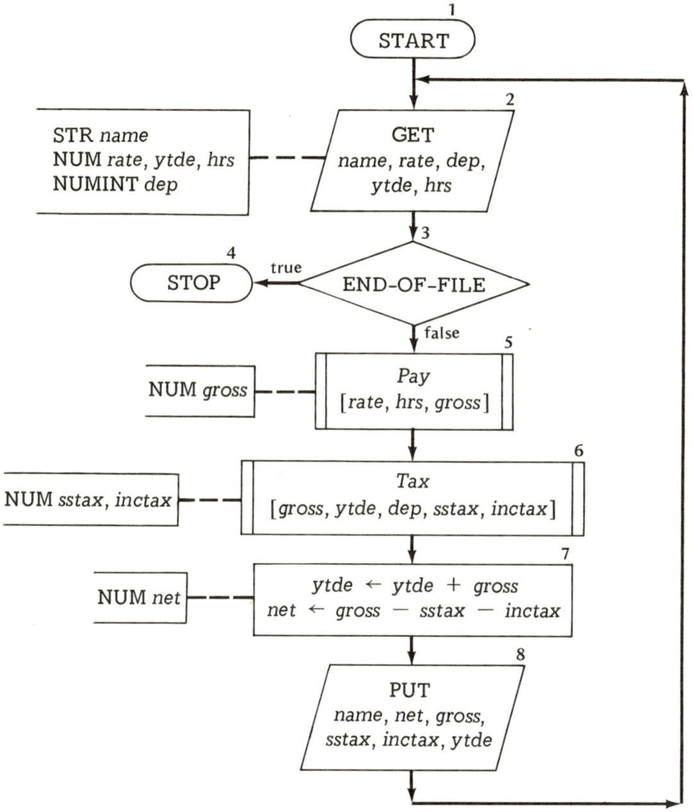

Figure 9.2 Flowchart for the Gross Pay Subalgorithm

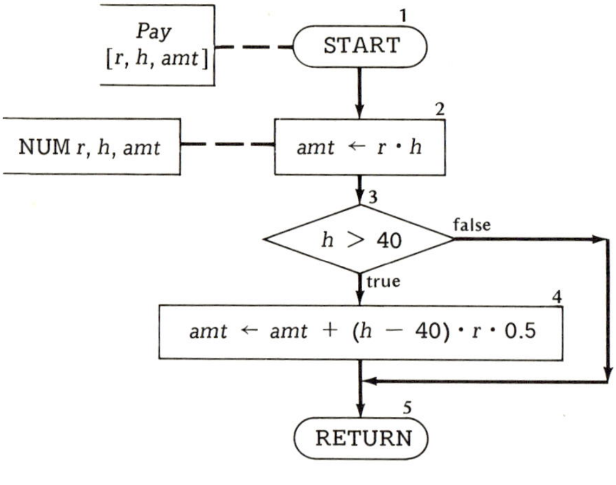

Figure 9.3 Flowchart for the Payroll Tax Subalgorithm

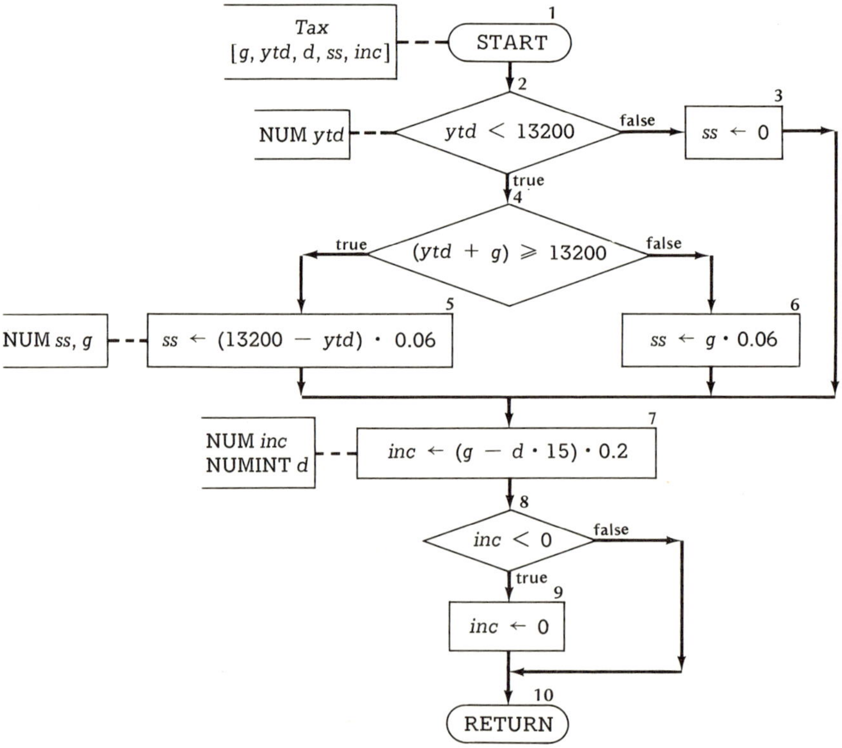

6. *gross* is the gross pay for the current pay period.
7. *sstax* is the social security tax for the current pay period.
8. *inctax* is the income tax for the current pay period.
9. *net* is the net or take home pay for the current pay period.

The FORTRAN program segments associated with these three flowcharts appear in Fig. 9.4. Also included in that figure is sample output, which was the result of program execution using as input records:

```
••••••••••••••••••••••••••••••••••••••••••••••••••
JOHN DOE                 2.0 3    7200.0      45.0
BOB LOW                  7.0 4   13100.0      40.0
VERN MOE                 1.5 8    4000.0      44.0
LARGE TOE               10.0 2   14100.0      35.0
••••••••••••••••••••••••••••••••••••••••••••••••••
```

The logic of the program follows that of the algorithm flowcharts and thus needs very little explanation. Notice that the flowchart string variable *name* has a real array as its program counterpart. The reason is that we want to be able to process names that contain up to twenty characters.

The actual parameters for the invocation of the subroutine named PAY are RATE, HRS, and GROSS. The corresponding formal parameters in the subroutine are in order, R, H, and AMT. The actual parameters RATE and HRS are used to output values to the subprogram, while GROSS is used to return the value of the result from the subroutine. For the subprogram with the entry point name TAX, the actual parameters are GROSS, YTDE, DEP, SSTAX, and INCTAX. The formal parameters that go with these actual parameters are G, YTD, D, SS, and INC, respectively. The actual parameters GROSS, YTDE, and DEP are used to output values to the subroutine while SSTAX and INCTAX are used to return results from the subroutine.

Figure 9.4 FORTRAN Program for the Flowcharts of Figures 9.1, 9.2, and 9.3

```
C   ***** PROGRAM FOR ALGORITHM OF FIGURE 9.4M ***************************
      REAL NAME(5),RATE,YTDE,HRS,GROSS,SSTAX,INCTAX,NET
      INTEGER DEP
  501 FORMAT('1',27X,'PAYROLL PROCESSING RESULTS',/,1X,80('-'),/,4X,
     * 'EMPLOYEE NAME',7X,'NET PAY',4X,'GROSS PAY',4X,'S S TAX',5X,
     * 'INC TAX',4X,'YTD EARNGS',/,1X,20('-'),5(2X,10('-')))
  502 FORMAT(5A4,F5.2,I2,2F10.2)
  503 FORMAT(1X,5A4,5('   $',F9.2))
      WRITE(6,501)
   10 READ(5,502,END=999) NAME,RATE,DEP,YTDE,HRS
      CALL PAY(RATE,HRS,GROSS)
      CALL TAX(GROSS,YTDE,DEP,SSTAX,INCTAX)
      YTDE=YTDE+GROSS
      NET=GROSS-SSTAX-INCTAX
      WRITE(6,503) NAME,NET,GROSS,SSTAX,INCTAX,YTDE
      GO TO 10
  999 STOP
      END
C   ***** SUBPROGRAM FOR SUBALGORITHM OF FIGURE 9.5M *******************
      SUBROUTINE PAY(R,H,AMT)
      REAL R,H,AMT
      AMT=R*H
      IF(H.GT.40.0) AMT=AMT+(H-40.0)*R*0.5
      RETURN
      END
C   ***** SUBPROGRAM FOR SUBALGORITHM OF FIGURE 9.6M *******************
      SUBROUTINE TAX(G,YTD,D,SS,INC)
      REAL YTD,SS,G,INC
      INTEGER D
      IF(YTD.LT.13200.0) GO TO 10
      SS=0.0
      GO TO 20
   10 IF((YTD+G).GE.13200.0) GO TO 15
      SS=G*0.06
      GO TO 20
   15 SS=(13200.0-YTD)*0.06
   20 INC=(G-FLOAT(D*15))*0.2
      IF(INC.LT.0.0) INC=0.0
      RETURN
      END
```

Figure 9.4 (Continued)

PAYROLL PROCESSING RESULTS

EMPLOYEE NAME	NET PAY	GROSS PAY	S S TAX	INC TAX	YTD EARNGS
JOHN DOE	$ 79.30	$ 95.00	$ 5.70	$ 10.00	$ 7295.00
BOB LOW	$ 230.00	$ 280.00	$ 6.00	$ 44.00	$ 13380.00
VERN MOE	$ 64.86	$ 69.00	$ 4.14	$ 0.00	$ 4069.00
LARGE TOE	$ 286.00	$ 350.00	$ 0.00	$ 64.00	$ 14450.00

9.3 FUNCTION SUBPROGRAMS

Function subprograms in FORTRAN are quite similar to subroutines except for the manner in which they are invoked. Whereas a subroutine is invoked explicitly in a CALL statement, a function subprogram is invoked implicitly by using its entry name in an arithmetic expression. In addition, a function subprogram returns a constant as a value to the point of invocation, something not done by a subroutine. The constant returned is specified by the value that has been most recently assigned to the entry point name of the function subprogram.

As an example, Fig. 9.5 contains an algorithm flowchart for the problem of: (1) inputting the symbols in a Roman number, (2) invoking a function subalgorithm to convert the Roman number to its decimal equivalent, and (3) outputting the Roman number and its decimal equivalent. The function subalgorithm for performing the conversion is given in Fig. 9.6.* Notice that the value of the variable *Sum* is the one that is returned to the point of invocation. In addition, the variable *err* has its value changed within the subalgorithm to

*For those using the main text, Figs. 9.5 and 9.6 correspond with the flowcharts in Figs. 9.9M and 9.10M, respectively.

Figure 9.5 Flowchart for the Roman Number Conversion Invoking Algorithm

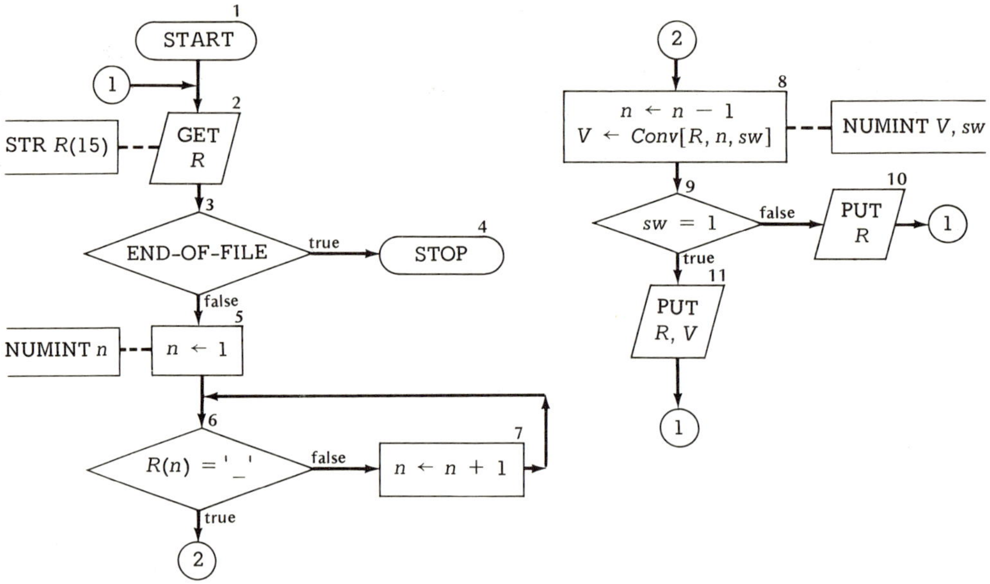

indicate whether the return is normal (conversion was successful) or abnormal (an illegal Roman digit was encountered).

The FORTRAN program for performing Roman number conversion is given in Fig. 9.7. The input records that produced the sample output shown in this figure are not displayed since the output contains the input values. Notice that the actual parameter R is an array variable and so is the corresponding formal parameter, S. Also observe that the variables RI, RV, RX, RL, RC, RD, and RM are required to store the string constants for the seven Roman numerals since FORTRAN does not allow string constants to appear in IF statements. Similarly, the variable BLANK is used instead of a string constant in the main program segment. In both cases, these variables

Figure 9.6 Flowchart for the Roman Number Conversion Subalgorithm

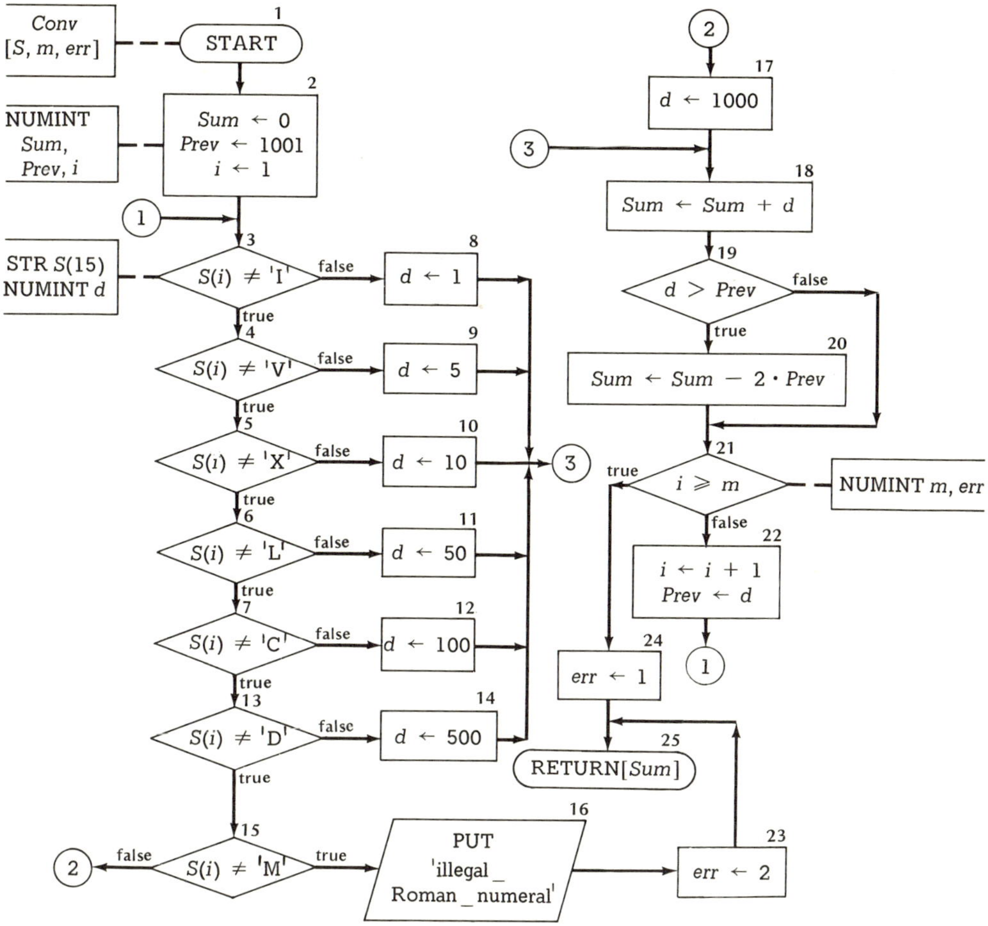

are initialized with their string constant values in DATA statements. Finally, notice that the subprogram entry point name has been declared in the main program segment to be of type integer because it returns an integer value. In addition, the subprogram is declared to be of type integer in the FUNCTION statement because it returns an integer value as the value of the entry point name CONV.

Figure 9.7 FORTRAN Program for the Flowcharts of Figures 9.5 and 9.6

```
C   ***** PROGRAM FOR ALGORITHM OF FIGURE 9.9 ***************************
      INTEGER R(15),N,V,SW,BLANK,CONV
      DATA BLANK/' '/
  501 FORMAT('1    ROMAN NUMBER EQUIVALENTS',/,1X,29('-'),/,2X,'ROMAN N'
     * 'UMBER',5X,'DEC. EQUIV.',/,1X,15('-'),3X,11('-'))
  502 FORMAT(15A1)
  503 FORMAT(1X,15A1,I11)
      WRITE(6,501)
    1 READ(5,502,END=999) R
      DO 10 N=1,15
   10   IF(R(N).EQ.BLANK) GO TO 15
   15 N=N-1
      V=CONV(R,N,SW)
      IF(SW.EQ.1) GO TO 20
      WRITE(6,503) R
      GO TO 1
   20 WRITE(6,503) R,V
      GO TO 1
  999 STOP
      END
```

Figure 9.7 (Continued)

```
C   ***** SUBPROGRAM FOR SUBALGORITHM OF FIGURE 9.10M ******************
          INTEGER FUNCTION CONV(S,M,ERR)
          INTEGER S(15),SUM,PREV,I,D,M,ERR,RI,RV,RX,RL,RC,RD,RM
          DATA RI,RV,RX,RL,RC,RD,RM/'I','V','X','L','C','D','M'/
      501 FORMAT(' ILLEGAL ROMAN NUMERAL')
          SUM=0
          PREV=1001
          DO 40 I=1,M
            IF(S(I).NE.RI) GO TO 10
            D=1
            GO TO 3
       10   IF(S(I).NE.RV) GO TO 15
            D=5
            GO TO 3
       15   IF(S(I).NE.RX) GO TO 20
            D=10
            GO TO 3
       20   IF(S(I).NE.RL) GO TO 25
            D=50
            GO TO 3
       25   IF(S(I).NE.RC) GO TO 30
            D=100
            GO TO 3
       30   IF(S(I).NE.RD) GO TO 35
            D=500
            GO TO 3
       35   IF(S(I).NE.RM) GO TO 50
            D=1000
        3   SUM=SUM+D
            IF(D.GT.PREV) SUM=SUM-2*PREV
       40   PREV=D
          ERR=1
       45 CONV=SUM
          RETURN
       50 WRITE(6,501)
          ERR=2
          GO TO 45
          END
```

Figure 9.7 (Continued)

```
   ROMAN NUMBER EQUIVALENTS
-----------------------------
 ROMAN NUMBER     DEC. EQUIV.
--------------    -----------
MDVC                  1595
DM                     500
MDCCCCLXXIIII         1974
XXXIX                   39
```

PROBLEMS

For problems 1 through 7: (1) develop subalgorithm and invoking algorithm flowcharts, (2) write the corresponding FORTRAN program segments, and (3) test the program using input records you create. All of these problems correspond with problems in Ch. 9 of the main text (the corresponding main-text problem numbers are given in parentheses). Therefore, those using the main text should already have completed the algorithm flowchart development phase.

1. (Prob. 1) An education professor often needs the range of scores on examinations, where the range is defined to be the largest score less the smallest score. The invoking algorithm should be used to: (a) input the test scores into an array, (b) output the test scores, (c) invoke a general subalgorithm that finds both the maximum and minimum values in the set, and (d) outputs the maximum and minimum values followed by the range. Assume that the number of scores in each set is unknown but not greater than 500. Also, each data set except the last is followed by the value 999.

2. (Prob. 3) An English professor needs a subalgorithm that scans a sequence of characters until it finds a substring of those characters. When the substring is found, the subalgorithm should record the position of the leftmost character of the substring in the string, counting from the left of the string (assume that the leftmost character in the string is numbered 1). If the substring is not found in the character sequence, a value of zero should be recorded. Thus, for the character sequence

TOM AND BILL, the value recorded for the substring AND would be 5 because AND begins in the fifth position from the left of the string. The invoking algorithm should: (a) input a value for the number of characters in the character sequence; (b) input the characters in the sequence into a one-dimensional string array, with one character per element; (c) input a value for the number of characters in the substring; (d) input the characters in the substring into a one-dimensional string array, with one character per element; (e) invoke a general subalgorithm that performs the scan and returns the pointer as described above; and (f) outputs the character sequence, the substring, and the pointer value.

3. (Prob. 4) Expand the payroll problem of Section 9.2 to include deductions for: (a) union dues, (b) payroll savings, (c) hospitalization insurance, and (d) retirement. Each of these deductions are optional and may be subscribed to in any combination. Union dues are a flat $5 per month, whereas payroll savings can be any amount desired by the employee. Hospitalization insurance is $10 plus $1.50 for each dependent up to a maximum of three dependents. Retirement is computed as a flat 6 percent of gross pay. Develop general subalgorithms for computing: (a) hospitalization insurance, (b) retirement, and (c) year-to-date earnings and net pay. Also revise the invoking algorithm accordingly.

4. (Prob. 5) A chemist often needs to look up in a table the values of certain functions for a given argument. The invoking algorithm should: (a) input the table values into a two-dimensional array, the first column of which contains the list argument values and the second column of which has the function values; (b) input search argument values and invoke a function subalgorithm that returns the appropriate function value; and (c) output the search argument and function values. Assume that any search argument value not equal to one of the list argument values is in error.

5. (Prob. 6) A mathematician wants a subalgorithm that can compute an approximation to the cube root of a number z using the iterative formula

$$x_{i+1} = (2 \cdot x_i + z/x_i^2)/3$$

The invoking algorithm should: (a) input the value of z and a critical value of the maximum relative difference that will be allowed for a good approximation, (b) invoke the cube-root-function subalgorithm, and (c) output the value of z and the approximation returned by the subalgorithm.

6. (Prob. 7) Modify the algorithm and subalgorithm of Figs. 9.5 and 9.6 so that the subalgorithm is used only for converting a Roman numeral into its decimal equivalent. That is, the subalgorithm will return a value *d* that represents the decimal equivalent for some Roman numeral.

7. (Prob. 8) Develop a function subalgorithm that converts a Roman number to its decimal equivalent. The formal parameter list should be assumed to be the same as the one for the subalgorithm of Fig. 9.6. However, the subalgorithm for this problem should cause the string that contains the Roman numerals to be scanned from right to left during the conversion operation. Assume that the algorithm of Fig. 9.5 is used to invoke the subalgorithm you design.

SUMMARY

1. A subalgorithm is an algorithm that is subordinate to another algorithm and that provides a solution to a class of subproblems. Similarly, a FORTRAN subprogram is a program segment that is subordinate to another program segment.

2. An algorithm (or program segment) that calls upon a subalgorithm (or a subprogram) to solve a subproblem is called an invoking algorithm (or program segment).

3. A subalgorithm (or subprogram) that is called upon to solve a subproblem is called the invoked subalgorithm (or subprogram).

4. The point where execution of a subalgorithm (or subprogram) may begin is called an entry point. The entry name of a subalgorithm (or subprogram) must be unique.

5. A parameter list that is used in the invoking algorithm (or program segment) is called the actual parameter list. An actual parameter list in our flowchart language is enclosed in square brackets and may contain:
   a. Arithmetic expressions.
   b. String variables or constants.
   In FORTRAN, actual parameter lists can contain only arithmetic expressions and are enclosed between a pair of parentheses.

6. A formal parameter list is given along with the name of an entry point in a subalgorithm. A formal parameter list in our flowchart language is enclosed in square brackets and may contain

a. Arithmetic variable names.
b. String variable names.

In FORTRAN, formal parameter lists are enclosed within parentheses and are restricted to being numeric variables.

7. The actual and formal parameters are related to each other in a one-to-one correspondence based upon their relative positions in the parameter lists.

8. An explicitly invoked subalgorithm (or subprogram) is called a general subalgorithm (or subroutine subprogram). A general subalgorithm (or subroutine subprogram) is invoked by the appearance in a predefined process box (or a CALL statement) of an entry point name followed by an actual parameter list.

9. An implicitly invoked subalgorithm (or subprogram) is called a function subalgorithm (or subprogram). It is invoked by the appearance in an arithmetic expression of an entry point name followed by an actual parameter list.

10. A function subalgorithm (or subprogram) always returns a numeric constant to the point in the invoking algorithm (or program segment) expression where it was invoked. Results may also be returned to the invoking algorithm (or program segment) through the actual parameter list, as in the case of a general subalgorithm (or subroutine subprogram).

CHAPTER 10

FORTRAN PROGRAMMING IN THE PHYSICAL SCIENCES, MATHEMATICS, AND ENGINEERING

Problems in engineering and the physical sciences have in common that they are by nature mathematical. Furthermore, they are often problems that require a great deal of computation. In fact, the amount of computation required in solving most such problems is usually so great that a computer provides the only means of solution. Typical problems include finding the roots of an equation, solving systems of simultaneous equations, and evaluating definite integrals.

Many of the algorithms used to solve mathematical problems are designed to provide approximate rather than exact solutions. The reason that methods which yield approximate results are used is that algorithms which provide exact results are analytical rather than numerical in nature. Since analytical algorithms are usually very difficult (if not impossible) to design, numerical algorithms that yield approximate solutions are generally used.

In this chapter we are going to examine algorithms for solving problems from several areas relevant to engineers, mathematicians, and physical scientists. However, just as some of the solution methods that we examined in previous chapters are relevant to engineers and physical scientists, solution methods in this chapter have applications in business and the social sciences. Thus we are being too restrictive if we state that these problems and their associated algorithms pertain only to engineers or physical scientists. In this chapter we are going to cover rounding errors, digital graphing, methods for finding the roots of an equation, and the generation of random numbers (which is important to the solution of problems using simulation techniques).

10.1 ROUNDING ERRORS

In earlier chapters we observed that computers can only represent finite approximations to real numbers. That is, a limitation exists on the number of significant digits that the computer representation of a real number may contain. Thus, while floating-point numbers on many current computers can attain values as large in magnitude as 10^{75}, these numbers can often have a maximum of only sixteen significant decimal digits. The rest of the digits in the number will be implied zeros that are produced by a scale factor that is stored as part of the number.

Real constants or variables in most FORTRAN dialects have only six to eight significant decimal digits. This results in a considerable amount of rounding error in many computations, particularly those involving approximate algorithms. As a result, most FORTRAN dialects provide for double precision constants and variables. These double precision constants and variables will usually contain a maximum of at least sixteen significant decimal digits. FORTRAN double precision constants are written just like E-type real constants, except that the letter E is replaced by the letter D. Examples of double precision constants are:

```
2.5678901234567890+05
  -1.5678901230 4
    85.67890-12
    -5.67890-4
```

In most FORTRAN dialects the REAL type statement that has been used up to this point declares variables to be floating-point values with from six to eight significant decimal digits. In order to increase the maximum number of significant digits to at least sixteen, the type statement DOUBLE PRECISION must be used. An example of such a type statement would be:

```
DOUBLE PRECISION  A,B(100),C(5,3),R
```

When using double precision variables and constants, the FORTRAN numeric functional operators for double precision arguments must be used. For most of the functional operators, the double precision versions use the same names as their real counterparts, except that the letter D is used as a prefix to the name. For example, the functional operator for obtaining the square root of a double precision value is DSQRT.

10.2 THE DIGITAL GRAPH-PLOTTING PROGRAM

The solution of some mathematical problems, such as finding the roots of an equation, is often made easier by graphing a function. Although an accurate plot of a continuous function is often desirable, an approximation to the graph of a function is adequate for the analysis of most problems. Since computers are finite machines, we must be satisfied in computer-controlled graphing with approximations to continuous functions. Devices are available which plot continuous graphs of functions. These devices are rather expensive, however, and thus are not found in most computer installations. Therefore, we will use a line printer for producing a digital graph of a function.

In digital graphing, it is best to plot the y axis horizontally on the continuous forms of the printer and to plot the x axis vertically. One reason for this is that the function $y=f(x)$ may assume the same value for more than one value of x. Therefore, plotting the y axis horizontally requires that only one data point be printed per line of output. A second reason is that the number of print positions on a single line is fixed, whereas there is virtually no limit on the number of lines that can be printed. Therefore, the density of the plot (i.e., the number of data points printed in a given portion of the domain of $f(x)$) and the length of the domain of $f(x)$ plotted can be varied much more easily when the x axis is plotted vertically.

The concept of digital plotting is easy to understand. In each line we output to the printer we will print one symbol that represents a value of $f(x)$ for some value of x. Before we begin the plotting process, we must compute all of the data points that are to be used in the plot. The reason for this is that we must know the maximum and minimum value of $f(x)$ in the portion of the domain of the function to be plotted in order to divided the print line into m equal-length intervals. The values of x for which values of $f(x)$ are to be computed is determined by inputting the upper and lower limits of the portion of the domain of the function to be plotted and the number of data points n to be included in the plot. Given this information, a value of $f(x)$ is computed at equal intervals over this domain of $f(x)$, where the interval is taken as the upper minus the lower limit divided by $(n - 1)$. Once the data points have been generated, a line is printed for each data point with one symbol being placed in the print line position that corresponds with the interval of the range associated with that data point.

The algorithm flowchart in Fig. 10.1* is designed to produce a digital graph of a function that is given by a subalgorithm. In Fig 10.2† is a subalgorithm flowchart that provides three sample

---

*For those using the main text, this flowchart is the same one that appears in Fig. 10.5M.

†For those using the main text, this flowchart is the same one that appears in Fig. 10.6M.

Figure 10.1 Flowchart for the Graph-Plotting Algorithm

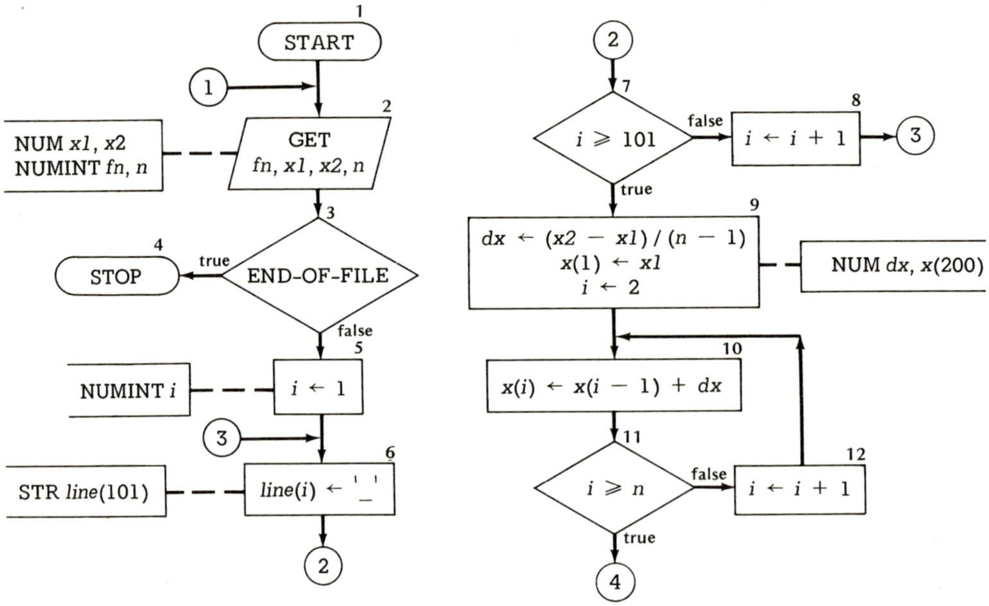

functions that can be plotted. For a function to be plotted, all that is necessary is to write an assignment statement with an expression for that function and insert it into the subalgorithm.

In Fig. 10.3 is a FORTRAN program that has program segments for this algorithm and subalgorithm. Also contained in that figure is a subprogram designed to print a descriptive header for the graph to be output. Note that this graph header subprogram does not have a corresponding algorithm flowchart. Figure 10.4 contains a graph that is the output from this program for the third function. The input record that produced this sample output was:

```
••••••••••••••••••••••••••••••••••••••••••••••
3          -2.0          4.0  41
••••••••••••••••••••••••••••••••••••••••••••••
```

For a function to be inserted into the subroutine named HEADER, it must be broken up into five string constants of no more than four characters each. This set of string constants is then inserted at the proper point in the second DATA statement in the

Figure 10.1 (Continued)

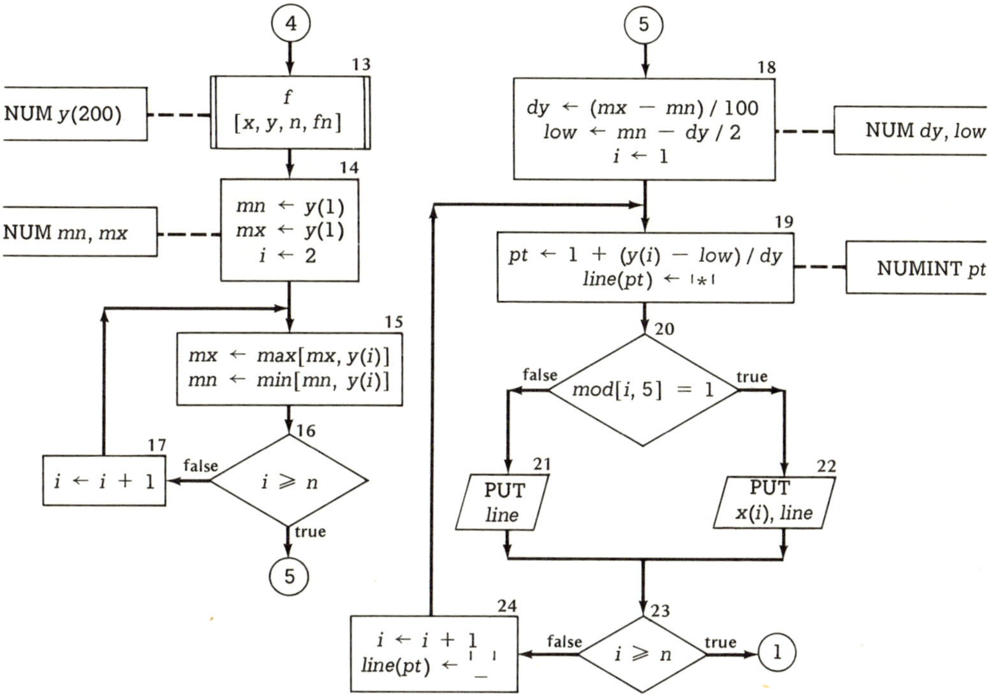

Figure 10.2 Flowchart for the Subalgorithm for Graph-Plotting Functions

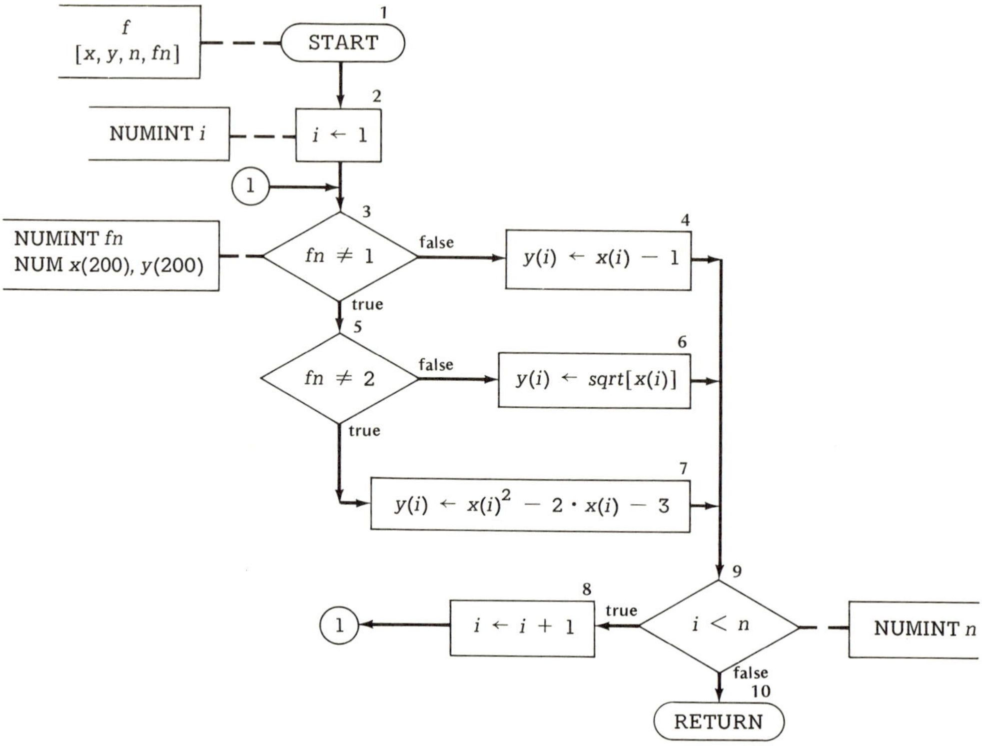

subprogram. Also note the use of the array DISP to display the values on the *y* axis of the graph. These values are generated by the DO-loop in the subprogram. The periods of the *y* axis scale were output from the array named PERIOD, which was initialized in the first DATA statement. Notice the use of the repeat constant 21 before the string constant '.' in this DATA statement. The use of a repeat constant in this case is equivalent to having written twenty-one consecutive string constants each containing the symbol for a period. In general, a repeat constant may be used in a DATA statement by placing an unsigned positive integer constant, followed by an asterisk, ahead of a constant.

Figure 10.3 FORTRAN Program for the Flowcharts of Figures 10.1 and 10.2

```
C   ***** PROGRAM FOR ALGORITHM OF FIGURE 10.5M *************************
      REAL X1,X2,DX,X(200),Y(200),MN,MX,DY,LOW
      INTEGER FN,N,I,LINE(101),PT,BLANK,AST
      DATA BLANK,AST/' ','*'/
  501 FORMAT(I1,2E12.5,I4)
  502 FORMAT(16X,101A1)
  503 FORMAT(E11.3,5X,101A1)
    1 READ(5,501,END=999) FN,X1,X2,N
      DO 10 I=1,101
   10   LINE(I)=BLANK
      DX=(X2-X1)/FLOAT(N-1)
      X(1)=X1
      DO 15 I=2,N
   15   X(I)=X(I-1)+DX
      CALL F(X,Y,N,FN)
      MN=Y(1)
      MX=Y(1)
      DO 20 I=2,N
        MX=AMAX1(MX,Y(I))
   20   MN=AMIN1(MN,Y(I))
      DY=(MX-MN)/100.0
      LOW=MN-DY/2.0
      CALL HEADER(MN,DY,FN)
      DO 30 I=1,N
        PT=1+IFIX((Y(I)-LOW)/DY)
        LINE(PT)=AST
        IF(MOD(I,5).EQ.1) GO TO 25
        WRITE(6,502) LINE
        GO TO 30
   25   WRITE(6,503) X(I),LINE
   30   LINE(PT)=BLANK
      GO TO 1
  999 STOP
      END
```

Figure 10.3 (Continued)

```
C   ***** SUBPROGRAM FOR SUBALGORITHM OF FIGURE 10.6M *******************
      SUBROUTINE F(X,Y,N,FN)
      REAL X(200),Y(200)
      INTEGER I,FN,N
      DO 20 I=1,N
        IF(FN.NE.1) GO TO 10
        Y(I)=X(I)-1.0
        GO TO 20
   10   IF(FN.NE.2) GO TO 15
        Y(I)=SQRT(X(I))
        GO TO 20
   15   Y(I)=X(I)**2-2.0*X(I)-3.0
   20   CONTINUE
      RETURN
      END
C   ***** SUBPROGRAM FOR PRINTING GRAPH HEADER     ************************
      SUBROUTINE HEADER(MN,DY,FN)
      REAL DISP(6),PRNT(5,3),MN,DY
      INTEGER PERIOD(21),RN,I
      DATA PERIOD/21*'.'/
      DATA PRNT/'F(X)','=X-1',' ',' ',' ','F(X)','=SQR','T(X)',' ',' ',
     * 'F(X)','=X**','2-2*','X-3',' '/
  501 FORMAT('1',45X,'PLOT OF',1X,5A4,//,57X,'Y AXIS',/,11X,110('-'),/,
     * 11X,6(E10.3,10X),/,16X,21(A1,4X),/,3X,'X AXIS',/,1X,10('-'))
      DO 10 I=1,6
   10   DISP(I)=MN+FLOAT((I-1)*20)*DY
      WRITE(6,501) (PRNT(I,FN),I=1,5),DISP,PERIOD
      RETURN
      END
```

The main program segment logic follows that of the flowchart of Fig. 10.1 and should thus be easy to follow. Therefore, it will not be discussed. Note that in dialects that do not include the MOD functional operator, MOD(I,5) can be replaced by the FORTRAN integer expression I-5*(I/5), since it produces equivalent results for positive values of I.

Figure 10.4 Output Generated by the Program of Figure 10.3

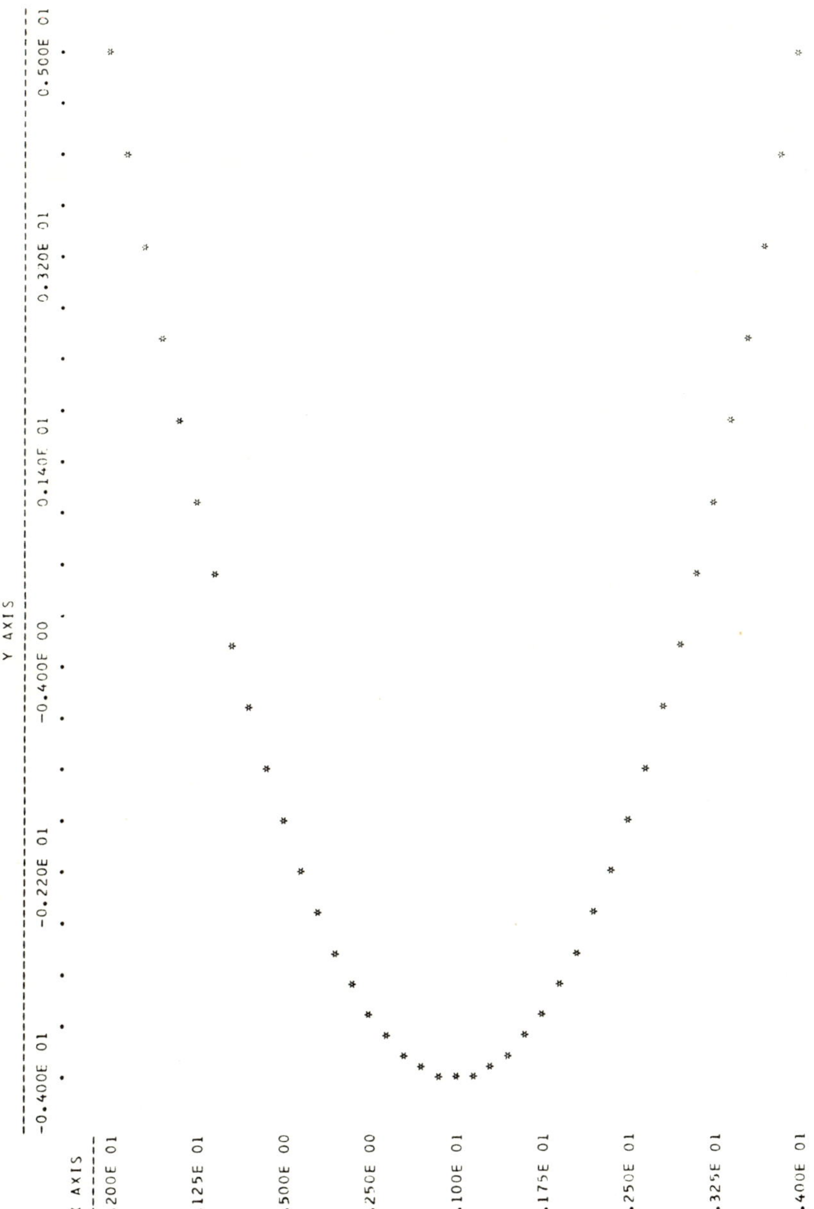

10.3 THE ROOTS-OF-AN-EQUATION PROGRAM

A problem that occurs often in applied mathematics is that of locating the roots of an equation. The roots of an equation are defined as those values of x for which an equation of the form $f(x)=0$ is satisfied. The method we will use for finding approximations to the real roots of an equation of the form $f(x)=0$ is the bisection method. We will assume that the functions we deal with are continuous in the neighborhood of interest in applying this method.

The logic of the bisection method for finding approximations to the real roots of an equation is very easy to understand. It reduces to simply beginning with an interval that is assumed to contain one real root x of the function. This interval is then bisected repeatedly until the interval converges on the root. The method of bisection is based upon the fact that if a function crosses the x axis once in an interval bounded by u and v, the signs of $f(u)$ and $f(v)$ will not be the same.

An algorithm flowchart for the method of bisection appears in Fig. 10.5.* In Fig. 10.6† is a subalgorithm flowchart that provides three sample functions of the equations to be solved. For an equation to be solved, one simply needs to insert an assignment statement into this subalgorithm for the function that describes the equation.

---

*For those using the main text, this flowchart is the same one that appears in Fig. 10.10M.

†For those using the main text, this flowchart is the same one that appears in Fig. 10.11M.

Figure 10.5 Flowchart for the Roots-of-an-Equation Invoking Algorithm

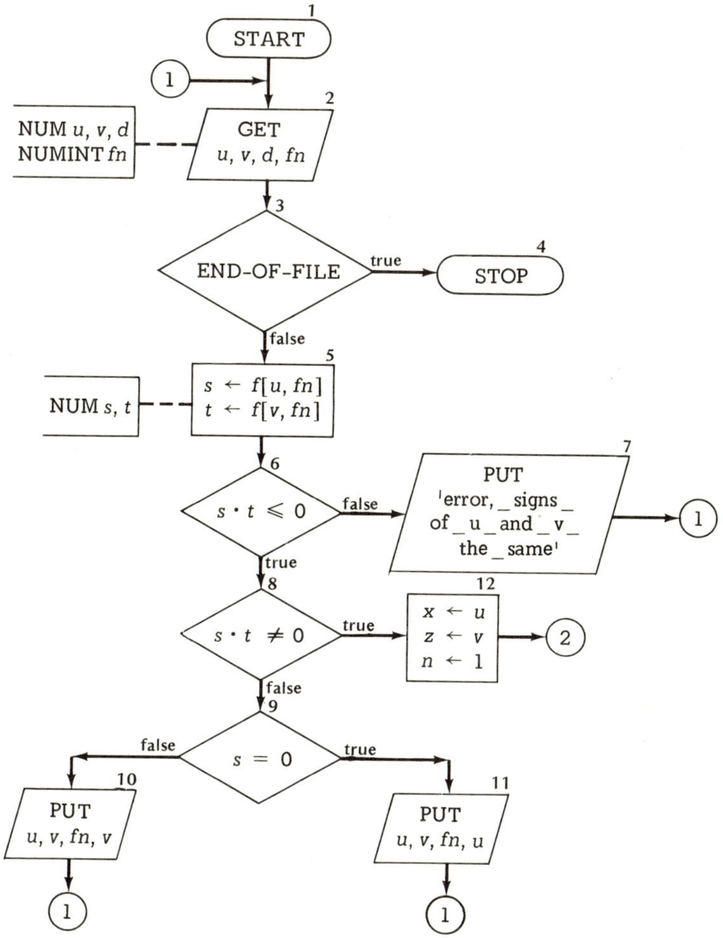

Figure 10.5 (Continued)

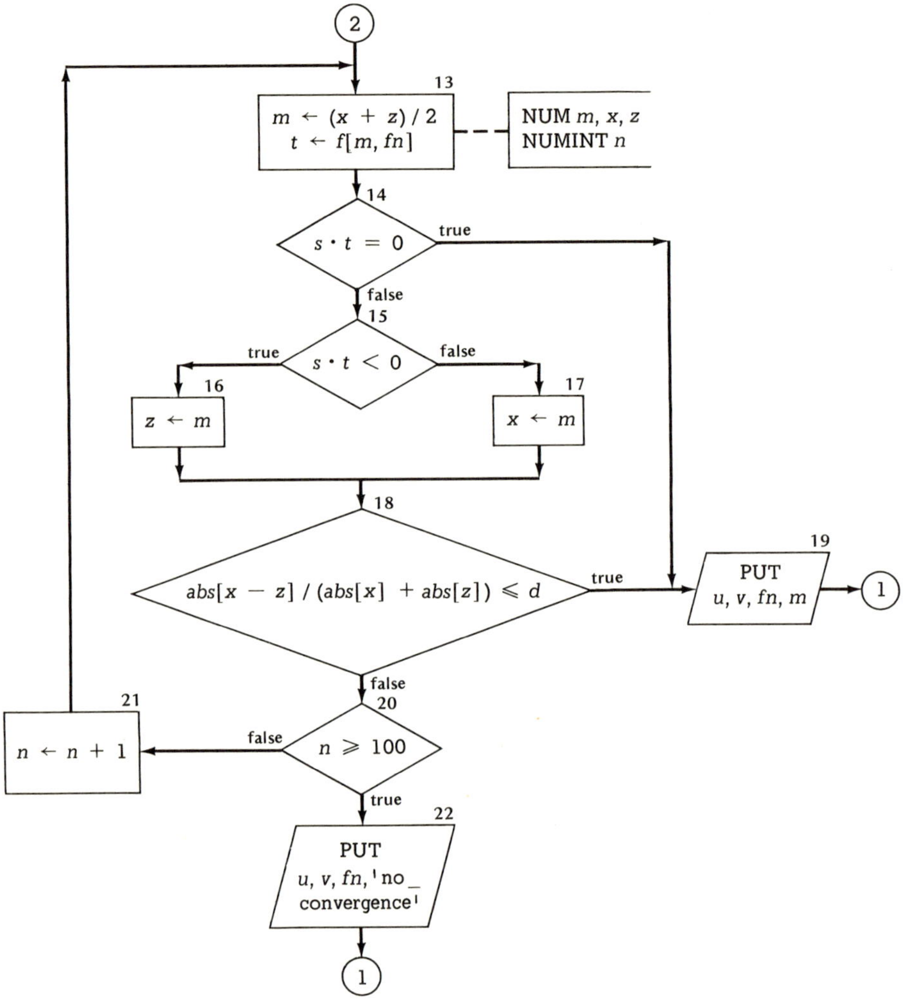

Figure 10.6 Flowchart for the Function Subalgorithm

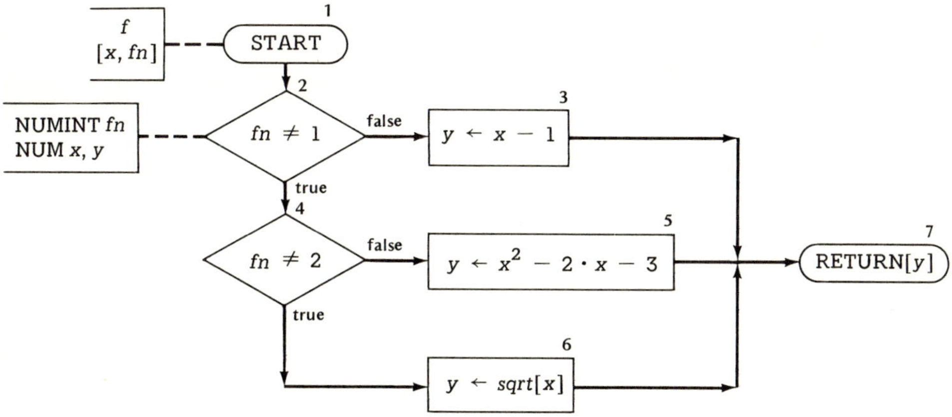

In Fig. 10.7 we have a FORTRAN program for the flowcharts of Figs. 10.5 and 10.6. Also contained in this program is sample output and a subroutine named OUTPUT, which produces output lines. As in the case of HEADER in the previous section, any function to be plotted needs to be inserted into the DATA statement of OUTPUT expressed as five string constants.

The sample output shown in Fig. 10.7 was produced by executing the program for the following input records:

```
.......................................
       0.0          3.0        0.001 1
      -2.0          0.0        0.001 2
       0.0          5.0        0.001 2
    -100.0        -50.0        0.001 2
.......................................
```

Since the program logic follows that of the flowcharts, it will not be discussed further.

Figure 10.7 FORTRAN Program for the Flowcharts of Figures 10.5 and 10.6

```
C   ***** PROGRAM FOR ALGORITHM OF FIGURE 10.10M ************************
      REAL U,V,D,S,T,M,X,Z,F
      INTEGER FN,N
  501 FORMAT('1',20X,'EQUATION SOLUTIONS',/,2X,55('-'),/,5X,'U',7X,'V',
     * 12X,'FUNCTION',15X,'ROOT',/,2(2X,6('-')),4X,20('-'),5X,12('-'))
  502 FORMAT(3E12.5,I2)
      WRITE(6,501)
    1 READ(5,502,END=999) U,V,D,FN
      S=F(U,FN)
      T=F(V,FN)
      IF(S*T.LE.0.0) GO TO 10
      CALL OUTPUT(U,V,FN,0.0,3)
      GO TO 1
   10 IF(S*T.NE.0.0) GO TO 20
      IF(S.EQ.0.0) GO TO 15
      CALL OUTPUT(U,V,FN,V,1)
      GO TO 1
   15 CALL OUTPUT(U,V,FN,U,1)
      GO TO 1
   20 X=U
      Z=V
      DO 30 N=1,100
         M=(X+Z)/2.0
         T=F(M,FN)
         IF(S*T.EQ.0.0) GO TO 35
         IF(S*T.LT.0.0) GO TO 25
         X=M
         GO TO 30
   25    Z=M
   30    IF(ABS(X-Z)/(ABS(X)+ABS(Z)).LE.D) GO TO 35
      CALL OUTPUT(U,V,FN,0.0,2)
      GO TO 1
   35 CALL OUTPUT(U,V,FN,M,1)
      GO TO 1
  999 STOP
      END
```

Figure 10.7 (Continued)

```
C    ***** SUBPROGRAM FOR SUBALGORITHM OF FIGURE 10.11M *****************
      REAL FUNCTION F(X,FN)
      REAL X,Y
      INTEGER FN
      IF(FN.NE.1) GO TO 10
      Y=X-1.0
      GO TO 20
   10 IF(FN.NE.2) GO TO 15
      Y=X**2-2.0*X-3.0
      GO TO 20
   15 Y=SQRT(X)
   20 F=Y
      RETURN
      END
C    ***** SUBPROGRAM FOR PRINTING OUTPUT LINES     **********************
      SUBROUTINE OUTPUT(U,V,FN,VALUE,TYPE)
      REAL U,V,VALUE,PRNT(5,3)
      INTEGER FN,TYPE,I
      DATA PRNT/'F(X)','=X-1',' ',' ',' ','F(X)','=X**','2-2*','X-3',
     * ' ','F(X)','=SQR','T(X)',' ',' '/
  501 FORMAT(2F8.2,4X,5A4,E17.5)
  502 FORMAT(2F8.2,4X,5A4,2X,'NO CONVERGENCE')
  503 FORMAT(2F8.2,4X,5A4,2X,'ERROR, SIGNS OF U AND V THE SAME')
      IF(TYPE.NE.1) GO TO 10
      WRITE(6,501) U,V,(PRNT(I,FN),I=1,5),VALUE
      GO TO 20
   10 IF(TYPE.NE.2) GO TO 15
      WRITE(6,502) U,V,(PRNT(I,FN),I=1,5)
      GO TO 20
   15 WRITE(6,503) U,V,(PRNT(I,FN),I=1,5)
   20 RETURN
      END
```

EQUATION SOLUTIONS

U	V	FUNCTION	ROOT
0.00	3.00	F(X)=X-1	0.10005E 01
-2.00	0.00	F(X)=X**2-2*X-3	-0.10000E 01
0.00	5.00	F(X)=X**2-2*X-3	0.30029E 01
-100.00	-50.00	F(X)=X**2-2*X-3	ERROR, SIGNS OF U AND V THE SAME

10.4 THE RANDOM NUMBER PROGRAM

There is one problem area we have not touched on that has relevance to almost any field of study. This technique is called the Monte Carlo method and involves the use of probability concepts in problem solution. The term "Monte Carlo" is used because the concepts involved were first studied as they relate to games of chance (e.g., poker, black jack, and roulette). Because of the large volume of computations usually involved, Monte Carlo methods are not practical in problem solving unless a computer is available.

Central to Monte Carlo methods is the use of random numbers. A random number is simply a value of a random variable generated by a random process. Since the physical processes that generate random numbers are difficult to harness to a digital computer, we are going to use pseudo-random numbers in doing our Monte Carlo work. A *pseudo-random number* is a number that behaves as though it is a random number but which is produced by a repeatable process. Throughout the remainder of this section, we will call pseudo-random numbers simply random numbers.

The most frequently used type of random number is one that is uniformly distributed over the unit interval. By this we mean that the values assumed by the random variable x can vary over the interval $0 \leq x \leq 1$ and all values in that interval have an equal probability of occurring. The probability density function for the uniform distribution is:

$$\begin{aligned} f(x) &= 1 \quad \text{for} \quad 0 \leq x \leq 1 \\ &= 0 \quad \text{for} \quad x < 0, \quad x > 1 \end{aligned}$$

A flowchart for a function subalgorithm that generates uniform random numbers appears in Fig. 10.8.* The method used in this subalgorithm will not be discussed because it is beyond the scope of this book. Before invoking this subalgorithm the first time, a value of 4097 must be assigned to *L* in the invoking algorithm. After the first invocation, the variable *L* simply has the value that it was assigned from the preceding invocation.

A FORTRAN program that produces a table of sixty uniform random numbers is given in Fig. 10.9. The subprogram in this figure is the one that corresponds with the subalgorithm flowchart of Fig. 10.8 Notice the evident randomness of the values in the table and the fact that they lie on the interval $0 < R < 1$.

The first executable statement in the subprogram RN follows the first step in the flowchart. That is, the previous value of L is multiplied by the integer constant 20613. By the very nature of its design, a computer with a 32-bit integer word will perform arithmetic

Figure 10.8 Flowchart for the Random Number Subalgorithm

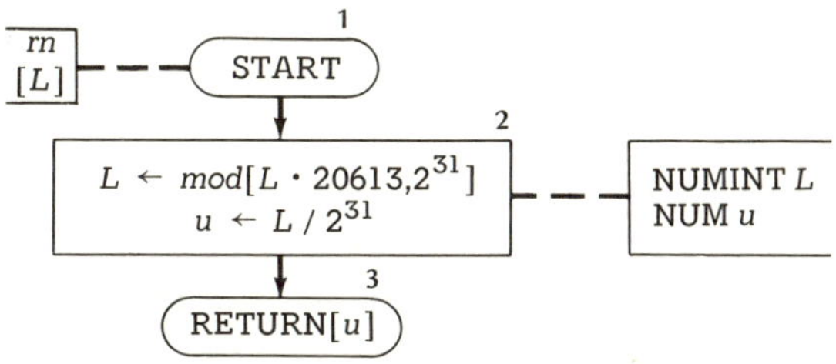

*For those using the main text, this flowchart is the same one that appears in Fig. 10.17M.

Figure 10.9 FORTRAN Program for the Random Number Problem

```
C    ***** DRIVER PROGRAM FOR SUBALGORITHM OF FIGURE 10.17M *************
          REAL R(6),RN
          INTEGER L,I,J
  501     FORMAT('1',11X,'UNIFORM RANDOM NUMBERS',/,2X,46('-'))
  502     FORMAT(6F8.4)
          L=4097
          WRITE(6,501)
          DO 15 I=1,10
            DO 10 J=1,6
   10         R(J)=RN(L)
   15       WRITE(6,502) R
          STOP
          END
C    ***** SUBPROGRAM FOR SUBALGORITHM OF FIGURE 10.17M ****************
          REAL FUNCTION RN(L)
          REAL U
          INTEGER L
          L=L*20613
          IF(L.LT.0) L=L+2147483647+1
          U=FLOAT(L)*4.656613E-10
          RN=U
          RETURN
          END
```

UNIFORM RANDOM NUMBERS

0.0393	0.6222	0.8539	0.5306	0.6903	0.3838
0.3880	0.8386	0.6791	0.0578	0.7028	0.9088
0.8644	0.3326	0.8098	0.6194	0.5767	0.7752
0.2122	0.2926	0.8072	0.9637	0.5030	0.3773
0.0610	0.9398	0.5664	0.1407	0.2490	0.8568
0.7548	0.2414	0.9944	0.6979	0.4173	0.0613
0.7274	0.9397	0.1555	0.6695	0.9449	0.0362
0.1804	0.2953	0.0088	0.5978	0.1457	0.1823
0.8581	0.1411	0.8328	0.7017	0.0106	0.2834
0.0628	0.5979	0.2287	0.2581	0.2092	0.2415

mod 2^{31}, with one exception: The sign bit might be changed in the multiplication operation to indicate that the result is negative. Should this happen, the sign bit can be changed to indicate a positive value by adding 2^{31} to the result. Thus, when the product is negative, it is made positive by having 2^{31} added to it. Since the largest integer that can be stored in a 32-bit-wordlength machine is $2^{31}-1$, however, the quantity $2^{31}-1$ (2147483647) must first be added to the product, and then 1 is added to this sum. This is done in the IF statement.

Finally, in the statement following the IF statement the random number is placed on the interval $0<R<1$ by dividing the product by 2^{31}. This is accomplished in the program by multiplying the value of L (converted to real mode) by 2^{-31} (which is approximately 4.656613E-10). The resulting product is then assigned to the variable U, which in turn is assigned to the entry-point name RN for return to the point of invocation.

When the computer being used has other than 32-bit binary integer values, then the constants in the subprogram RN need to be changed. The values to be used for several of the more popular word sizes are:

	First Multiplier	Value Added	Second Multiplier
16-bit word	253	32767	3.0517578E-5
32-bit word	20613	2147483647	4.656613E-10
36-bit word	131069	34359738367	2.9103830E-11

PROBLEMS

Problems 1 and 2 relate to algorithm and subalgorithm flowcharts in the main text. For those not using the main text, these problems should be ignored.

1. Write the FORTRAN program that corresponds with the algorithm flowchart of Fig. 10.15M. Notice that a subprogram for the subalgorithm of Fig. 10.11M and an output subroutine are also required. Use input records you create to test your program.

2. Write the FORTRAN program that corresponds with the algorithm flowchart of Fig. 10.20M. Notice that a subprogram for the subalgorithm of Fig. 10.17M is also required. Use input records you create to test your program.

For problems 3 through 10: (1) develop an algorithm flowchart, (2) write a corresponding FORTRAN program, and (3) test the program using input data records that you create. All of these problems correspond with problems in Ch. 10 of the main text (the corresponding main-text problem numbers are given in parentheses). Therefore, those using the main text should already have completed the algorithm flowchart development phase.

3. (Prob. 7) The solutions to two transcendental equations or a polynomial and a transcendental equation are often difficult to obtain analytically. The points of intersection can be approximated rather accurately, however, by plotting the equations on one graph and observing the points of intersection. Develop an algorithm that plots either one or two functions of one variable on one graph. When two functions are plotted, a list should be printed below the graph of the values of x for which the values of $f(x)$ fell into the same interval for both functions. Use an asterisk as the symbol for plotting the first function and a plus sign as the symbol for graphing the second function.

4. (Prob. 9) Modify the algorithm of Fig. 10.5 so that new initial values of u and v are generated should the test in box 6 show the signs of $f(u)$ and $f(v)$ are the same. Assume at first that there are two roots in the interval. Thus you should move u and v closer together. If after trying four new intervals the signs are still the same, begin widening the interval, beginning from the original values of u and v. This widening process should also be attempted four times.

5. (Prob. 10) An iterative method for finding approximations to the roots of an equation involves the Newton-Raphson method. This method involves taking an initial approximation x_1 and using the equation

$$x_{i+1} = x_i - f(x_i)/f'(x_i)$$

to generate successive approximations to the root. Develop an algorithm for finding approximations to roots using the Newton-Raphson method. Algorithm input should consist of an initial approximation, a maximum relative absolute difference, and an integer value that points to a function in a subalgorithm such as the one in Fig. 10.6. The formula in Problem 27 of Ch. 5 should be used to compute the relative absolute difference between two successive approximations. Be sure to include a test to be sure that $f'(x_i)$ does not become smaller than 10^{-6} because a small denominator can cause the method to fail.

6. (Prob. 13) The solution of two simultaneous equations represented by the functions $f(x)$ and $g(x)$ can be obtained by developing a third function $h(x)=f(x)-g(x)$ and solving for $h(x)=0$. Assume that $f(x)$ is contained in one function subalgorithm f and $g(x)$ in another function subalgorithm g. Modify the algorithm of Fig. 10.5 so that the solution of two simultaneous equations is found given the endpoints u and v of an interval in which they intersect.

7. (Prob. 15) One method of approximating the roots of an equation is the secant method. It uses the iterative formula

$$x_{i+1} = x_i - f(x_i)/m$$

where $m=[f(x_i)-f(x_{i-1})]/(x_i-x_{i-1})$. Use the secant method to develop an algorithm that finds a satisfactory approximation to the root of an equation.

8. (Prob. 23) Develop an algorithm for dealing at random four bridge hands of thirteen cards each. Assume that the cards of a deck are numbered from 1 to 52 and draw uniformly distributed random integers x from the interval $1 \leq x \leq 52$ in generating the bridge hands. Output, however, should include the suit and face value of the cards.

9. (Prob. 24) The probability of various five-card stud-poker hands can be approximated using the Monte Carlo method. Develop an algorithm that randomly generates hands of five cards each and counts the number of full houses, straights, flushes, and so on. Then the algorithm should use these counts to develop the respective probabilities of obtaining a particular hand.

10. (Prob. 25) Develop an algorithm that simulates the rolling of a pair of dice and counts the number of times each different point count (2 points, 3 points, ..., 12 points) comes face up. Then use these frequencies to compute the probability of the various outcomes.

APPENDIXES

APPENDIX A

CLASSIFICATION AND INDEX OF FORTRAN KEYWORDS AND/OR STATEMENTS USED IN THIS BOOK

Keyword or Statement	FORTRAN Functional Operator	Statement		Text Reference Section
		Executable	Nonexecutable	
ABS	X			4.3.1
ALOG	X			4.3.1
ALOG10	X			4.3.1
AMAX1	X			4.3.1
AMIN1	X			4.3.1
assignment		X		4.3
CALL		X		9.1
CONTINUE		X		5.1
DATA			X	4.3.2
DO		X		5.1
DOUBLE PRECISION			X	10.1
END			X	4.1
EXP	X			4.3.1
FLOAT	X			4.3.1
FORMAT			X	4.4
FUNCTION			X	9.1
GO TO		X		4.5
IABS	X			4.3.1
IF		X		4.5
IFIX	X			4.3.1
INTEGER			X	4.2.2
MAX0	X			4.3.1
MIN0	X			4.3.1
MOD	X			4.3.1
READ		X		4.4
REAL			X	4.2.2
RETURN		X		9.1
SQRT	X			4.3.1
STOP		X		4.3
SUBROUTINE			X	9.1
WRITE		X		4.4

APPENDIX B

FORTRAN NUMERIC FUNCTIONAL OPERATORS

Operation	*Name*	*Type of Argument Expression*	*Number of Argument Expressions*	*Type of Resulting Value*
Absolute value	ABS	Real	1	Real
	IABS	Integer	1	Integer
Natural logarithm	ALOG	Real	1	Real
Base-10 logarithm	ALOG10	Real	1	Real
Exponential	EXP	Real	1	Real
Maximum value	AMAX1	Real	≥ 2	Real
	MAX0	Integer	≥ 2	Integer
Minimum value	AMIN1	Real	≥ 2	Real
	MIN0	Integer	≥ 2	Integer
Modulus	AMOD	Real	2	Real
	MOD	Integer	2	Integer
Trigonometric cosine	COS	Real	1	Real
Trigonometric sine	SIN	Real	1	Real
Trigonometric tangent	TAN	Real	1	Real
Square root	SQRT	Real	1	Real
Type conversion	FLOAT	Integer	1	Real
	IFIX	Real	1	Integer

APPENDIX C

UNFORMATTED INPUT/OUTPUT IN FORTRAN

Some FORTRAN dialects provide statements that permit input/output without the use of FORMAT statements. These input/output statements are very handy to use for debugging a program or for first learning the FORTRAN language. However, options are severely limited when using unformatted input/output statements. For one thing, these statements do not provide for the input or output of string constants. Two of these forms will be examined in this appendix.

C.1 WATFOR/WATFIV Unformatted Input/Output

The WATFOR/WATFIV dialects permit the use of the READ and PRINT statements for the unformatted input/output of integer or real constants.* The general form of the unformatted input statement is

READ,*variable list*

where *variable list* is a list of variable names. The variable names in *variable list* must be separated by commas, and the comma preceding the first variable in the list is required. Moreover, *variable list* can contain implied DO statements.

Execution of a READ statement causes as many input records to be read as are necessary to input the number of values associated with the variables in the data list. When a READ statement is executed, the search for constants always begins with a new input record. The data constants are entered into input records in a free format; that is, the values may be placed in any columns of the record. Each constant must be separated from the following constant by: (1) one or more blank spaces, or (2) a comma. It is not necessary for the first constant to begin in column 1 of the input record. The constant values are assigned to the variables in the variable list in the order

---

*Double precision and complex constants can also be handled by unformatted input/output statements in WATFOR/WATFIV. However, they will not be discussed in this book.

in which they are found in input records.

The general form of the unformatted output statement is

PRINT,*variable list*

where *variable list* is as defined above for the READ statement. Execution of a PRINT statement causes the values of the variables in *variable list* to be output, using as many lines as are necessary. The constants are separated by several blank spaces, and a new line is begun for each execution of a PRINT statement.

Figure C.1 contains the listing of a program and sample output designed to illustrate the use of unformatted input/output statements in WATFOR/WATFIV. A listing of the input records used to produce the sample output follows:

```
.........................................................
10,-576345,5.67,0.432E-4
   4     6.3   -8.57E+04   -95.6783    4876.5E+12
   5                              657
  893,   -1245,8,-2.3        4.5,6.7     82.5
96.7
-8.52      1000
.........................................................
```

The first input record is read by the first READ statement, the second by the second READ statement, and the last four input records are read by the third READ statement. Notice that as many records will be read as are needed to input the number of data constants required for the variables in the variable list. Also observe the free use of blank spaces that is permitted in input records.

C.2 NAMELIST Unformatted Input/Output

A number of FORTRAN dialects permit the use of the NAMELIST statement for the unformatted input/output of integer or real constants. The general form of the unformatted input statement is

READ(*device*,*name*)

where *device* is the number of an input device (as described in Sec. 4.4), and *name* is the name of a variable list, as given in a NAMELIST statement. The general form of the NAMELIST statement is

NAMELIST/*name*/*variable list*

Figure C.1 Program to Illustrate WATFOR/WATFIV Input and Output

```
C   ***** EXAMPLES OF WATFOR UNFORMATTED I/O ******
      REAL D,E(4),F(2,3),G
      INTEGER A,B,C(5),I,J
      READ,A,B,D,G
      PRINT,A,D,G,B
      READ,A,(E(I),I=1,A)
      PRINT,A,(E(I),I=1,4)
      READ,C,((F(I,J),J=1,3),I=1,2),B
      PRINT,((F(I,J),J=1,3),I=1,2),B
      STOP
      END
```

```
        10   0.5670000E 01   0.4319999E-04      -576345
         4   0.6300000E 01  -0.8570000E 05  -0.9567830E 02   0.4876502E 16
-0.2300000E 01   0.4500000E 01   0.6700000E 01   0.8250000E 02   0.9670000E 02  -0.8520000E 01         1000
```

where *name* is the name used to reference a particular *variable list* and *variable list* is a list of scalar or array variable names. The variable names in *variable list* must be separated by commas, and the slashes enclosing *name* are required. Implied DO-loops cannot be used in the *variable list* of a NAMELIST statement.

Data constants to be input appear in input records in groups. Column 1 of a record must always be blank. The first element in a record must be the symbol & in column 2 (in some dialects the symbol $ is used instead of the &), immediately followed by a *group name*. The group names chosen are associated with the *names* used in NAMELIST statements to identify particular *variable lists*.

Following the *group name* (beginning in the second record of an input group) appears a list consisting of variable names and data constants. When the variable name is a simple scalar variable name, then it should be followed by an equal sign and a single constant. An array name, on the other hand, should appear unsubscripted* and should be followed by an equal sign and a list of constants. The constants in the list for an array name must be separated by commas. In addition, a variable name must be separated from a preceding input element by a comma. The last entry in each record in a group must be a constant followed by a comma. Each input group must be terminated by a record containing the sequence &END appearing in columns 2 through 5 (in $ dialects, a single symbol $ is used instead of &END). There may be as many records as needed in an input group.

Execution of a READ statement causes a scan of input groups to begin, with the scan continuing until the first group is found whose *group name* is the same as the variable list *name* used in the READ statement. When such a group is found, the data values are placed in the locations associated with the variable names given on the cards and in the *variable list*. A variable name cannot appear in an input group that is not given in the *variable list* of the same name.

The general form of the unformatted output statement is

WRITE(*device*,*name*)

where *device* is the number of an output device and *name* is as defined above for the READ statement. Execution of the WRITE statement causes the values of the variables in the *variable list* identified by *name* to be output in a manner similar to the appearance

---

*If an array name appears in an input group with a subscript, some dialects will begin inputting values into the array beginning with that element. Any subscript value used in an input group must be an unsigned positive integer constant.

of input groups. As many lines as may be required will be output.

Figure C.2 contains the listing of a program and sample output designed to illustrate the use of the NAMELIST unformatted input/output statements. A listing of the input records used to produce the sample output follows:

```
.................................................
&INPUT
A=10,B=-576345,D=5.67,G=0.432E-4
&END
&TESTR
A=4,E=6.3,-8.57E+04,-95.6783,4876.5E+12
&END
&INNER
C=5,657,893,-1245,8,F=-2.3,4.5,
6.7,82.5,96.7,
-8.52,B=1000
&END
.................................................
```

The three input groups are read in order by their respective READ statements. Notice that if an input group with a fourth *group name* had preceded the first of the three groups given above, it would have been ignored. This is because the first READ statement in the program did not use a NAMELIST *name* that referenced that *group name*.

Figure C.2 Program to Illustrate NAMELIST Input and Output

```
C  ***** EXAMPLES OF USE OF NAMELIST STATEMENTS **
      REAL D,E(4),F(2,3),G
      INTEGER A,B,C(5),I,J
      NAMELIST /INPUT/A,B,D,G
      NAMELIST /OUTPUT/A,D,G,B
      NAMELIST /TESTR/A,E
      NAMELIST /OUTER/A,E
      NAMELIST /INNER/C,F,B
      NAMELIST /DOWNR/F,B,C
      READ(5,INPUT)
      WRITE(6,OUTPUT)
      READ(5,TESTR)
      WRITE(6,OUTER)
      READ(5,INNER)
      WRITE(6,DOWNR)
      STOP
      END
```

```
&OUTPUT
A=          10,D=  5.6699991    ,G= 0.43199994E-04,B=     -576345
&END
&OUTER
A=           4,E=  6.2999992    , -85700.000     , -95.678299     , 0.48764973E 16
&END
&DOWNR
F= -2.2999992     ,  4.5000000     ,  6.6999998     ,  82.500000     ,  96.699997     , -8.5199995    ,B=        1000,C=           5,
          657,          893,        -1245,            8
&END
```

APPENDIX D

ADDITIONAL FORTRAN FEATURES

There are some features common to many FORTRAN dialects that have not been discussed in the body of this text. Some of these features will be introduced in this appendix, while others (for example, the COMMON, EQUIVALENCE, and IMPLICIT statements) will not be discussed at all.

D.1 The Computed and Assigned GO TO Statements

A second version of the GO TO statement in FORTRAN is the computed GO TO statement. The general form is

GO TO (*label list*), *v*

where *label list* is a list of statement labels and *v* is any simple integer variable. The comma preceding *v* must always be included, and the values in *label list* must be separated from each other with commas. In addition, the value *n* assumed by *v* must satisfy $1 \le n \le m$, where *m* is the number of labels in *label list*. Execution of a computed GO TO statement causes a branch to be taken to the statement with the *n*th label in *label list*, where *n* is the value of *v*. For example, execution of the statement

```
GO TO(5,3,18,10),SW
```

causes an unconditional branch to: (1) statement 5 for SW=1, (2) statement 3 for SW=2, (3) statement 18 for SW=3, and (4) statement 10 for SW=4. In this example, SW must be an integer variable and must have a value that is not less than 1 nor greater than 4. The first executable statement following a computed GO TO must have a statement label.

Many FORTRAN dialects permit a third form of GO TO statement, the assigned GO TO. The general form of the assigned GO TO statement is

GO TO *v*, (*label list*)

where *v* is a simple integer variable and *label list* is a list of statement labels. Execution of an assigned GO TO statement causes a branch to the statement with a label equal to the value of v.

The value must be assigned to v using a special statement, whose general form is

ASSIGN *label* TO *v*

where *label* is any statement label known in this program segment and v is the integer variable defined above for the assigned GO TO. The value assigned to v for use in a particular assigned GO TO statement must be one of the values given in the *label list* for that statement. As an example, execution of the statements

```
ASSIGN 25 TO SW
GO TO SW,(5,10,25,17,18)
```

will cause a branch to statement 25. Had the ASSIGN statement been

```
ASSIGN 13 TO SW
```

then an error would occur in this example since 13 is not in the *label list* of the assigned GO TO statement. Both the ASSIGN and assigned GO TO statements are executable.

D.2 The Arithmetic IF Statement

The second version of the conditional branch statement is the arithmetic IF statement, which is available in all FORTRAN dialects. The arithmetic IF statement has the general form

IF (*arithmetic expression*) n_1, n_2, n_3

where *arithmetic expression* is any FORTRAN arithmetic expression as described in Sec. 4.3.1, and n_1, n_2, and n_3 are statement labels. Execution of an arithmetic IF statement causes the evaluation of the arithmetic expression to a constant value, which is then compared to zero. A branch is taken to statement n_1, n_2, or n_3, respectively, when that value is: (1) less than zero, (2) equal to zero, or (3) greater than zero. In the flowchart language, the arithmetic IF statement is described by the sequence

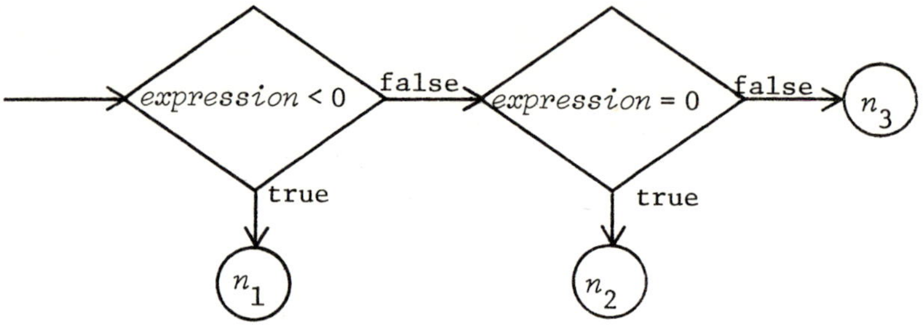

where *expression* is any arithmetic expression. As an example, execution of the statement

```
IF(A-X) 5,30,20
```

causes a branch to statement 5, 30, or 20, depending on whether: (1) A < X; (2) A = X, or (3) A > X, respectively.

Two-way branches can be effected by simply making two of the three labels the same. For example, the statement

```
IF(B**2-4.0*A*C) 20,35,35
```

causes a branch to statement 20 when B**2 < 4.0*A*C, and to statement 35 when B**4 ≥ 4.0*A*C. As with the GO TO statements, the first executable statement following an arithmetic IF statement must have a statement label. Otherwise, there is no way of executing that statement since the arithmetic IF statement always branches to one of the statements referenced by the three labels. Also notice that, for most dialects, all three labels must be present in the arithmetic IF statement.

D.3 Logical and Complex Data and Storage Allocation Sizes

Two types of constants available in many FORTRAN dialects are the *logical* and *complex* constants. A logical constant consists of either the value *true* or the value *false*. In FORTRAN, these values are written as .TRUE. and .FALSE., respectively. (The pair of periods around the value is required.) Logical variables may be declared in LOGICAL type statements, just as integer variables are declared in INTEGER type statements. Logical expressions can be formed by combining logical variables and logical constants using the logical operators .AND., .OR., and .NOT., together with the relational operators given in Fig. 4.10. The logical value resulting from evaluation of a logical expression may be assigned to a logical variable in an assignment statement. It may also be used in logical IF statements. Logical constants may also be input and output as the letters T and F. The format specification L*w* is used for the input and output of logical constant values. These values are always assumed to be right-justified in a field of width *w*.

In mathematics, a complex constant consists of a number of the form $a + b \cdot i$, where $i = \sqrt{-1}$. The FORTRAN representation of a complex constant takes the form of a pair of real constants separated by a comma and enclosed in parentheses. Examples would be

```
(-8.3E21,45.67E3)
(2.35,-75.4E-2)
(0.0,4.67)
```

Variables may also be made complex simply by being declared in a COMPLEX type statement.

In addition, complex expressions can be formed, in which complex variables and complex constants are combined using the FORTRAN arithmetic operators. The complex constant which results from evaluating a complex expression can be used in an assignment statement to assign a value to a complex variable. It can also be used as an actual or formal parameter, or in an IF statement for decision purposes. Furthermore, complex numeric functional operators are available in many dialects for many of the common functions. The names for these operators are usually the same as those for real arguments, except that a prefix C is included. Thus, the square root functional operator for a complex argument is CSQRT. To input or output complex values, they are simply read or printed as two real constants. Note that in the input/output of complex constants, the parentheses and separating comma do not appear.

An option available in some FORTRAN dialects is the declaration of the amount of storage allocated to variables.* Half-word integers can be declared by using INTEGER*2 instead of INTEGER in a type statement. Thus, the statements

```
INTEGER*2  A,B,C
INTEGER  D,E
```

declare A, B, and C to be integer variables, with the value of each variable being stored in a half word (2 bytes) of storage, and D and E to be integer variables whose values are each stored in a full word (4 bytes) of storage. Similarly, a length factor is permitted in REAL type statements. A type statement that begins with REAL*8 is equivalent to the type statement beginning with DOUBLE PRECISION.

---

*The discussion in this paragraph relates to the FORTRAN dialects for the IBM System/360 and 370 computer series.

APPENDIX E

WATFOR ERROR-DIAGNOSTIC MESSAGES

```
'ASSIGN STATEMENTS AND VARIABLES'
AS-2    'ATTEMPT TO REDEFINE AN ASSIGNED VARIABLE IN AN ARITHMETIC STATEMENT'
AS-3    'ASSIGNED VARIABLE USED IN AN ARITHMETIC EXPRESSION'
AS-4    'ASSIGNED VARIABLE CANNOT BE HALF WORD INTEGER'
AS-5    'ATTEMPT TO REDEFINE AN ASSIGN VARIABLE IN AN INPUT LIST'

'BLOCK DATA STATEMENTS'
BD-0    'EXECUTABLE STATEMENT IN BLOCK DATA SUBPROGRAMME'
BD-1    'IMPROPER BLOCK DATA STATEMENT'

'CARD FORMAT AND CONTENTS'
CC-0    'COLUMNS 1-5 OF CONTINUATION CARD NOT BLANK'
           PROBABLE CAUSE - STATEMENT PUNCHED TO LEFT OF COLUMN 7
CC-1    'TOO MANY CONTINUATION CARDS (MAXIMUM OF 5)'
CC-2    'INVALID CHARACTER IN FORTRAN STATEMENT '$' INSERTED IN SOURCE LISTING'
CC-3    'FIRST CARD OF A PROGRAMME IS A CONTINUATION CARD'
           PROBABLE CAUSE - STATEMENT PUNCHED TO LEFT OF COLUMN 7
CC-4    'STATEMENT TOO LONG TO COMPILE (SCAN-STACK OVERFLOW)'
CC-5    'BLANK CARD ENCOUNTERED'
CC-6    'KEYPUNCH USED DIFFERS FROM KEYPUNCH SPECIFIED ON JOB CARD'
CC-7    'FIRST CHARACTER OF STATEMENT NOT ALPHABETIC'
CC-8    'INVALID CHARACTER(S) CONCATENTATED WITH FORTRAN KEYWORD'
CC-9    'INVALID CHARACTERS IN COL 1-5. STATEMENT NUMBER IGNORED'
           PROBABLE CAUSE - STATEMENT PUNCHED TO LEFT OF COLUMN 7

'COMMON'
CM-0    'VARIABLE PREVIOUSLY PLACED IN COMMON'
CM-1    'NAME IN COMMON LIST PREVIOUSLY USED AS OTHER THAN VARIABLE'
CM-2    'SUBPROGRAMME PARAMETER APPEARS IN COMMON STATEMENT'
CM-3    'INITIALIZING OF COMMON SHOULD BE DONE IN A BLOCK DATA SUBPROGRAMME'
CM-4    'ILLEGAL USE OF BLOCK NAME'

'FORTRAN CONSTANTS'
CN-0    'MIXED REAL*4,REAL*8 IN COMPLEX CONSTANT'
CN-1    'INTEGER CONSTANT GREATER THAN 2,147,483,647 (2**31-1)'
CN-2    'EXPONENT OVERFLOW OR UNDERFLOW CONVERTING CONSTANT IN SOURCE STATEMENT'
CN-3    'EXPONENT ON REAL CONSTANT GREATER THAN 99'
CN-4    'REAL CONSTANT HAS MORE THAN 16 DIGITS, TRUNCATED TO 16'
CN-5    'INVALID HEXADECIMAL CONSTANT'
CN-6    'ILLEGAL USE OF DECIMAL POINT'
CN-8    'CONSTANT WITH E-TYPE EXPONENT HAS MORE THAN 7 DIGITS, ASSUME D-TYPE'
CN-9    'CONSTANT OR STATEMENT NUMBER GREATER THAN 99999'

'COMPILER ERRORS'
CP-0    'DETECTED IN PHASE RELOC'
CP-1    'DETECTED IN PHASE LINKR'
CP-2    'DUPLICATE PSEUDO STATEMENT NUMBERS'
CP-4    'DETECTED IN PHASE ARITH'
CP-5    'COMPILER INTERRUPT'

'DATA STATEMENT'
DA-0    'REPLICATION FACTOR GREATER THAN 32767, ASSUME 32767'
DA-1    'NON-CONSTANT IN DATA STATEMENT'
DA-2    'MORE VARIABLES THAN CONSTANTS IN DATA STATEMENT'
DA-3    'ATTEMPT TO INITIALIZE A SUBPROGRAMME PARAMETER IN A DATA STATEMENT'
DA-4    'NON-CONSTANT SUBSCRIPTS IN A DATA STATEMENT INVALID IN /360 FORTRAN'
DA-5    '/360 FORTRAN DOES NOT HAVE IMPLIED DO IN DATA STATEMENT'
DA-6    'NON-AGREEMENT BETWEEN TYPE OF VARIABLE AND CONSTANT IN DATA STATEMENT'
```

```
DA-7    'MORE CONSTANTS THAN VARIABLES IN DATA STATEMENT'
DA-8    'VARIABLE PREVIOUSLY INITIALIZED. LATEST VALUE USED'
             CHECK COMMON/EQUIVALENCED VARIABLES
DA-9    'INITIALIZING BLANK COMMON NOT ALLOWED IN /360 FORTRAN'
DA-A    'INVALID DELIMITER IN CONSTANT LIST PORTION OF DATA STATEMENT'
DA-B    'TRUNCATION OF LITERAL CONSTANT HAS OCCURRED'

'DIMENSION STATEMENTS'
DM-0    'NO DIMENSIONS SPECIFIED FOR A VARIABLE IN A DIMENSION STATEMENT'
DM-1    'OPTIONAL LENGTH SPECIFICATION IN DIMENSION STATEMENT IS ILLEGAL'
DM-2    'INITIALIZATION IN DIMENSION STATEMENT IS ILLEGAL'
DM-3    'ATTEMPT TO RE-DIMENSION A VARIABLE'
DM-4    'ATTEMPT TO DIMENSION AN INITIALIZED VARIABLE'

'DO LOOPS'
DO-0    'ILLEGAL STATEMENT USED AS OBJECT OF DO'
DO-1    'ILLEGAL TRANSFER INTO THE RANGE OF A DO-LOOP'
DO-2    'OBJECT OF A DO STATEMENT HAS ALREADY APPEARED'
DO-3    'IMPROPERLY NESTED DO-LOOPS'
DO-4    'ATTEMPT TO REDEFINE A DO-LOOP PARAMETER WITHIN RANGE OF LOOP'
DO-5    'INVALID DO-LOOP PARAMETER'
DO-6    'TOO MANY NESTED DO'S (MAXIMUM OF 20)'
DO-7    'DO-PARAMETER IS UNDEFINED OR OUTSIDE RANGE'
DO-8    'THIS DO LOOP WILL TERMINATE AFTER FIRST TIME THROUGH'
DO-9    'ATTEMPT TO REDEFINE A DO-LOOP PARAMETER IN AN INPUT LIST'

'EQUIVALENCE AND/OR COMMON'
EC-0    'TWO EQUIVALENCED VARIABLES APPEAR IN COMMON'
EC-1    'COMMON BLOCK HAS DIFFERENT LENGTH THAN IN A PREVIOUS SUBPROGRAMME'
EC-2    'COMMON AND/OR EQUIVALENCE CAUSES INVALID ALIGNMENT. EXECUTION SLOWED'
             REMEDY - ORDER VARIABLES IN DESCENDING ORDER BY LENGTH
EC-3    'EQUIVALENCE EXTENDS COMMON DOWNWARDS'
EC-7    'COMMON/EQUIVALENCE STATEMENT DOES NOT PRECEDE PREVIOUS USE OF VARIABLE'
EC-8    'VARIABLE USED WITH NON-CONSTANT SUBSCRIPT IN COMMON/EQUIVALENCE LIST'
EC-9    'A NAME SUBSCRIPTED IN AN EQUIVALENCE STATEMENT WAS NOT DIMENSIONED'

'END STATEMENTS'
EN-0    'NO END STATEMENT IN PROGRAMME -- END STATEMENT GENERATED'
EN-1    'END STATEMENT USED AS STOP STATEMENT AT EXECUTION'
EN-2    'IMPROPER END STATEMENT'
EN-3    'FIRST STATEMENT OF SUBPROGRAMME IS END STATEMENT'

'EQUAL SIGNS'
EQ-6    'ILLEGAL QUANTITY ON LEFT OF EQUALS SIGN'
EQ-8    'ILLEGAL USE OF EQUAL SIGN'
EQ-A    'MULTIPLE ASSIGNMENT STATEMENTS NOT IN /360 FORTRAN'

'EQUIVALENCE STATEMENTS'
EV-0    'ATTEMPT TO EQUIVALENCE A VARIABLE TO ITSELF'
EV-1    'ATTEMPT TO EQUIVALENCE A SUBPROGRAMME PARAMETER'
EV-2    'LESS THAN 2 MEMBERS IN AN EQUIVALENCE LIST'
EV-3    'TOO MANY EQUIVALENCE LISTS (MAX = 255)'
EV-4    'PREVIOUSLY EQUIVALENCED VARIABLE RE-EQUIVALENCED INCORRECTLY'

'POWERS AND EXPONENTIATION'
EX-0    'ILLEGAL COMPLEX EXPONENTIATION'
EX-2    'I**J WHERE I=J=0'
EX-3    'I**J WHERE I=0, J.LT.0'
EX-6    '0.0**Y WHERE Y.LE.0.0'
```

```
EX-7    '0.0**J WHERE J=0'
EX-8    '0.0**J WHERE J.LT.0'
EX-9    'X**Y WHERE X.LT.0.0, Y.NE.0.0'

'ENTRY STATEMENT'
EY-0    'SUBPROGRAMME NAME IN ENTRY STATEMENT PREVIOUSLY DEFINED'
EY-1    'PREVIOUS DEFINITION OF FUNCTION NAME IN AN ENTRY IS INCORRECT'
EY-2    'USE OF SUBPROGRAMME PARAMETER INCONSISTENT WITH PREVIOUS ENTRY POINT'
EY-3    'ARGUMENT NAME HAS APPEARED IN AN EXECUTABLE STATEMENT'
         BUT WAS NOT A SUBPROGRAMME PARAMETER
EY-4    'ENTRY STATEMENT NOT PERMITTED IN MAIN PROGRAMME'
EY-5    'ENTRY POINT INVALID INSIDE A DO-LOOP'
EY-6    'VARIABLE WAS NOT PREVIOUSLY USED AS A PARAMETER - PARAMETER ASSUMED'

'FORMAT'
  SOME FORMAT ERROR MESSAGES GIVE CHARACTERS IN WHICH ERROR WAS DETECTED
FM-0    'INVALID CHARACTER IN INPUT DATA'
FM-2    'NO STATEMENT NUMBER ON A FORMAT STATEMENT'
FM-5    'FORMAT SPECIFICATION AND DATA TYPE DO NOT MATCH'
FM-6    'INCORRECT SEQUENCE OF CHARACTERS IN INPUT DATA'
FM-7    'NON-TERMINATING FORMAT'

FT-0    'FIRST CHARACTER OF VARIABLE FORMAT NOT A LEFT PARENTHESIS'
FT-1    'INVALID CHARACTER ENCOUNTERED IN FORMAT'
FT-2    'INVALID FORM FOLLOWING A SPECIFICATION'
FT-3    'INVALID FIELD OR GROUP COUNT'
FT-4    'A FIELD OR GROUP COUNT GREATER THAN 255'
FT-5    'NO CLOSING PARENTHESIS ON VARIABLE FORMAT'
FT-6    'NO CLOSING QUOTE IN A HOLLERITH FIELD'
FT-7    'INVALID USE OF COMMA'
FT-8    'INSUFFICIENT SPACE TO COMPILE A FORMAT STATEMENT (SCAN-STACK OVERFLOW)'
FT-9    'INVALID USE OF P SPECIFICATION'
FT-A    'CHARACTER FOLLOWS CLOSING RIGHT PARENTHESIS'
FT-B    'INVALID USE OF PERIOD(.)'
FT-C    'MORE THAN THREE LEVELS OF PARENTHESES'
FT-D    'INVALID CHARACTER BEFORE A RIGHT PARENTHESIS'
FT-E    'MISSING OR ZERO LENGTH HOLLERITH ENCOUNTERED'
FT-F    'NO CLOSING RIGHT PARENTHESIS'

'FUNCTIONS AND SUBROUTINES'
FN-0    'NO ARGUMENTS IN A FUNCTION STATEMENT'
FN-3    'REPEATED ARGUMENT IN SUBPROGRAMME OR STATEMENT FUNCTION DEFINITION'
FN-4    'SUBSCRIPTS ON RIGHT HAND SIDE OF STATEMENT FUNCTION'
              PROBABLE CAUSE - VARIABLE TO LEFT OF = NOT DIMENSIONED
FN-5    'MULTIPLE RETURNS ARE INVALID IN FUNCTION SUBPROGRAMMES'
FN-6    'ILLEGAL LENGTH MODIFIER IN TYPE FUNCTION STATEMENT'
FN-7    'INVALID ARGUMENT IN ARITHMETIC OR LOGICAL STATEMENT FUNCTION'
FN-8    'ARGUMENT OF SUBPROGRAMME IS SAME AS SUBPROGRAMME NAME'

'GO TO STATEMENTS'
GO-0    'STATEMENT TRANSFERS TO ITSELF OR A NON-EXECUTABLE STATEMENT'
GO-1    'INVALID TRANSFER TO THIS STATEMENT'
GO-2    'INDEXED OF COMPUTED 'GOTO' IS NEGATIVE,ZERO OR UNDEFINED'
GO-3    'ERROR IN VARIABLE OF 'GO TO' STATEMENT'
GO-4    'INDEX OF ASSIGNED 'GO TO' IS UNDEFINED OR NOT IN RANGE'

'HOLLERITH CONSTANTS'
HO-0    'ZERO LENGTH SPECIFIED FOR H-TYPE HOLLERITH'
HO-1    'ZERO LENGTH QUOTE-TYPE HOLLERITH'
```

```
HO-2   'NO CLOSING QUOTE OR NEXT CARD NOT CONTINUATION CARD'
HO-3   'HOLLERITH CONSTANT SHOULD APPEAR ONLY IN CALL STATEMENT'
HO-4   'UNEXPECTED HOLLERITH OR STATEMENT NUMBER CONSTANT'

'IF STATEMENTS (ARITHMETIC AND LOGICAL)'
IF-0   'STATEMENT INVALID AFTER A LOGICAL IF'
IF-3   'ARITHMETIC OR INVALID EXPRESSION IN LOGICAL IF'
IF-4   'LOGICAL, COMPLEX, OR INVALID EXPRESSION IN ARITHMETIC IF'

'IMPLICIT STATEMENT'
IM-0   'INVALID MODE SPECIFIED IN AN IMPLICIT STATEMENT'
IM-1   'INVALID LENGTH SPECIFIED IN AN IMPLICIT OR TYPE STATEMENT'
IM-2   'ILLEGAL APPEARANCE OF $ IN A CHARACTER RANGE'
IM-3   'IMPROPER ALPHABETIC SEQUENCE IN CHARACTER RANGE'
IM-4   'SPECIFICATION MUST BE SINGLE ALPHABETIC CHARACTER, 1ST CHARACTER USED'
IM-5   'IMPLICIT STATEMENT DOES NOT PRECEDE OTHER SPECIFICATION STATEMENTS'
IM-6   'ATTEMPT TO ESTABLISH THE TYPE OF A CHARACTER MORE THAN ONCE'
IM-7   '/360 FORTRAN ALLOWS ONE IMPLICIT STATEMENT PER PROGRAMME'
IM-8   'INVALID ELEMENT IN IMPLICIT STATEMENT'
IM-9   'INVALID DELIMITER IN IMPLICIT STATEMENT'

'INPUT/OUTPUT'
IO-0   'MISSING COMMA IN I/O LIST OF I/O OR DATA STATEMENT'
IO-2   'STATEMENT NUMBER IN I/O STATEMENT NOT A FORMAT STATEMENT NUMBER'
IO-3   'FORMATTED LINE TOO LONG FOR I/O DEVICE (RECORD LENGTH EXCEEDED)'
IO-6   'VARIABLE FORMAT NOT AN ARRAY NAME'
IO-8   'INVALID ELEMENT IN INPUT LIST OR DATA LIST'
IO-9   'TYPE OF VARIABLE UNIT NOT INTEGER IN I/O STATEMENTS'
IO-A   'HALF-WORD INTEGER VARIABLE USED AS UNIT IN I/O STATEMENTS'
IO-B   'ASSIGNED INTEGER VARIABLE USED AS UNIT IN I/O STATEMENTS'
IO-C   'INVALID ELEMENT IN AN OUTPUT LIST'
IO-D   'MISSING OR INVALID UNIT IN I/O STATEMENT'
IO-E   'MISSING OR INVALID FORMAT IN READ/WRITE STATEMENT'
IO-F   'INVALID DELIMITER IN SPECIFICATION PART OF I/O STATEMENT'
IO-G   'MISSING STATEMENT NUMBER AFTER END= OR ERR='
IO-H   '/360 FORTRAN DOESN'T ALLOW END/ERR RETURNS IN WRITE STATEMENTS'
IO-J   'INVALID DELIMITER IN I/O LIST'
IO-K   'INVALID DELIMITER IN STOP, PAUSE, DATA, OR TAPE CONTROL STATEMENT'

'JOB CONTROL CARDS'
JB-1   'JOB CARD ENCOUNTERED DURING COMPILATION'
JB-2   'INVALID OPTION(S) SPECIFIED ON JOB CARD'
JB-3   'UNEXPECTED CONTROL CARD ENCOUNTERED DURING COMPILATION'

'JOB TERMINATION'
KO-0   'JOB TERMINATED IN EXECUTION BECAUSE OF COMPILE TIME ERROR'
KO-1   'FIXED-POINT DIVISION BY ZERO'
KO-2   'FLOATING-POINT DIVISION BY ZERO'
KO-3   'TOO MANY EXPONENT OVERFLOWS'
KO-4   'TOO MANY EXPONENT UNDERFLOWS'
KO-5   'TOO MANY FIXED-POINT OVERFLOWS'
KO-6   'JOB TIME EXCEEDED'
KO-7   'COMPILER ERROR - INTERRUPTION AT EXECUTION TIME,RETURN TO SYSTEM'
KO-8   'INTEGER IN INPUT DATA IS TOO LARGE (MAXIMUM IS 2147483647)'

'LOGICAL OPERATIONS'
LG-2   '.NOT. USED AS A BINARY OPERATOR'

'LIBRARY ROUTINES'
```

```
LI-0    'ARGUMENT OUT OF RANGE DGAMMA OR GAMMA. (1.382E-76 .LT. X .LT. 57.57)'
LI-1    'ABSOLUTE VALUE OF ARGUMENT .GT. 174.673, SINH,COSH,DSINH,DCOSH'
LI-2    'SENSE LIGHT OTHER THAN 0,1,2,3,4 FOR SLITE OR 1,2,3,4 FOR SLITET'
LI-3    'REAL PORTION OF ARGUMENT .GT. 174.673, CEXP OR CDEXP'
LI-4    'ABS(AIMAG(Z)) .GT. 174.673 FOR CSIN, CCOS, CDSIN OR CDCOS OF Z'
LI-5    'ABS(REAL(Z)) .GE. 3.537E15 FOR CSIN, CCOS, CDSIN OR CDCOS OF Z'
LI-6    'ABS(AIMAG(Z)) .GE. 3.537E15 FOR CEXP OR CDEXP OF Z'
LI-7    'ARGUMENT .GT. 174.673, EXP OR DEXP'
LI-8    'ARGUMENT IS ZERO, CLOG, CLOG10, CDLOG OR CDLG10'
LI-9    'ARGUMENT IS NEGATIVE OR ZERO, ALOG, ALOG10, DLOG OR DLOG10'
LI-A    'ABS(X) .GE. 3.537E15 FOR SIN, COS, DSIN OR DCOS OF X'
LI-B    'ABSOLUTE VALUE OF ARGUMENT .GT. 1, FOR ARSIN, ARCOS, DARSIN OR DARCOS'
LI-C    'ARGUMENT IS NEGATIVE, SQRT OR DSQRT'
LI-D    'BOTH ARGUMENTS OF DATAN2 OR ATAN2 ARE ZERO'
LI-E    'ARGUMENT TOO CLOSE TO A SINGULARITY, TAN, COTAN, DTAN OR DCOTAN'
LI-F    'ARGUMENT OUT OF RANGE DLGAMA OR ALGAMA. (0.0  .LT. X .LT. 4.29E73)'
LI-G    'ABSOLUTE VALUE OF ARGUMENT .GE. 3.537E15, TAN, COTAN, DTAN, DCOTAN'
LI-H    'FEWER THAN TWO ARGUMENTS FOR ONE OF MINO, MIN1, AMINO, ETC.'

'MIXED MODE'
MD-2    'RELATIONAL OPERATOR HAS A LOGICAL OPERAND'
MD-3    'RELATIONAL OPERATOR HAS A COMPLEX OPERAND'
MD-4    'MIXED MODE - LOGICAL WITH ARITHMETIC'
MD-5    'WARNING - SUBSCRIPT IS COMPLEX. REAL PART USED'

'MEMORY OVERFLOW'
MO-0    'SYMBOL TABLE OVERFLOWS OBJECT CODE. SOURCE ERROR CHECKING CONTINUES'
MO-1    'INSUFFICIENT MEMORY TO ASSIGN ARRAY STORAGE. JOB ABANDONED'
MO-2    'SYMBOL TABLE OVERFLOWS COMPILER, JOB ABANDONED'
MO-3    'DATA AREA OF SUBPROGRAMME TOO LARGE -- SEGMENT SUBPROGRAMME'
MO-4    'GETMAIN CANNOT PROVIDE BUFFER FOR WATLIB'

'PARENTHESES'
PC-0    'UNMATCHED PARENTHESES'
PC-1    'INVALID PARENTHESIS COUNT'

'PAUSE, STOP STATEMENTS'
PS-0    'STOP WITH OPERATOR MESSAGE NOT ALLOWED. SIMPLE STOP ASSUMED'
PS-1    'PAUSE WITH OPERATOR MESSAGE NOT ALLOWED. TREATED AS CONTINUE'

'RETURN STATEMENT'
RE-0    'FIRST CARD OF SUBPROGRAMME IS A RETURN STATEMENT'
RE-1    'RETURN I, WHERE I IS ZERO,NEGATIVE OR TOO LARGE'
RE-2    'MULTIPLE RETURN NOT VALID IN FUNCTION SUBPROGRAMME'
RE-3    'VARIABLE IN MULTIPLE RETURN IS NOT A SIMPLE INTEGER VARIABLE'
RE-4    'MULTIPLE RETURN NOT VALID IN MAIN PROGRAMME'

'ARITHMETIC AND LOGICAL STATEMENT FUNCTIONS'
   PROBABLE CAUSE OF SF ERRORS - VARIABLE ON LEFT OF = WAS NOT DIMENSIONED
SF-1    'PREVIOUSLY REFERENCED STATEMENT NUMBER ON STATEMENT FUNCTION'
SF-2    'STATEMENT FUNCTION IS THE OBJECT OF A LOGICAL IF STATEMENT'
SF-3    'RECURSIVE STATEMENT FUNCTION, NAME APPEARS ON BOTH SIDES OF ='
SF-5    'ILLEGAL USE OF A STATEMENT FUNCTION'

'SUBPROGRAMMES'
SR-0    'MISSING SUBPROGRAMME'
SR-2    'SUBPROGRAMME ASSIGNED DIFFERENT MODES IN DIFFERENT PROGRAMME SEGMENTS'
SR-4    'INVALID TYPE OF ARGUMENT IN SUBPROGRAMME REFERENCE'
SR-5    'SUBPROGRAMME ATTEMPTS TO REDEFINE A CONSTANT,TEMPORARY OR DO PARAMETER'
```

```
SR-6   'ATTEMPT TO USE SUBPROGRAMME RECURSIVELY'
SR-7   'WRONG NUMBER OF ARGUMENTS IN SUBPROGRAMME REFERENCE'
SR-8   'SUBPROGRAMME NAME PREVIOUSLY DEFINED -- FIRST REFERENCE USED'
SR-9   'NO MAIN PROGRAMME'
SR-A   'ILLEGAL OR BLANK SUBPROGRAMME NAME'

'SUBSCRIPTS'
SS-0   'ZERO SUBSCRIPT OR DIMENSION NOT ALLOWED'
SS-1   'SUBSCRIPT OUT OF RANGE'
SS-2   'INVALID VARIABLE OR NAME USED FOR DIMENSION'

'STATEMENTS AND STATEMENT NUMBERS'
ST-0   'MISSING STATEMENT NUMBER'
ST-1   'STATEMENT NUMBER GREATER THAN 99999'
ST-3   'MULTIPLY-DEFINED STATEMENT NUMBER'
ST-4   'NO STATEMENT NUMBER ON STATEMENT FOLLOWING TRANSFER STATEMENT'
ST-5   'UNDECODEABLE STATEMENT'
ST-7   'STATEMENT NUMBER SPECIFIED IN A TRANSFER IS A NON-EXECUTABLE STATEMENT'
ST-8   'STATEMENT NUMBER CONSTANT MUST BE IN A CALL STATEMENT'
ST-9   'STATEMENT SPECIFIED IN A TRANSFER STATEMENT IS A FORMAT STATEMENT'
ST-A   'MISSING FORMAT STATEMENT'

'SUBSCRIPTED VARIABLES'
SV-0   'WRONG NUMBER OF SUBSCRIPTS'
SV-1   'ARRAY NAME OR SUBPROGRAMME NAME USED INCORRECTLY WITHOUT LIST'
SV-2   'MORE THAN 7 DIMENSIONS NOT ALLOWED'
SV-3   'DIMENSION TOO LARGE'
SV-4   'VARIABLE WITH VARIABLE DIMENSIONS IS NOT A SUBPROGRAMME PARAMETER'
SV-5   'VARIABLE DIMENSION NEITHER SIMPLE INTEGER VARIABLE NOR S/P PARAMETER'

'SYNTAX ERRORS'
SX-0   'MISSING OPERATOR'
SX-1   'SYNTAX ERROR-SEARCHING FOR SYMBOL,NONE FOUND'
SX-2   'SYNTAX ERROR-SEARCHING FOR CONSTANT,NONE FOUND'
SX-3   'SYNTAX ERROR-SEARCHING FOR SYMBOL OR CONSTANT,NONE FOUND'
SX-4   'SYNTAX ERROR-SEARCHING FOR STATEMENT NUMBER,NONE FOUND'
SX-5   'SYNTAX ERROR-SEARCHING FOR SIMPLE INTEGER VARIABLE,NONE FOUND'
SX-C   'ILLEGAL SEQUENCE OF OPERATORS IN EXPRESSION'
SX-D   'MISSING OPERAND OR OPERATOR'

'I/O OPERATIONS'
UN-0   'CONTROL CARD ENCOUNTERED ON UNIT 5 DURING EXECUTION'
            PROBABLE CAUSE - MISSING DATA OR IMPROPER FORMAT STATEMENTS
UN-1   'END OF FILE ENCOUNTERED'
UN-2   'I/O ERROR'
UN-3   'DATA SET REFERENCED FOR WHICH NO DD CARD SUPPLIED'
UN-4   'REWIND, ENDFILE, BACKSPACE REFERENCES UNIT 5, 6, 7'
UN-5   'ATTEMPT TO READ ON UNIT 5 AFTER IT HAS HAD END-OF-FILE'
UN-6   'UNIT NUMBER IS NEGATIVE,ZERO,GREATER THAN 7 OR UNDEFINED'
UN-7   'TOO MANY PAGES'
UN-8   'ATTEMPT TO DO SEQUENTIAL I/O ON A DIRECT ACCESS FILE'
UN-9   'WRITE REFERENCES 5 OR READ REFERENCES 6, 7'
UN-A   'ATTEMPT TO READ MORE DATA THAN CONTAINED IN LOGICAL RECORD'
UN-B   'TOO MANY PHYSICAL RECORDS IN A LOGICAL RECORD.INCREASE RECORD LENGTH.'
UN-C   'I/O ERROR ON WATLIB'
UN-D   'RECFM OTHER THAN V IS SPECIFIED FOR I/O WITHOUT FORMAT CONTROL'

'UNDEFINED VARIABLES'
UV-0   'UNDEFINED VARIABLE - SIMPLE VARIABLE'
```

```
UV-1   'UNDEFINED VARIABLE - EQUIVALENCED, COMMONED, OR DUMMY PARAMETER'
UV-2   'UNDEFINED VARIABLE - ARRAY MEMBER'
UV-3   'UNDEFINED VARIABLE - ARRAY NAME WHICH WAS USED AS A DUMMY PARAMETER'
UV-4   'UNDEFINED VARIABLE - SUBPROGRAMME NAME USED AS DUMMY PARAMETER'
UV-5   'UNDEFINED VARIABLE - ARGUMENT OF THE LIBRARY SUBPROGRAMME NAMED'
UV-6   'VARIABLE FORMAT CONTAINS UNDEFINED CHARACTER(S)'

'VARIABLE NAMES'
VA-0   'ATTEMPT TO REDEFINE TYPE OF A VARIABLE NAME'
VA-1   'SUBROUTINE NAME OR COMMON BLOCK NAME USED INCORRECTLY'
VA-2   'NAME LONGER THAN SIX CHARACTERS. TRUNCATED TO SIX'
VA-3   'ATTEMPT TO REDEFINE THE MODE OF A VARIABLE NAME'
VA-4   'ATTEMPT TO REDEFINE THE TYPE OF A VARIABLE NAME'
VA-6   'ILLEGAL USE OF A SUBROUTINE NAME'
VA-8   'ATTEMPT TO USE A PREVIOUSLY DEFINED NAME AS FUNCTION OR ARRAY'
VA-9   'ATTEMPT TO USE A PREVIOUSLY DEFINED NAME AS A STATEMENT FUNCTION'
VA-A   'ATTEMPT TO USE A PREVIOUSLY DEFINED NAME AS A SUBPROGRAMME NAME'
VA-B   'NAME USED AS A COMMON BLOCK PREVIOUSLY USED AS A SUBPROGRAMME NAME'
VA-C   'NAME USED AS SUBPROGRAMME PREVIOUSLY USED AS A COMMON BLOCK NAME'
VA-D   'ILLEGAL DO-PARAMETER,ASSIGNED OR INITIALIZED VARIABLE IN SPECIFICATION'
VA-E   'ATTEMPT TO DIMENSION A CALL-BY-NAME PARAMETER'

'EXTERNAL STATEMENT'
XT-0   'INVALID ELEMENT IN EXTERNAL LIST'
XT-1   'INVALID DELIMITER IN EXTERNAL STATEMENT'
XT-2   'SUBPROGRAMME PREVIOUSLY EXTERNALLED'
```

APPENDIX F

WATFIV ERROR-DIAGNOSTIC MESSAGES

```
    /360 WATFIV COMPILER ERROR MESSAGES

'ASSEMBLER LANGUAGE SUBPROGRAMMES'
AL-0    'MISSING END CARD ON ASSEMBLY LANGUAGE OBJECT DECK'
AL-1    'ENTRY-POINT OR CSECT NAME IN AN OBJECT DECK WAS PREVIOUSLY
        DEFINED.FIRST DEFINITION USED'

'BLOCK DATA STATEMENTS'
BD-0    'EXECUTABLE STATEMENTS ARE ILLEGAL IN BLOCK DATA SUBPROGRAMS'
BD-1    'IMPROPER BLOCK DATA STATEMENT'

'CARD FORMAT AND CONTENTS'
CC-0    'COLUMNS 1-5 OF CONTINUATION CARD ARE NOT BLANK.
        PROBABLE CAUSE STATEMENT PUNCHED TO LEFT OF COLUMN 7'
CC-1    'LIMIT OF 5 CONTINUATION CARDS EXCEEDED'
CC-2    'INVALID CHARACTER IN FORTRAN STATEMENT.
         A '$' WAS INSERTED IN THE SOURCE LISTING'
CC-3    'FIRST CARD OF A PROGRAM IS A CONTINUATION CARD.
        PROBABLE CAUSE STATEMENT PUNCHED TO LEFT OF COLUMN 7'
CC-4    'STATEMENT TOO LONG TO COMPILE (SCAN-STACK OVERFLOW)'
CC-5    'A BLANK CARD WAS ENCOUNTERED'
CC-6    'KEYPUNCH USED DIFFERS FROM KEYPUNCH SPECIFIED ON JOB CARD'
CC-7    'THE FIRST CHARACTER OF THE STATEMENT WAS NOT ALPHABETIC'
CC-8    'INVALID CHARACTER(S) ARE CONCATENATED WITH THE FORTRAN KEYWORD'
CC-9    'INVALID CHARACTERS IN COLUMNS 1-5.STATEMENT NUMBER IGNORED.
        PROBABLE CAUSE STATEMENT PUNCHED TO LEFT OF COLUMN 7'

'COMMON'
CM-0    'THE VARIABLE IS ALREADY IN COMMON'
CM-1    'OTHER COMPILERS MAY NOT ALLOW COMMONED VARIABLES TO BE INITIALIZED IN
        OTHER THAN A BLOCK DATA SUBPROGRAM'
CM-2    'ILLEGAL USE OF A COMMON BLOCK OR NAMELIST NAME'

'FORTRAN TYPE CONSTANTS'
CN-0    'MIXED REAL*4,REAL*8 IN COMPLEX CONSTANT REAL*8 ASSUMED FOR BOTH'
CN-1    'AN INTEGER CONSTANT MAY NOT BE GREATER THAN 2,147,483,647 (2**31-1)'
CN-2    'EXPONENT ON A REAL CONSTANT IS GREATER THAN 2 DIGITS'
CN-3    'A REAL CONSTANT HAS MORE THAN 16 DIGITS.IT WAS TRUNCATED TO 16'
CN-4    'INVALID HEXADECIMAL CONSTANT'
CN-5    'ILLEGAL USE OF A DECIMAL POINT'
CN-6    'CONSTANT WITH MORE THAN 7 DIGITS BUT E-TYPE EXPONENT,ASSUMED TO BE
        REAL*4'
CN-7    'CONSTANT OR STATEMENT NUMBER GREATER THAN 99999'
CN-8    'AN EXPONENT OVERFLOW OR UNDERFLOW OCCURRED WHILE CONVERTING A CONSTANT
        IN A SOURCE STATEMENT'

'COMPILER ERRORS'
CP-0    'COMPILER ERROR - LANDR/ARITH'
CP-1    'COMPILER ERROR.LIKELY CAUSE MORE THAN 255 DO STATEMENTS'
CP-4    'COMPILER ERROR - INTERRUPT AT COMPILE TIME,RETURN TO SYSTEM'

'CHARACTER VARIABLE'
CV-0    'A CHARACTER VARIABLE IS USED WITH A RELATIONAL OPERATOR'
CV-1    'LENGTH OF A CHARACTER VALUE ON RIGHT OF EQUAL SIGN EXCEEDS THAT ON
        LEFT. TRUNCATION WILL OCCUR'
CV-2    'UNFORMATTED CORE-TO-CORE I/O NOT IMPLEMENTED'

'DATA STATEMENT'
DA-0    'REPLICATION FACTOR IS ZERO OR GREATER THAN 32767.
```

```
    /360 WATFIV COMPILER ERROR MESSAGES
         IT IS ASSUMED TO BE 32767'
DA-1     'MORE VARIABLES THAN CONSTANTS'
DA-2     'ATTEMPT TO INITIALIZE A SUBPROGRAM PARAMETER IN A DATA STATEMENT'
DA-3     'OTHER COMPILERS MAY NOT ALLOW NON-CONSTANT SUBSCRIPTS IN DATA
         STATEMENTS'
DA-4     'TYPE OF VARIABLE AND CONSTANT DO NOT AGREE.  (MESSAGE ISSUED ONCE FOR
         AN ARRAY)'
DA-5     'MORE CONSTANTS THAN VARIABLES'
DA-6     'A VARIABLE WAS PREVIOUSLY INITIALIZED.THE LATEST VALUE IS USED.
         CHECK COMMONED AND EQUIVALENCED VARIABLES'
DA-7     'OTHER COMPILERS MAY NOT ALLOW INITIALIZATION OF BLANK COMMON'
DA-8     'A LITERAL CONSTANT HAS BEEN TRUNCATED'
DA-9     'OTHER COMPILERS MAY NOT ALLOW IMPLIED DO-LOOPS IN DATA STATEMENTS'

'DEFINE FILE STATEMENTS'
DF-0     'THE UNIT NUMBER IS MISSING'
DF-1     'INVALID FORMAT TYPE'
DF-2     'THE ASSOCIATED VARIABLE IS NOT A SIMPLE INTEGER VARIABLE'
DF-3     'NUMBER OF RECORDS OR RECORD SIZE IS ZERO OR GREATER THAN 32767'

'DIMENSION STATEMENTS'
DM-0     'NO DIMENSIONS ARE SPECIFIED FOR A VARIABLE IN A DIMENSION STATEMENT'
DM-1     'THE VARIABLE HAS ALREADY BEEN DIMENSIONED'
DM-2     'CALL-BY-LOCATION PARAMETERS MAY NOT BE DIMENSIONED'
DM-3     'THE DECLARED SIZE OF ARRAY EXCEEDS SPACE PROVIDED BY CALLING ARGUMENT'

'DO LOOPS'
DO-0     'THIS STATEMENT CANNOT BE THE OBJECT OF A DO-LOOP'
DO-1     'ILLEGAL TRANSFER INTO THE RANGE OF A DO-LOOP'
DO-2     'THE OBJECT OF THIS DO-LOOP HAS ALREADY APPEARED'
DO-3     'IMPROPERLY NESTED DO-LOOPS'
DO-4     'ATTEMPT TO REDEFINE A DO-LOOP PARAMETER WITHIN THE RANGE OF THE LOOP'
DO-5     'INVALID DO-LOOP PARAMETER'
DO-6     'ILLEGAL TRANSFER TO A STATEMENT WHICH IS INSIDE THE RANGE OF A DO-LOOP'
DO-7     'A DO-LOOP PARAMETER IS UNDEFINED OR OUT OF RANGE'
DO-8     'BECAUSE OF ONE OF THE PARAMETERS,THIS DO-LOOP WILL TERMINATE AFTER THE
         FIRST TIME THROUGH'
DO-9     'A DO-LOOP PARAMETER MAY NOT BE REDEFINED IN AN INPUT LIST'
DO-A     'OTHER COMPILERS MAY NOT ALLOW THIS STATEMENT TO END A DO-LOOP'

'EQUIVALENCE AND/OR COMMON'
EC-0     'EQUIVALENCED VARIABLE APPEARS IN A COMMON STATEMENT'
EC-1     'A COMMON BLOCK HAS A DIFFERENT LENGTH THAN IN A PREVIOUS
         SUBPROGRAM GREATER LENGTH USED'
EC-2     'COMMON AND/OR EQUIVALENCE CAUSES INVALID ALIGNMENT.
         EXECUTION SLOWED.REMEDY ORDER VARIABLES BY DECREASING LENGTH'
EC-3     'EQUIVALENCE EXTENDS COMMON DOWNWARDS'
EC-4     'A SUBPROGRAM PARAMETER APPEARS IN A COMMON OR EQUIVALENCE STATEMENT'
EC-5     'A VARIABLE WAS USED WITH SUBSCRIPTS IN AN EQUIVALENCE STATEMENT BUT HAS
         NOT BEEN PROPERLY DIMENSIONED'

'END STATEMENTS'
EN-0     'MISSING END STATEMENT END STATEMENT GENERATED'
EN-1     'AN END STATEMENT WAS USED TO TERMINATE EXECUTION'
EN-2     'AN END STATEMENT CANNOT HAVE A STATEMENT NUMBER. STATEMENT NUMBER
         IGNORED'
EN-3     'END STATEMENT NOT PRECEDED BY A TRANSFER'
```

```
    /360 WATFIV COMPILER ERROR MESSAGES
'EQUAL SIGNS'
EQ-0    'ILLEGAL QUANTITY ON LEFT OF EQUALS SIGN'
EQ-1    'ILLEGAL USE OF EQUAL SIGN'
EQ-2    'OTHER COMPILERS MAY NOT ALLOW MULTIPLE ASSIGNMENT STATEMENTS'
EQ-3    'MULTIPLE ASSIGNMENT IS NOT IMPLEMENTED FOR CHARACTER VARIABLES'

'EQUIVALENCE STATEMENTS'
EV-0    'ATTEMPT TO EQUIVALENCE A VARIABLE TO ITSELF'
EV-2    'A MULTI-SUBSCRIPTED EQUIVALENCED VARIABLE HAS BEEN INCORRECTLY
        RE-EQUIVALENCED.REMEDY DIMENSION THE VARIABLE FIRST'

'POWERS AND EXPONENTIATION'
EX-0    'ILLEGAL COMPLEX EXPONENTIATION'
EX-1    'I**J WHERE I=J=0'
EX-2    'I**J WHERE I=0, J.LT.0'
EX-3    '0.0**Y WHERE Y.LE.0.0'
EX-4    '0.0**J WHERE J=0'
EX-5    '0.0**J WHERE J.LT.0'
EX-6    'X**Y WHERE X.LT.0.0, Y.NE.0.0'

'ENTRY STATEMENT'
EY-0    'ENTRY-POINT NAME WAS PREVIOUSLY DEFINED'
EY-1    'PREVIOUS DEFINITION OF FUNCTION NAME IN AN ENTRY IS INCORRECT'
EY-2    'THE USAGE OF A SUBPROGRAM PARAMETER IS INCONSISTENT WITH A PREVIOUS
        ENTRY-POINT'
EY-3    'A PARAMETER HAS APPEARED IN A EXECUTABLE STATEMENT BUT IS NOT A
        SUBPROGRAM PARAMETER'
EY-4    'ENTRY STATEMENTS ARE INVALID IN THE MAIN PROGRAM'
EY-5    'ENTRY STATEMENT INVALID INSIDE A DO-LOOP'

'FORMAT'
   SOME FORMAT ERROR MESSAGES GIVE CHARACTERS IN WHICH ERROR WAS DETECTED
FM-0    'IMPROPER CHARACTER SEQUENCE OR INVALID CHARACTER IN INPUT DATA'
FM-1    'NO STATEMENT NUMBER ON A FORMAT STATEMENT'
FM-2    'FORMAT CODE AND DATA TYPE DO NOT MATCH'
FM-4    'FORMAT PROVIDES NO CONVERSION SPECIFICATION FOR A VALUE IN I/O LIST'
FM-5    'AN INTEGER IN THE INPUT DATA IS TOO LARGE.
         (MAXIMUM=2,147,483,647=2**31-1)'
FM-6    'A REAL NUMBER IN THE INPUT DATA IS OUT OF MACHINE RANGE (1.E-78,1.E+75)'
FM-7    'UNREFERENCED FORMAT STATEMENT'
FT-0    'FIRST CHARACTER OF VARIABLE FORMAT IS NOT A LEFT PARENTHESIS'
FT-1    'INVALID CHARACTER ENCOUNTERED IN FORMAT'
FT-2    'INVALID FORM FOLLOWING A FORMAT CODE'
FT-3    'INVALID FIELD OR GROUP COUNT'
FT-4    'A FIELD OR GROUP COUNT GREATER THAN 255'
FT-5    'NO CLOSING PARENTHESIS ON VARIABLE FORMAT'
FT-6    'NO CLOSING QUOTE IN A HOLLERITH FIELD'
FT-7    'INVALID USE OF COMMA'
FT-8    'FORMAT STATEMENT TOO LONG TO COMPILE (SCAN-STACK OVERFLOW)'
FT-9    'INVALID USE OF P FORMAT CODE'
FT-A    'INVALID USE OF PERIOD(.)'
FT-B    'MORE THAN THREE LEVELS OF PARENTHESES'
FT-C    'INVALID CHARACTER BEFORE A RIGHT PARENTHESIS'
FT-D    'MISSING OR ZERO LENGTH HOLLERITH ENCOUNTERED'
FT-E    'NO CLOSING RIGHT PARENTHESIS'
FT-F    'CHARACTERS FOLLOW CLOSING RIGHT PARENTHESIS'
FT-G    'WRONG QUOTE USED FOR KEY-PUNCH SPECIFIED'
FT-H    'LENGTH OF HOLLERITH EXCEEDS 255'
```

```
/360 WATFIV COMPILER ERROR MESSAGES

'FUNCTIONS AND SUBROUTINES'
FN-1    'A PARAMETER APPEARS MORE THAN ONCE IN A SUBPROGRAM OR STATEMENT
        FUNCTION DEFINITION'
FN-2    'SUBSCRIPTS ON RIGHT-HAND SIDE OF STATEMENT FUNCTION.
         PROBABLE CAUSE VARIABLE TO LEFT OF EQUAL SIGN NOT DIMENSIONED'
FN-3    'MULTIPLE RETURNS ARE INVALID IN FUNCTION SUBPROGRAMS'
FN-4    'ILLEGAL LENGTH MODIFIER'
FN-5    'INVALID PARAMETER'
FN-6    'A PARAMETER HAS THE SAME NAME AS THE SUBPROGRAM'

'GO TO STATEMENTS'
GO-0    'THIS STATEMENT COULD TRANSFER TO ITSELF'
GO-1    'THIS STATEMENT TRANSFERS TO A NON-EXECUTABLE STATEMENT'
GO-2    'ATTEMPT TO DEFINE ASSIGNED GOTO INDEX IN AN ARITHMETIC STATEMENT'
GO-3    'ASSIGNED GOTO INDEX MAY BE USED ONLY IN ASSIGNED GOTO AND ASSIGN
        STATEMENTS'
GO-4    'THE INDEX OF AN ASSIGNED GOTO IS UNDEFINED OR OUT OF RANGE,OR INDEX OF
        COMPUTED GOTO IS UNDEFINED'
GO-5    'ASSIGNED GOTO INDEX MAY NOT BE AN INTEGER*2 VARIABLE'

'HOLLERITH CONSTANTS'
HO-0    'ZERO LENGTH SPECIFIED FOR H-TYPE HOLLERITH'
HO-1    'ZERO LENGTH QUOTE-TYPE HOLLERITH'
HO-2    'NO CLOSING QUOTE OR NEXT CARD NOT A CONTINUATION CARD'
HO-3    'UNEXPECTED HOLLERITH OR STATEMENT NUMBER CONSTANT'

'IF STATEMENTS (ARITHMETIC AND LOGICAL)'
IF-0    'AN INVALID STATEMENT FOLLOWS THE LOGICAL IF'
IF-1    'ARITHMETIC OR INVALID EXPRESSION IN LOGICAL IF'
IF-2    'LOGICAL,COMPLEX OR INVALID EXPRESSION IN ARITHMETIC IF'

'IMPLICIT STATEMENT'
IM-0    'INVALID DATA TYPE'
IM-1    'INVALID OPTIONAL LENGTH'
IM-3    'IMPROPER ALPHABETIC SEQUENCE IN CHARACTER RANGE'
IM-4    'A SPECIFICATION IS NOT A SINGLE CHARACTER.THE FIRST CHARACTER IS USED'
IM-5    'IMPLICIT STATEMENT DOES NOT PRECEDE OTHER SPECIFICATION STATEMENTS'
IM-6    'ATTEMPT TO DECLARE THE TYPE OF A CHARACTER MORE THAN ONCE'
IM-7    'ONLY ONE IMPLICIT STATEMENT PER PROGRAM SEGMENT ALLOWED. THIS ONE
        IGNORED'

'INPUT/OUTPUT'
IO-0    'I/O STATEMENT REFERENCES A STATEMENT WHICH IS NOT A FORMAT STATEMENT'
IO-1    'A VARIABLE FORMAT MUST BE AN ARRAY NAME'
IO-2    'INVALID ELEMENT IN INPUT LIST OR DATA LIST'
IO-3    'OTHER COMPILERS MAY NOT ALLOW EXPRESSIONS IN OUTPUT LISTS'
IO-4    'ILLEGAL USE OF END= OR ERR= PARAMETERS'
IO-5    'INVALID UNIT NUMBER'
IO-6    'INVALID FORMAT'
IO-7    'ONLY CONSTANTS,SIMPLE INTEGER*4 VARIABLES,AND CHARACTER VARIABLES ARE
        ALLOWED AS UNIT'
IO-8    'ATTEMPT TO PERFORM I/O IN A FUNCTION WHICH IS CALLED IN AN OUTPUT
        STATEMENT'
IO-9    'UNFORMATTED WRITE STATEMENT MUST HAVE A LIST'

'JOB CONTROL CARDS'
JB-0    'CONTROL CARD ENCOUNTERED DURING COMPILATION
```

```
    /360 WATFIV COMPILER ERROR MESSAGES
        PROBABLE CAUSE MISSING $ENTRY CARD'
JB-1    'MIS-PUNCHED JOB OPTION'

'JOB TERMINATION'
KO-0    'SOURCE ERROR ENCOUNTERED WHILE EXECUTING WITH RUN=FREE'
KO-1    'LIMIT EXCEEDED FOR FIXED-POINT DIVISION BY ZERO'
KO-2    'LIMIT EXCEEDED FOR FLOATING-POINT DIVISION BY ZERO'
KO-3    'EXPONENT OVERFLOW LIMIT EXCEEDED'
KO-4    'EXPONENT UNDERFLOW LIMIT EXCEEDED'
KO-5    'FIXED-POINT OVERFLOW LIMIT EXCEEDED'
KO-6    'JOB-TIME EXCEEDED'
KO-7    'COMPILER ERROR - EXECUTION TIME RETURN TO SYSTEM'
KO-8    'TRACEBACK ERROR. TRACEBACK TERMINATED'
KO-9    'CANNOT OPEN WATFIV.ERRTEXTS. RUN TERMINATED'
KO-A    'I/O ERROR ON TEXT FILE'

'LOGICAL OPERATIONS'
LG-0    '.NOT. WAS USED AS A BINARY OPERATOR'

'LIBRARY ROUTINES'
LI-0    'ARGUMENT OUT OF RANGE DGAMMA OR GAMMA. (1.382E-76 .LT. X .LT. 57.57)'
LI-1    'ABSOLUTE VALUE OF ARGUMENT .GT. 174.673, SINH,COSH,DSINH,DCOSH'
LI-2    'SENSE LIGHT OTHER THAN 0,1,2,3,4 FOR SLITE OR 1,2,3,4 FOR SLITET'
LI-3    'REAL PORTION OF ARGUMENT .GT. 174.673, CEXP OR CDEXP'
LI-4    'ABS(AIMAG(Z)) .GT. 174.673 FOR CSIN, CCOS, CDSIN OR CDCOS OF Z'
LI-5    'ABS(REAL(Z)) .GE. 3.537E15 FOR CSIN, CCOS, CDSIN OR CDCOS OF Z'
LI-6    'ABS(AIMAG(Z)) .GE. 3.537E15 FOR CEXP OR CDEXP OF Z'
LI-7    'ARGUMENT .GT. 174.673, EXP OR DEXP'
LI-8    'ARGUMENT IS ZERO, CLOG, CLOG10, CDLOG OR CDLG10'
LI-9    'ARGUMENT IS NEGATIVE OR ZERO, ALOG, ALOG10, DLOG OR DLOG10'
LI-A    'ABS(X) .GE. 3.537E15 FOR SIN, COS, DSIN OR DCOS OF X'
LI-B    'ABSOLUTE VALUE OF ARGUMENT .GT. 1, FOR ARSIN, ARCOS, DARSIN OR DARCOS'
LI-C    'ARGUMENT IS NEGATIVE, SQRT OR DSQRT'
LI-D    'BOTH ARGUMENTS OF DATAN2 OR ATAN2 ARE ZERO'
LI-E    'ARGUMENT TOO CLOSE TO A SINGULARITY, TAN, COTAN, DTAN OR DCOTAN'
LI-F    'ARGUMENT OUT OF RANGE DLGAMA OR ALGAMA. (0.0 .LT. X .LT. 4.29E73)'
LI-G    'ABSOLUTE VALUE OF ARGUMENT .GE. 3.537E15, TAN, COTAN, DTAN, DCOTAN'
LI-H    'LESS THAN TWO ARGUMENTS FOR ONE OF MINO,MIN1,AMINO,ETC.'

'MIXED MODE'
MD-0    'RELATIONAL OPERATOR HAS LOGICAL OPERAND'
MD-1    'RELATIONAL OPERATOR HAS COMPLEX OPERAND'
MD-2    'MIXED MODE - LOGICAL OR CHARACTER WITH ARITHMETIC'
MD-3    'OTHER COMPILERS MAY NOT ALLOW SUBSCRIPTS OF TYPE COMPLEX,LOGICAL OR
        CHARACTER'

'MEMORY OVERFLOW'
MO-0    'INSUFFICIENT MEMORY TO COMPILE THIS PROGRAM.REMAINDER WILL BE ERROR
        CHECKED ONLY'
MO-1    'INSUFFICIENT MEMORY TO ASSIGN ARRAY STORAGE. JOB ABANDONED'
MO-2    'SYMBOL TABLE EXCEEDS AVAILABLE SPACE,JOB ABANDONED'
MO-3    'DATA AREA OF SUBPROGRAM EXCEEDS 24K -- SEGMENT SUBPROGRAM'
MO-4    'INSUFFICIENT MEMORY TO ALLOCATE COMPILER WORK AREA OR WATLIB BUFFER'

'NAMELIST STATEMENTS'
NL-0    'NAMELIST ENTRY MUST BE A VARIABLE,NOT A SUBPROGRAM PARAMETER'
NL-1    'NAMELIST NAME PREVIOUSLY DEFINED'
NL-2    'VARIABLE NAME TOO LONG'
```

```
    /360 WATFIV COMPILER ERROR MESSAGES
NL-3    'VARIABLE NAME NOT FOUND IN NAMELIST'
NL-4    'INVALID SYNTAX IN NAMELIST INPUT'
NL-6    'VARIABLE INCORRECTLY SUBSCRIPTED'
NL-7    'SUBSCRIPT OUT OF RANGE'

'PARENTHESES'
PC-0    'UNMATCHED PARENTHESIS'
PC-1    'INVALID PARENTHESIS NESTING IN I/O LIST'

'PAUSE, STOP STATEMENTS'
PS-0    'OPERATOR MESSAGES NOT ALLOWED SIMPLE STOP ASSUMED FOR STOP,
        CONTINUE ASSUMED FOR PAUSE'

'RETURN STATEMENT'
RE-1    'RETURN I, WHERE I IS OUT OF RANGE OR UNDEFINED'
RE-2    'MULTIPLE RETURN NOT VALID IN FUNCTION SUBPROGRAM'
RE-3    'VARIABLE IS NOT A SIMPLE INTEGER'
RE-4    'A MULTIPLE RETURN IS NOT VALID IN THE MAIN PROGRAM'

'ARITHMETIC AND LOGICAL STATEMENT FUNCTIONS'
    PROBABLE CAUSE OF SF ERRORS - VARIABLE ON LEFT OF = WAS NOT DIMENSIONED
SF-1    'A PREVIOUSLY REFERENCED STATEMENT NUMBER APPEARS ON A STATEMENT
        FUNCTION DEFINITION'
SF-2    'STATEMENT FUNCTION IS THE OBJECT OF A LOGICAL IF STATEMENT'
SF-3    'RECURSIVE STATEMENT FUNCTION DEFINITION NAME APPEARS ON BOTH SIDES OF
        EQUAL SIGN.LIKELY CAUSE VARIABLE NOT DIMENSIONED'
SF-4    'A STATEMENT FUNCTION DEFINITION APPEARS AFTER THE FIRST EXECUTABLE
        STATEMENT'
SF-5    'ILLEGAL USE OF A STATEMENT FUNCTION NAME'

'SUBPROGRAMS'
SR-0    'MISSING SUBPROGRAM'
SR-1    'SUBPROGRAM REDEFINES A CONSTANT,EXPRESSION,DO-PARAMETER OR ASSIGNED
        GOTO INDEX'
SR-2    'THE SUBPROGRAM WAS ASSIGNED DIFFERENT TYPES IN DIFFERENT PROGRAM
        SEGMENTS'
SR-3    'ATTEMPT TO USE A SUBPROGRAM RECURSIVELY'
SR-4    'INVALID TYPE OF ARGUMENT IN REFERENCE TO A SUBPROGRAM'
SR-5    'WRONG NUMBER OF ARGUMENTS IN A REFERENCE TO A SUBPROGRAM'
SR-6    'A SUBPROGRAM WAS PREVIOUSLY DEFINED. THE FIRST DEFINITION IS USED'
SR-7    'NO MAIN PROGRAM'
SR-8    'ILLEGAL OR MISSING SUBPROGRAM NAME'
SR-9    'LIBRARY PROGRAM WAS NOT ASSIGNED THE CORRECT TYPE'
SR-A    'METHOD FOR ENTERING SUBPROGRAM PRODUCES UNDEFINED VALUE FOR
        CALL-BY-LOCATION PARAMETER'

'SUBSCRIPTS'
SS-0    'ZERO SUBSCRIPT OR DIMENSION NOT ALLOWED'
SS-1    'ARRAY SUBSCRIPT EXCEEDS DIMENSION'
SS-2    'INVALID SUBSCRIPT FORM'
SS-3    'SUBSCRIPT IS OUT OF RANGE'

'STATEMENTS AND STATEMENT NUMBERS'
ST-0    'MISSING STATEMENT NUMBER'
ST-1    'STATEMENT NUMBER GREATER THAN 99999'
ST-2    'STATEMENT NUMBER HAS ALREADY BEEN DEFINED'
ST-3    'UNDECODEABLE STATEMENT'
ST-4    'UNNUMBERED EXECUTABLE STATEMENT FOLLOWS A TRANSFER'
```

```
    /360 WATFIV COMPILER ERROR MESSAGES
ST-5    'STATEMENT NUMBER IN A TRANSFER IS A NON-EXECUTABLE STATEMENT'
ST-6    'ONLY CALL STATEMENTS MAY CONTAIN STATEMENT NUMBER ARGUMENTS'
ST-7    'STATEMENT SPECIFIED IN A TRANSFER STATEMENT IS A FORMAT STATEMENT'
ST-8    'MISSING FORMAT STATEMENT'
ST-9    'SPECIFICATION STATEMENT DOES NOT PRECEDE STATEMENT FUNCTION DEFINITIONS
        OR EXECUTABLE STATEMENTS'
ST-A    'UNREFERENCED STATEMENT FOLLOWS A TRANSFER'

'SUBSCRIPTED VARIABLES'
SV-0    'THE WRONG NUMBER OF SUBSCRIPTS WERE SPECIFIED FOR A VARIABLE'
SV-1    'AN ARRAY OR SUBPROGRAM NAME IS USED INCORRECTLY WITHOUT A LIST'
SV-2    'MORE THAN 7 DIMENSIONS ARE NOT ALLOWED'
SV-3    'DIMENSION OR SUBSCRIPT TOO LARGE (MAXIMUM 10**8-1)'
SV-4    'A VARIABLE USED WITH VARIABLE DIMENSIONS IS NOT A SUBPROGRAM PARAMETER'
SV-5    'A VARIABLE DIMENSION IS NOT ONE OF SIMPLE INTEGER VARIABLE,SUBPROGRAM
        PARAMETER,IN COMMON'

'SYNTAX ERRORS'
SX-0    'MISSING OPERATOR'
SX-1    'EXPECTING OPERATOR'
SX-2    'EXPECTING SYMBOL'
SX-3    'EXPECTING SYMBOL OR OPERATOR'
SX-4    'EXPECTING CONSTANT'
SX-5    'EXPECTING SYMBOL OR CONSTANT'
SX-6    'EXPECTING STATEMENT NUMBER'
SX-7    'EXPECTING SIMPLE INTEGER VARIABLE'
SX-8    'EXPECTING SIMPLE INTEGER VARIABLE OR CONSTANT'
SX-9    'ILLEGAL SEQUENCE OF OPERATORS IN EXPRESSION'
SX-A    'EXPECTING END-OF-STATEMENT'

'TYPE STATEMENTS'
TY-0    'THE VARIABLE HAS ALREADY BEEN EXPLICITLY TYPED'
TY-1    'THE LENGTH OF THE EQUIVALENCED VARIABLE MAY NOT BE CHANGED.
        REMEDY  INTERCHANGE TYPE AND EQUIVALENCE STATEMENTS'

'I/O OPERATIONS'
UN-0    'CONTROL CARD ENCOUNTERED ON UNIT 5 AT EXECUTION.
        PROBABLE CAUSE MISSING DATA OR INCORRECT FORMAT'
UN-1    'END OF FILE ENCOUNTERED (IBM CODE IHC217)'
UN-2    'I/O ERROR (IBM CODE IHC218)'
UN-3    'NO DD STATEMENT WAS SUPPLIED (IBM CODE IHC219)'
UN-4    'REWIND,ENDFILE,BACKSPACE REFERENCES UNIT 5, 6 OR 7'
UN-5    'ATTEMPT TO READ ON UNIT 5 AFTER IT HAS HAD END-OF-FILE'
UN-6    'AN INVALID VARIABLE UNIT NUMBER WAS DETECTED (IBM CODE IHC220)'
UN-7    'PAGE-LIMIT EXCEEDED'
UN-8    'ATTEMPT TO DO DIRECT ACCESS I/O ON A SEQUENTIAL FILE OR VICE VERSA.
        POSSIBLE MISSING DEFINE FILE STATEMENT (IBM CODE IHC231)'
UN-9    'WRITE REFERENCES 5 OR READ REFERENCES 6 OR 7'
UN-A    'DEFINE FILE REFERENCES A UNIT PREVIOUSLY USED FOR SEQUENTIAL I/O (IBM
        CODE IHC235)'
UN-B    'RECORD SIZE FOR UNIT EXCEEDS 32767,OR DIFFERS FROM DD STATEMENT
        SPECIFICATION (IBM CODES IHC233,IHC237)'
UN-C    'FOR DIRECT ACCESS I/O THE RELATIVE RECORD POSITION IS NEGATIVE,ZERO,OR
        TOO LARGE (IBM CODE IHC232)'
UN-D    'AN ATTEMPT WAS MADE TO READ MORE INFORMATION THAN LOGICAL RECORD
        CONTAINS (IBM CODE IHC236)'
UN-E    'FORMATTED LINE EXCEEDS BUFFER LENGTH (IBM CODE IHC212)'
UN-F    'I/O ERROR - SEARCHING LIBRARY DIRECTORY'
```

```
    /360 WATFIV COMPILER ERROR MESSAGES
UN-G    'I/O ERROR - READING LIBRARY'
UN-H    'ATTEMPT TO DEFINE THE OBJECT ERROR FILE AS A DIRECT ACCESS FILE
        (IBM CODE IHC234)'
UN-I    'RECFM IS NOT V(B)S FOR I/O WITHOUT FORMAT CONTROL   (IBM CODE IHC214)'
UN-J    'MISSING DD CARD FOR WATLIB.NO LIBRARY ASSUMED'
UN-K    'ATTEMPT TO READ OR WRITE PAST THE END OF CHARACTER VARIABLE BUFFER'
UN-L    'ATTEMPT TO READ ON AN UNCREATED DIRECT ACCESS FILE (IHC236)'

'UNDEFINED VARIABLES'
UV-0    'VARIABLE IS UNDEFINED'
UV-3    'SUBSCRIPT IS UNDEFINED'
UV-4    'SUBPROGRAM IS UNDEFINED'
UV-5    'ARGUMENT IS UNDEFINED'
UV-6    'UNDECODABLE CHARACTERS IN VARIABLE FORMAT'

'VARIABLE NAMES'
VA-0    'A NAME IS TOO LONG.IT HAS BEEN TRUNCATED TO SIX CHARACTERS'
VA-1    'ATTEMPT TO USE AN ASSIGNED OR INITIALIZED VARIABLE OR DO-PARAMETER IN A
        SPECIFICATION STATEMENT'
VA-2    'ILLEGAL USE OF A SUBROUTINE NAME'
VA-3    'ILLEGAL USE OF A VARIABLE NAME'
VA-4    'ATTEMPT TO USE THE PREVIOUSLY DEFINED NAME AS A FUNCTION OR AN ARRAY'
VA-5    'ATTEMPT TO USE A PREVIOUSLY DEFINED NAME AS A SUBROUTINE'
VA-6    'ATTEMPT TO USE A PREVIOUSLY DEFINED NAME AS A SUBPROGRAM'
VA-7    'ATTEMPT TO USE A PREVIOUSLY DEFINED NAME AS A COMMON BLOCK'
VA-8    'ATTEMPT TO USE A FUNCTION NAME AS A VARIABLE'
VA-9    'ATTEMPT TO USE A PREVIOUSLY DEFINED NAME AS A VARIABLE'
VA-A    'ILLEGAL USE OF A PREVIOUSLY DEFINED NAME'

'EXTERNAL STATEMENT'
XT-0    'A VARIABLE HAS ALREADY APPEARED IN AN EXTERNAL STATEMENT'
```

INDEX

435